City College
and the
Jewish Poor

Compton Hall and Chemistry Building, CCNY. *Archives, The City College, City University of New York*

Sherry Gorelick

City College and the Jewish Poor

Education in New York, 1880–1924

Rutgers University Press

New Brunswick, New Jersey

A Dreamer's Journey by Morris Raphael Cohen, copyright © 1949, renewed 1977 by The Free Press, a Division of Macmillan Publishing Co., Inc. is reprinted with permission of Macmillan Publishing Co., Inc.

Library of Congress Cataloging in Publication Data
Gorelick, Sherry.
    City College and the Jewish poor.

    Bibliography: p.
    Includes index.
    1. Jews in New York (City)—Education.   2. Jews in New York (City)—Economic conditions.   3. New York (City). City College.   4. Occupational mobility—New York (City)   I. Title.
LC743.N5G67   371.97'924'07471   80-22128
ISBN 0–8135–0905–X

Jacket photograph courtesy of Photoworld/F. P. G.

Dedicated to

SAMUEL H. GORELICK

1908–1967

worker, builder, Russian Jewish immigrant
a good man, a gentle man
who left me a legacy,
the best lesson of my education:

Social justice cannot exist
where social classes exist.

Contents

Acknowledgments

Now, in these days of attack on public education at all levels, I want to state my debts. The people of the City and State of New York gave me most of my education: elementary, high school, and college. At the peak of its greatest expansion, the City University gave me my first teaching job. But now the public schools suffer gross neglect. In 1976, tuition was imposed on the City University, ending 129 years of free education. Teachers were fired, budgets cut, and whole schools dismantled. Without free higher education in New York City, it would have been very difficult for me and for many others to have gone much past high school. I wish that tuition-free, public higher education were still there for others as it was for us.

In a way this book is a work of self-clarification, and much of my life is in it. My father, Samuel H. Gorelick, taught me class consciousness, unionism, and respect for labor, a lesson that outlasted twenty-two years of American education. My mother, Emma S. Gorelick, translated Yiddish works for me, explained many points of Jewish practice and religious law, discussed many of the issues involved, and helped proofread. An Orthodox Jew, she has set an example of dignity and courage by her insistence, all her life, on standing for her convictions even under hostile conditions. Most important, by her warm and loving support for a project with which she most assuredly disagrees, she has taught me a lesson in the combination of love, strong conviction, and respect for differences.

Monica Jardine, relentless, driving friend, forced me to face the importance of racism and ethnicity—to do precisely the study I needed to do—to analyze the Jewish question when such study was equally unfashionable among mainstream academics and Marxists.

Maarten de Kadt has read this work in its many metamorphoses and helped to move it along. He has lent it his clear methodological sense. He took on more than his share of the mechanics of our life, deftly managed my attacks of self-doubt, discussed City College and the Eastern European Jews in greater detail than he ever would have chosen on his own, and lightened these long months of monolithic work-madness with his wonderful irrepressible humor.

I learned a lot from people who read various versions of this work, or corrected chapters, or taught me new ways of thinking: Hal Benenson, Lourdes Benería, Ivar Berg, Constance Blake, Edmund Braun, Amy Bridges, Penny Ciancanelli, Sarah Eisenstein, Beverly Elkan, Herbert Gans, Eli Ginsberg, Philip Harvey, Irving Louis Horowitz, Morris Laub, Stephen Steinberg, and Linda Schneider.

Librarians are magicians: they pull rare bits out of top hats. For their good-humored and knowledgeable assistance I am grateful to Sol Becker of the Municipal Reference and Research Library, Florence Wilkinson of Teachers College Library, Alice Bonnell of the Columbiana Collection, and, most particularly, Alan Streit and Barbara Dunlap of the City College Archives and Catheryn O'Dea of the Professional Library of the New York Board of Education. Ms. O'Dea supplemented her librarian's skills with her considerable personal knowledge of the position of teachers in New York City. Ms. Dunlap searched for photos and facts with electric enthusiasm for CCNY's history and a happy sharing in its display.

Ernie Hill typed the manuscript with enthusiasm, skill, good conversation, and a twinkle in his eye. Lisa Duggan did copy editing under crazy pressure skillfully and with reassurances. Anonymous reviewers for Rutgers University Press gave me excellent advice. Marlie Wasserman, editor for the Press, has been sympathetic and supportive. Leslie Mitchner, Joe Esposito, and Dariel Mayer at the Press combined a warm, patient, and collaborative spirit with sure knowledge of their craft. I am grateful to all of these people, and to many whom I do not know and may never meet, who taught me many things and helped in the emotional, intellectual, personal, and political process of developing this work.

City College
and the
Jewish Poor

Sweatshop, c. 1909–1914. *Lewis Hine/International Museum of Photography at George Eastman House*

1

Uneasy Questions on the Mobility Miracle

Around the world, wherever they went, the Jews of Eastern Europe became in large proportions businessmen. Too, wherever they went, they showed a fierce passion to have their children educated and become professionals.

—Nathan Glazer and
Daniel P. Moynihan,
Beyond the Melting Pot

The rise in socio-economic status of the Eastern European Jews and their descendants is, in fact, the greatest collective Horatio Alger story in American immigration history.

—Milton Gordon,
Assimilation in American Life

The truth about Jewish mobility is neither as simple nor as bland as most people believe. Many people believe that the Jews have made a remarkable success of themselves in the United States, rising from rags to riches because of their "passion" for education. The sojourn of the Jews in poverty was brief, people commonly believe, because of the opportunities America offered, and because Jewish culture uniquely prepared the Jews to take advantage of those opportunities. Most important in their culture was their traditional reverence for book learning.

As with most widely held beliefs, there is enough truth in this story to lead people to accept it. The children of Jewish immigrants did tend to go into non-manual occupations, although in the earlier generations their work was very far from the higher professions so often celebrated. The vast majority were still manual workers; some became businessmen, salesmen, or clerks; but a tiny proportion of this initial migration did go into professional work. Although the majority of Russian Jewish children, like most of the rest of the population at the turn of the century, dropped out of school at or before the legal school-leaving age, and less than 1 percent of Russian Jewish children entered college, these children, even in the earlier years, tended to stay in school slightly longer than other children. That trend increased in later generations. The present generation of Jews, one hundred years re-

moved from the first proletarian Jewish migration, is in fact dispropor-
tionately represented in the professions.

But this picture of the easy marriage of Jewish values and American
opportunities is oversimplified. It exaggerates the amount of mobility
in each generation without giving the meaning of mobility its measure.
It misrepresents the variety of Jewish culture, overestimates the opportunities, underestimates the struggle involved, and fails to explain
either the opportunities or the struggle. It takes as given just what
needs to be explained, and in so doing leaves out the drama of the vast
social processes that made Jewish social mobility possible.

Let us look more closely at this Horatio Alger tale, and then at some
inconvenient facts that beg us to rethink the story. The myth has two
main themes: American opportunities, and Jewish culture.

Nathan Glazer's comments are particularly relevant to the first
theme. Undoubtedly the foremost sociologist of ethnicity in the United
States, he argued in 1958 that the economic distribution of any
particular ethnic group would be determined by

> two factors . . . the character of the group at the time of its arrival,
> and the structure of economic opportunity in the country at the time
> of its arrival. . . . Between 1910 and 1950, the proportion of the
> population engaged in nonmanual work rose from 21 percent to 38
> percent. Certainly this offered great opportunity to the Jews. But
> one had to be of the proper social and psychological constitution to
> take advantage of it—which the Jewish immigrants were.[1]

Europe, people said, was fraught with discrimination and class
distinctions, but "America Is Different."[2] In New York City, where
the vast majority of poor Jews landed and lived, the City College
provided them with the opportunity to turn their passion for education
into "success." This was an oft-repeated claim, especially in the City
University controversies of the 1960s and 1970s. But a number of facts
just won't fit this picture.

When the first wave of Eastern European Jews began to arrive in the
United States in 1881, a migration of proletarians and peddlers,[3]
education was not a channel of social mobility. Most children were at
work in factories. When child labor and compulsory education laws
were finally passed, the New York City schools became so overcrowded that they turned children away, causing riots by parents.
There were no high schools in New York City, and few anywhere else.
Throughout the country, elementary schools did not teach the subjects
that colleges required for admission.

The College of the City of New York, now famed for its provision of educational opportunities to the poor, was then attended by the sons of the middle class. Only they could afford to undertake a course of study that was scarcely relevant to the world of work. The curriculum stressed Latin, Greek, and classical literature, with a smattering of more "modern" subjects. Only one out of every eleven entrants graduated. Most dropped out before graduation. Higher education all across the country was geared to giving cultural polish to men of independent means, men who would become lawyers, doctors, Christian ministers, or simply "cultivated gentlemen." Anyone seriously engaged in the accumulation of wealth generally scorned college.

City College had been created in 1847 as part of a movement to reform higher education by providing it with a curriculum that would prepare graduates for business-related occupations. But within one year the school developed a more traditional curriculum and began to imitate the older institutions. A classics-oriented faculty became entrenched and succeeded in curtailing educational innovation. The commercial course of study was abolished, and a pedagogy course was prevented. The requirements in Latin and Greek were expanded.

All through the nineteenth century, businessmen and educational reformers tried to transform the traditional college curriculum to make it more relevant to business. They tried to introduce modern, commercial languages like Spanish and French to replace Greek and Latin. They tried to introduce science, engineering, accounting, research. They had some success in the early nineteenth century but then ran aground. They were unable to budge the theologians, backed by religious congregations and wealthy cultural conservatives, bulwarks of the classical, Christian curriculum in U.S. colleges. As long as higher education remained leisure-class education, it could not serve as a channel of social mobility.

When the new Jewish immigrants first arrived in the 1880s, many of the occupations that their children would later enter did not yet exist. The institutions in which they were to study and work had not yet been created. The teaching profession was much smaller, both absolutely and in proportion to population, than it was to become. Educational administration was extremely simple and localized. Educational decision making was in the hands of community leaders or politicians, rather than salaried professionals. Social work, and its predecessor, social philanthropy, were yet to be developed. Accounting and bookkeeping involved relatively few people, and businesses were generally much smaller and less complex than in modern times.

Even law was not as important as it was to become with the battles of the great corporate giants.

In short, if the U.S. institutional structure had remained as it was when the Eastern European Jews arrived, the Jewish "passion for education" might have remained an unrequited love. Unlettered Jews might still have made their "success" in business, but the sons and daughters of the Jewish proletariat would have lived and died, as most children of the Jewish proletariat lived and died, as wage workers, peddlers, businessmen, salesmen, and a handful of clerks. But everything changed. It *had* to change. And Jewish immigrants were part of that change.

The second major theme in the mythical saga of Jewish mobility concerns Jewish culture. According to the saga, the Jews were able to seize the opportunities America offered because of their culture, which embodied "middle-class values" and a traditional love of learning. These values include "foresight, care, moderation . . . postponement of pleasure," and particularly a "strong emphasis on learning and study."[4]

> The Jews arrived in America with middle-class values already internalized. . . . It is these cultural values which account for the rapid rise of the Jewish group in occupational status and economic affluence. . . . The traditional stress and high evaluation placed upon Talmudic learning was easily transferred under new conditions to a desire for secular education.[5]

But when the Eastern Jews arrived higher education was generally not secular. It was Christian. Even at City College attendance at Chapel was mandatory until 1904. Once higher education was reformed, and the hold of theology over the curriculum was broken, the dominant content of secular social science came to be "scientific racism," in which the biological inferiority of the immigrants was "proven." These proofs were later attacked by environmentalists, who asserted that the inferiority of the immigrants was not biological: it was merely cultural. At the City College Jewish boys were taught that the immigrants were a social problem, that they "yield a disproportion of illiterates, diseased, insane, paupers and criminals," and "tend to embitter labor disputes."[6]

The transfer to secular learning cannot have been as easy as hanging up a prayer shawl and putting on academic robes. "One of the longest journeys in the world is the journey from Brooklyn to Manhattan," said Norman Podhoretz of his own cultural odyssey from the Jewish ghetto to acceptance in the literary world.[7] Whether Christian or secular, the culture of higher education was either hostile or irrelevant to Jewish immigrant culture.

Not only was the culture of higher education antithetical to immigrant culture; Jewish culture was itself undergoing enormous changes throughout the nineteenth century. Jews of Western Europe had begun to assimilate since the development of modern capitalism. In Eastern Europe movements directly antagonistic to traditional Jewish culture began: an "enlightenment" oriented to assimilation into Russian culture, Marxism, and a Jewish socialist labor movement.

Traditional Judaism, already weakened in Eastern Europe, was even more severely undermined when brought to North America. Factory work was not organized to honor Jewish holidays—even Jewish employers tried to lengthen Friday afternoon work into the Sabbath. Moreover, both the Jewish anarchists and the Jewish bourgeoisie were hostile to orthodoxy. The anarchists organized a Yom Kippur Ball; the liberals tried to close down the *hedarim* (see Glossary).

The German Jewish business class, long removed from traditional Jewish culture, was seeking cultural, social and economic assimilation into the North American business class. When they practiced a Jewish religion at all, it was Reform Judaism, which specifically repudiated orthodoxy. Religious orthodoxy, which embodies traditional culture, seemed to the German Jews to be "oriental," alien, and an embarrassment to American Jews. Although German Jews did express "middle-class values," love of learning was not one of them; they generally did not encourage their sons to go to college, preferring instead to have them join the family firm early. Dismayed by the culture of the Eastern European Jews, by both their traditional values and their socialism, the German Jews made great efforts to reform Jewish culture and remold it in more acceptable directions.

Socialism, favored by proletarianized Jewish immigrants, was a cultural passion which espoused neither traditional nor middle-class values. Jewish immigrants were active in the socialist movement, elected socialist candidates, formed socialist labor unions, and voted socialist long after the strength of the Socialist Party had waned among other groups. They created, on the Lower East Side, cultural institutions of their own. The Jewish labor movement and the predominance of Jews in the socialist movement were so important that the authors of major works on Jewish history find it hard to avoid mentioning them, but the role of socialism among the Jewish working class, and in the United States generally, tends to be discounted. Whether they remember Jewish socialism with a distant nostalgia, explain it away as an embarrassment of youth, or ignore it entirely, most scholars of Jewry have not seriously analyzed the importance of the socialist movement in the fate of the Jews.

But the socialist movement, and Jewish participation in it, were very important in Jewish mobility. The labor and socialist movements, in which Jews took part, created a social crisis. This social crisis led to the reform of educational institutions and the creation of new occupations which the children of immigrants then entered. Jewish mobility involved not merely cultural continuity; it involved social conflict and cultural change.

Myths and mystiques lead us into complacency. We become simpler than The Simple Son of the Passover Service: we become The One Who Wits Not to Ask.[8] In this book I raise questions that the mythology of Jewish mobility has kept us from asking.

- If there was great diversity in Jewish culture, why was the passion for education encouraged when other strivings were left unsatisfied? Why and how was Jewish culture channeled into the directions and forms that it took? What processes within the Jewish community, and what social and economic forces, reinforced and channeled education as an element within Jewish culture? How was the passion for education shaped?
- If there was a Jewish passion for education, why was it not disappointed? What conditions and what social changes were necessary for it to pay off? How did these changes come about? What was the role of the great social conflicts of the day, and what was the role of the Jewish immigrants themselves, in making Jewish mobility through education possible?
- What were the social forces that transformed occupations and shaped mobility? What was the role of the socialist and labor movements in that transformation?
- How much mobility was there through education? What exactly was the historical pattern of mobility, and what was the class distribution of Eastern European Jewish immigrants in the first five decades?
- How did the political, economic, and cultural conflicts of the turn of the century affect the culture of higher education? How did the culture of higher education affect the children of the Jewish working class? What, in short, was the psychological, political, and cultural meaning of Jewish mobility through education?

- How did the College of the City of New York come to serve as a vehicle for mobility? How did its transformation and its curriculum express the social forces of the time? How did the culture of City College reflect, and reflect on, the cultural environment of the Jewish ghetto?
- Finally, what are the implications of these conflicts, these experiences, and this apparent expansion of opportunity, for the present day?

A mystique has been created and recreated and retold and used against those ethnic groups who now attend or seek to attend the City University. A never-never land has been imagined in which docile Jews, living in safe slums, gratefully, respectfully, obediently lap up the gifts of Anglo-Saxon culture to the admiration and love of their teachers.[9] In this never-never land democratic and free institutions open gladly and bountifully to receive the hopes and passions of their eager entrants.

But this is not what happened. The Eastern Jews were not welcomed, and they were not docile. The mystique distorts Jewish culture, demeans the Eastern European Jews, and takes all the vitality out of the relationship between the Jews and education. The educational ladder that the Jews are said to have climbed was not there when the Eastern European Jews reached North America, and it was not created for them. The educational ladder and the occupational opportunities were created in part because of the Eastern Jews, but only by suppressing much of their culture and reshaping the rest. In large part the ladder and the opportunities were created in spite of them, in spite of what they wanted and created for themselves.

Part I

Social Conflict and
Jewish Mobility

Library of the Educational Alliance c. 1898. *Picture Collection, The Branch Libraries, The New York Public Library*

2

Remolding Jewish Culture

As compared to other groups a folk community has a greater consciousness of its identity and individuality, its historical experience, it is more integrated endogamous. . . . Jews differ from non-Jews in that Jews are more conscious of their mutual needs and more integrated about their group value system.

—S. Joseph Fauman[1]

"In the first revulsion," remarked Oscar Handlin, "it was hard to tell which was worse, the long-haired anarchist or the side-locked Chasidic rabbi."[2] The U.S. Jews of German extraction who looked with such refined contempt upon their East European coreligionists were neither anarchists nor Hasidim; they spoke no Yiddish, worshiped at Reform temples, and were regarded by the Orthodox as un-Jewish. The German Jews had not been unified among themselves, not even in the realm of religion.[3] Facing an influx of thousands of Jewish refugees from the Russian pogroms, the German Jews panicked. "The thoroughly acclimated American Jew," said *The Hebrew Standard* in June 1894, ". . .has no religious, social or intellectual sympathies with [the 'oriental' Jews]. He is closer to the Christian sentiment around him than to the Judaism of these miserable darkened Hebrews."[4]

As for the Eastern European Jews themselves, far from being the simple bearers of a unitary, integrated value system—a *shtetl* transplanted—they were the products of over a century of cultural conflict and cultural change. These cultural changes and these cultural conflicts between German and Eastern European Jews challenge the standard sociological belief that the Jews have been upwardly mobile because of their integrated and unchanging middle-class values.

The Jewish Passions

The Jews of Eastern Europe fought with each other about education, equality, privilege, price, and power. The Hasidic movement of the late eighteenth century was a revolt by impoverished Jewish workers

13

against education—against the "arid" Talmudic tradition, middle-class values, and the merchant class which used Talmudic scholarship as its aristocratic emblem. Hasidism expressed "contempt for mere study and Talmudic erudition" and emphasized instead ecstatic worship in which "the prayers of the poor and illiterate were of enduring value too, . . . if they were deeply felt and sincerely expressed."[5] The Hasidic movement advocated social equality and struggle against collaboration by wealthy Jews with czarist oppression.[6]

In the early nineteenth century the society of tailors of Kaidan, Lithuania, staged a revolt in favor of equality.

> On the first day of Rosh Hashanah . . . a tailor entered the synagogue with a satin skull cap under his hat, just like the important people wore.
>
> Immediately after the holidays the *Kahal* (the assembly) held a meeting and decided to punish the impudent tailor with a levy of ten pounds of candles for the synagogue. However, the entire "mob" took the side of the tailor and the first day of Succoth all the artisans came to the synagogue dressed from head to foot like the aristocrats. The latter were outraged at seeing this flaunting [sic] of propriety. They complained secretly to Count Chopsky, the squire of the town. He sent twenty of his retainers to publicly flog the audacious artisans. *Kahal* was taken to court, and after several years of litigation peace was concluded. The "mob" forgave the flogging and the *Kahal* granted the common people equality in clothing.[7]

Poor Jews resented not only the social snobbery and elitism of the wealthy, but also the discriminatory way in which the *Kehillah* (the corporate government of the Jews under the control of the czar) distributed the tax burden, set artisans' prices, and administered the czar's twenty-five year military service. Prices and taxes were set to benefit the merchants who ran the *Kehillah;* merchants' children went free while sons of the poor were drafted.

The wealthy used their military recruitment power to secure privileged sanctuary for their own families, and they also wielded it on behalf of their class interests as merchants, threatening with military service those artisans who protested the regulated price. Folk songs bitterly protested that

> Children are snatched from the schools
> And forced into soldiers' apparel
> With the aid of the rich and "respected"

. . . .

But the scurvy . . . aristocrats
They . . . must never be soldiers.[8]

Reflecting on these antagonisms and diverse cultural movements, Bernard Weinryb concluded that "an attempt to reconstruct the culture of the *shtetl* as an integral unity . . . can at best be regarded as a gross oversimplification."[9] How much more unlikely, then, is the attempt to project this supposed integrated value system beyond the *shtetl*, beyond Eastern Europe, beyond two millennia of Jewish history.[10] Jewish culture was far more complex than the few ethereal, changeless values which now bear the heavy burden of explaining the rise of the Jewish professor and the decline of the Jewish proletariat.

CULTURAL CONFLICT AND SOCIAL CHANGE IN EASTERN EUROPE

With the development of industrialization the conflicts between Jewish merchants and artisans took on the forms characteristic of the conflict between industrial capitalists and wage workers. Until then the Jews had continued their medieval occupations as merchants, petty traders, moneylenders, factors (of agricultural products), artisans, and stewards. It was the preservation of traditional Jewish functions under Russian feudalism that had kept Jewish orthodoxy from becoming assimilated into the "Western enlightenment," which the German Jews had undergone with their integration into Western European industrial capitalism.[11]

When defeat in the Crimean War shocked the czar into sponsoring limited industrialization, however, a small section of the Jews became industrialists. Based primarily in textiles and shoe and garment manufacturing, they were also engaged in smelting, brewing beer, and the processing or manufacture of tobacco, lumber, hides, soap, brick and tiles.[12] The Jewish working class, comprising factory workers, skilled and unskilled laborers, and artisans, began to organize a classical workers' movement.[13] Those universities fostering the "enlightenment" were partially opened to the children of that small Jewish industrial capitalist class, and the members of that class started to seek integration into Russian society.

But with discrimination thwarting the full integration of the Russified Jewish intellectuals into Russian society, many of these intellectuals turned toward the Jewish masses. "Traditional Judaism [faced] the challenge of such movements as the Haskalah [enlightenment], political Zionism, and Marxist socialism."[14] Those intellectuals who fostered the Haskalah believed that the famed "rules of reason" would create the brotherhood of Christian and Jew, if only "the old traditional folkways of the ghetto . . . and general secular ignorance" were abolished.[15] That is, they launched an explicit attack on Jewish tradition in the name of liberalism.

Some of the enlighteners became Marxists, and sought the integration of the Jews into a reconstructed Russian society. Many of the intellectuals, however, "forged an alliance with the Jewish masses to create specifically *Jewish* political movements,"[16] notably Russian Zionism and the Bund (The General Workers Union [Bund] in Russia, Poland and Lithuania). Founded in 1897 as a socialist organization with a Jewish national program dedicated to a "Russian state of the future, based on socialist principles [which] would guarantee to all nationalities, including the Jews, the right to maintain their national life through the creation of national cultural institutions," the Bund became an important force in the Jewish labor movement.[17]

But capitalism and feudalism were no more able to coexist peacefully in Russia than they had been able to share the same state in Western Europe in the earlier centuries. Beginning in the 1880s, feudal reaction sparked Russia's attempt to expunge capitalist reforms. Waves of worker and peasant unrest, channeled by czar and church into anti-Jewish riots, provoked the flight of four million Hasidim, Talmudists, enlighteners, assimilationist Marxists, Bundists, liberal Zionists, traditionalists, industrialists, wage workers, and petty traders.[18]

AMERICAN CONDITIONS AND JEWISH CULTURAL CONTINUITY

If Eastern European Jewish culture was neither integrated nor unchanging, neither did the divergent and mutually hostile cultural expressions migrate to the United States without changing. On the contrary, American conditions selectively reinforced certain characteristics and cultural tendencies and discouraged others.

Conditions in the United States generally did not favor orthodoxy. Religious men wrote home telling their *landsmen* not to come to "this *trefe* [impure] land." Certainly the tendency of even Jewish employers to lengthen Friday night work gradually until it extended beyond the hour of the beginning of Sabbath did not encourage piety. Herbert Gutman sees the threat to Jewish religious rhythms as part of the more general effort of capitalists to break down artisan (and peasant) habits and traditions in the interest of factory discipline and maximal productivity.[19] But orthodoxy held on, especially among those Jews who, as small shopkeepers or peddlers, could maintain the more traditional patterns in the framework of the more traditional pursuits.

"Whatever the proportions of the religious and radical elements among the immigrants to begin with," Nathan Glazer remarks, "there is no question that the impact of America (as indeed of the large cities of Eastern Europe) was to reduce the number of the Orthodox and increase the number of the radical."[20] Among the factors which worked *against* the maintenance of the Jewish socialist tradition were the possibilities for small trading and for contracting, and eventually for clerkship and educated pursuits. The wage differential between the "labor-short" United States and relatively populous Europe also played a role in stifling socialism, both in the United States and in Europe, where migration to the United States was seen as an escape from economic oppression.[21] Among the conditions that *reinforced* the Jewish labor movement and Jewish socialism were the conditions of work and life in sweatshop and ghetto, and the intense and increasing class conflict between the general American labor movement and the corporate class. For both labor and capital organized on a nationwide basis at the end of the nineteenth century, and the conflict between them was bloody, vicious, and far-reaching in its implications.

The dates of the great Jewish proletarian migration were also the dates of virtual insurgency in the labor movement, of the Haymarket Affair and the Homestead strike, of the rapid expansion and demise of the Knights of Labor, of the formation of the first lasting American labor unions, and of the organization of the Socialist Party. Even before the great migration these upheavals sent their ripples back to Russia, where the Hebrew socialist magazine discussed the American railroad strike of 1877, and to the Jewish working-class colony in London, where Morris Winchevksy, "the Father of Yiddish Literature," wrote the poem "Listen, Children, Something is Stirring" in response to the Haymarket Affair.[22]

In the United States the Eastern Jewish immigrants, both those who had been wage workers in Russia and those newly proletarianized on arrival, found themselves working sixteen to eighteen hours a day in dangerous sweatshops, and receiving, after an unpaid apprenticeship, five dollars per week from employers who overworked them in the heavy season and then laid them off in the slack season. The workers responded with work stoppages, meat riots, union organizing, and support for the socialist movement.

Meanwhile, the German Jewish *haute bourgeoisie* was busy floating bond issues in Germany, buying and selling railroad stock, attending the new Temple Emanu-El, forming the Ethical Culture Society and the Harmonie Club, and beginning to create a conception of its role as the leadership of the Jewish community. Thus Jewish culture at the turn of the century continued to be fundamentally divided by class. When the German Jewish bourgeoisie did begin to take the role of leaders of the Jewish community, they directed much of their efforts at remolding these hostile Jewish cultures into a single, more acceptable, unitary form under their own general leadership. Two relatively recent historical works, Moses Rischin's *The Promised City*, and Arthur Goren's *New York Jews and the Quest for Community*, have examined the effort of that German Jewish capitalist class to create a unified community which, contrary to the whole body of popular mythology and scholarly canon, simply did not exist at the turn of the century.[23]

By the 1950s, when the major works in the sociological literature on Jewish success were being written, the socialist component of Jewish culture received scarcely any emphasis, the decline of Yiddish and traditional Jewish values was beginning to be lamented, and reverence for education had become almost the defining characteristic of Jewish culture. Although these works reflect the social milieu of the period in which they were written, they also reflect a real change which had taken place in the content of the culture of most American Jews. The central question of this chapter is: What processes within the Jewish community, and what social and economic forces, reinforced and channeled education as an element within Jewish culture? In examining that cultural transformation this study will describe the process by which some of those in the Jewish business class became leaders of the Jewish community and forged education into an assimilative device to destroy both Orthodox traditionalism and socialism.

Institutions Created by the Eastern Jews

Culture is more than an idea system or an inventory of values. It involves a total and active pattern of responses to a total and often changing life situation. Culture involves habit, knowledge, personal connections, patterns of trust, advice, and conceptions of alternative courses of action when customary patterns are thwarted.

When customary courses of action fail to fit new circumstances, people generally perceive only a limited set of the possible alternative paths; that set is determined by culture in the form of limited knowledge, conceptions of propriety, and patterns of advice and influence. Even the latter are not purely normative, involving also knowledge, conceptions of cause and probable effect, and concrete practical aid. Each of these elements of culture influences the ways in which immigrants respond to the concrete circumstances they find; thus each of them—or rather all of them in interaction—influences the economic role of immigrants in a new country.[24]

Let us look somewhat more closely at the institutions that the Eastern Jewish immigrants created to express, reinforce, protect and modify two of the cultural strains of Eastern European Jewish culture— religious orthodoxy and socialism.[25] Each of these antagonistic Jewish cultural tendencies had its own version of the "passion for education," but the content, form, purpose, and meaning of "education" was quite different for each of them, and the institutions they initially established differed accordingly.

ORTHODOXY

As the religion of the *shtetl*, Eastern Jewish orthodoxy was a religion of traders, peddlers, and artisans living in small villages within an agricultural economy. Eastern Jews in New York City could no longer peddle to the peasants, but many of them did resume peddling, supplying small goods to the new proletariat. Even those who went to work in factories would be thrown back periodically into peddling as a result of the seasonal nature of the needle trades. Residing (for numerous reasons) in an ethnic enclave further reinforced traditional practices, as did the sense that they were in a hostile environment, a fact made most manifest in the hostility, contempt, and foreignness of the German Jewish "relief" agencies. But for the early Eastern European Jewish immigrants there were few institutions in which religious orthodoxy could be either expressed or transmitted to the next generation.

Those who had come from communities where "religious tradition interpenetrated every aspect of life"[26] found that everyday life in the United States was antagonistic to religious observance. The U.S. work week, pressing on for more and more production faster and faster, would not pause for traditional festivals, whether they were Slavic saints' days or Jewish celebrations for the birth of a son.[27] Sunday was the American Sabbath, if the work week paused for Sabbath at all, making Orthodox Jewish workers more dependent on Jewish-owned shops, or giving them added incentive to try to work for themselves.

For Saturday observers, the garment industry had the advantage of Jewish ownership, but the disadvantage of seasonal work, which pressed even pious bosses to steal minutes from the sacred Sabbath for profane profit. And the normal rhythms of life—which in Italy, Poland, and the Russian Pale had regulated and paced work and play, ritual and prayer—were broken by the lengthening, exhausting, all-consuming workday. The sweatshop overtook the *shtetl*, and the Eastern European Jewish workers had neither time nor money nor energy for the establishment of Orthodox educational institutions.

Thus although orthodoxy did keep a hold on many proletarianized Jews, it is not surprising that the more traditional Jewish occupations in trade and commerce were more conducive to the maintenance of traditional religious forms. The foundation of Yeshivat Etz Chaim in 1886 corroborates the point: its incorporators were a clothing dealer, a real estate dealer, an unpaid rabbi who supported himself by "customer peddling," another peddler, and several tailors.[28]

Despite the unpromising circumstances, the poverty of the Eastern Jews, and the hostility of the wealthy Jews, five "communally sponsored schools . . . for . . . Eastern European Jews" subsisted on the Lower East Side at the end of the nineteenth century, in addition to innumerable private schools of varying quality and even more numerous "itinerant *malamdim*" (religious tutors). Unlike the Machzikei Talmud Torah, an afternoon religious school designed merely to supplement public secular education, Etz Chaim was an all-day parochial school, reflecting the founders' "deep sense of alarm at the specter of 'secular' education which possessed a siren-like attraction for the young immigrants who strove desperately to learn the language and culture of the United States in order to become acceptable Americans."[29]

Day schools like Etz Chaim represented both continuity and adaptation—an effort to preserve a cultural world under consciously perceived new conditions, and an attempt to ward off alien influences by grudgingly incorporating, and perhaps encapsulating, them. They taught English, but stinted on the English department's budget. The English instructor was subject to suspicion, and the religious community rejoiced that, at the public examinations, one could "forget that we are on American soil." Yet a generation later several parents expressed pleasure that in addition to their comprehensive learning of the Torah, their children had "completed the public school curriculum in a short time and entered City College."[30]

Even before Americanization became a virtually obsessive goal of public education, the public educational system both reinforced and undermined orthodoxy. The Public School Society controversy of the 1840s—in which public funds were denied to schools run by the Hebrew Congregation, the Scotch Presbyterian Church, and the Roman Catholic Church—had resulted in the collapse of private schooling for Jewish children and in the sanctification of a subtly Christian and anti-Catholic secular schooling. Although this secular schooling was sufficiently foreign to constitute additional motivation to the newly arrived Orthodox parents for the support of private *hedarim,* it was certainly more secular than the Russian or Polish *gymnasium* had been,[31] and it was sufficiently nonsectarian to attract immigrant youngsters.

Moreover, public schooling increasingly reached into the *hedarim.* The New York compulsory education law of 1904 "imposed conditions and specified a secular curriculum that the traditional *heder,* which devoted full time to the sacred language, could not meet.[32] Nevertheless Orthodox schooling of various forms expanded gradually; in 1917, when Alexander Dushkin conducted his study of *Jewish Education in New York City,* there were 182 schools of various religious leanings serving 65,400 children.[33] This was part of the "oriental threat" which prompted the German Jewish business class first to attempt to supplant these *hedarim,* through the Educational Alliance, and later, through the *Kehillah,* to attempt to revive them in new forms mirroring Progressive educational ideas.

In addition to religious institutions and religious educational institutions, the Orthodox Jews formed self-help agencies as alternatives to the paternalistic, grudging, and often interfering charitable efforts of the German Jews. *Landtsmanschaften* were the characteristic form.[34] These too were part of the "oriental threat." "In the eyes of many German Jews," Goren reports, "the immigrant [welfare] agencies were ineffectual and even harmful." Said Louis Marshall, one of the German Jewish leaders most hostile to the Eastern Jewish efforts, "What we need is an organization to suppress unnecessary organizations."[35]

SOCIALISM AND THE LABOR COMMUNITY

While Orthodox Jews were attempting to reconstruct and preserve a traditional culture, the Jewish labor movement was creating a new one. Between 1880 and 1889, during the first nine years of substantial Russian Jewish presence in America, small unions appeared and disappeared in the predominantly Jewish trades of cloakmakers and dressmakers, men's tailors, ladies' garment workers, Jewish actors, typesetters, tinsmiths, and bookbinders. The United Hebrew Trades was organized under socialist auspices in 1888. Men's tailors staged a successful strike in 1884, and the cloakmakers brought the entire industry to a standstill in 1885.[36] Isaac Hourwich, refuting the Immigration Commission's charge that Eastern and Southern European immigrants impeded the organization of labor, pointed out that "the highest per cent of employees joining in strikes in 1887–1905 was found among clothing workers," who were predominantly Jewish with a substantial minority of Italian workers. "The percentage of thoroughly successful strikes of clothing workers for the period 1881–1905 was much above average."[37]

The Arbeiter Ring (Workmen's Circle), a mutual aid society organized in 1892 by rank-and-file workers, provided social services in a leftist ethnic atmosphere, combining social insurance, burial benefits, and social and cultural activities with support for striking workers and even for revolutionary activities in Russia.[38]

Jewish immigrants were also active in the socialist movement. They succeeded in electing Meyer London to Congress, and several other socialists to the New York State Assembly and to other local offices. The Jewish working-class electoral wards were the ones in which socialists scored electoral victories or at least received their highest votes; several of the Jewish unions were affiliated with the New York Socialist Party, and the Yiddish newspaper with the greatest readership was a socialist paper, the *Jewish Daily Forward.*

Oscar Handlin, Moses Rischin, and some other authors deride Jewish socialism as an infantile disorder from which Jews matured into Gomperism. Werner Cohn sees Jewish radicalism as no more than a complex result of anti-Semitism.[39] Handlin goes so far as to deny that Jews were ever interested in politics, "although occasionally a popular figure like Meyer London, through active communal service, built up a following of his own on the East Side of New York."[40] Handlin does not mention that London was a socialist or that he was one of two socialists elected to Congress, the other being Milwaukee's Victor Berger, also a Jew. Daniel Bell has gone one step further, denying that socialism was ever a workers' movement in America.[41] Bell's thesis has been explicitly and empirically refuted, however, by Melvyn Dubovsky in "Success and Failure of Socialism in New York City." Dubovsky marshals historical data, including detailed analyses of electoral returns, personal interviews, and archival materials, to show that Bell is incorrect, at least as far as New York Jews were concerned. Among New York Jews the Socialist Party had a mass, working-class base and strong links to the labor movement.

That the Jewish masses were oriented toward socialism may be gathered as well from the fact that the *Forward* had the largest circulation of the "dozen or so" Yiddish newspapers in New York, even though politically conservative and Orthodox papers were available to them. Handlin points out that

> the business of publishing a newspaper in these particular years grew increasingly expensive, and none could survive without a substantial circulation. . . . The widespread development of the weeklies revealed which attractions in the papers really induced the immigrants to part with their precious pennies for this new luxury. Not news for its own sake but the point of view of the newspaper was important.[42]

But he craftily avoids applying this insight to the popularity of the *Forward* and instead uses literary license to imply that its readership was conservative.

To their credit, Nathan Glazer and Howard Morley Sachar are among the authors who do not exhibit a similar need to deny the reality or importance of socialism among Jewish workers. "By 1910," wrote Sachar, "the American Socialist Party had solid anchorage in the East Side of New York, especially in the predominantly Jewish Twelfth Congressional District."[43] By now Irving Howe's *World of Our Fathers* and Nora Levin's *While Messiah Tarried* should be sufficient to convince all but the most die-hard liberal ideologues of the importance of socialism among Eastern European Jews. Howe correctly derides the efforts of "later sentimentalists" to transform bitter class conflicts into common communal spirit and to "dissolve the Jewish radical experience in the acids of retrospection."[44]

At first the Jewish socialists were preoccupied with the Russian revolutionary movement and had difficulty adapting to North American realities. There were numerous splits; the anarchists and socialists fought bitterly. Jewish workers generally showed the same tendency as American workers—to wage militant strikes but abandon unions as soon as the strikes were won. Many bitterly fought strikes were lost. But beginning in 1909 a series of well-organized strikes, sparked by young women in the shirtwaist industry followed by male cloakmakers and bakers, galvanized the Lower East Side and forced German Jewry to take notice. "By 1910 one could speak of a Jewish working class, structured, disciplined, self-conscious, and with a much stronger tie to socialist politics than characterized the American workers," says Irving Howe. "By 1910 the Jewish socialists had begun to deepen their roots in the East Side, breaking out of their earlier sectarianism and approaching the condition—as well as the problems—of a mass movement."[45] Although socialists were a minority, they cast an influence far beyond their own membership.

Even more than in Europe, the Jewish labor movement in America fostered a Yiddish cultural flowering: labor poetry, short stories, the famed Yiddish theatre, and translations of literary classics and of works in the social and natural sciences. The Yiddish press, Epstein points out, "combined the functions of a journal of opinion, a literary magazine and a people's college," and he notes that "for many years the *Forward* carried in its Sunday edition an educational supplement called People's College."[46] Abraham Cahan translated Karl Marx in the *Arbeiter Zeitung*. The Arbeiter Ring sponsored semimonthly educational meetings, including lectures on Darwinism.

In addition to educational and cultural activities in the newspapers and theatre, the labor community sponsored various forms of lectures and Marx study circles. Numerous educational societies and clubs were formed through which working-class Jews could teach themselves not only Marxism but also American history and English literature. The Lower East Side was intellectually and politically aflame:

> The younger [immigrants], for the most part socially-conscious and enthusiastic, embraced the new radical beliefs with the same passion as their fathers had the Torah. They formed the advanced guard of socialism and anarchism. They filled the lecture halls and propaganda meetings, and were the core of the numerous educational societies, clubs and dramatic groups. The long hours of hard labor did not prevent them from attending dances and balls given by the movement. And in spite of economic insecurity, their lives were full of excitement.[47]

The intellectual passion, the educational vitality, of the Lower East Side was proletarian and socialist.

These social and cultural activities of the Jewish labor movement were linked to strike activities which extended from the 1880s and 1890s through the Great Upheaval of 1908–1910 (moving on despite the protocol of labor peace and the setbacks and stalemates common to all social movements) through the 1920s and 1930s. They provided strong motivation for the reform activities of the German Jewish business class.

The Impact of the Jewish Bourgeoisie

At first the German Jewish business class extended charity and aid to the victims of the 1881 Russian pogroms, but as the flow of refugees continued, they generally became alarmed. In November 1881, the New York Jewish leadership complained to Jewish charities in Europe:

> You were to send us the strong and able bodies, willing to work and possessing a knowledge of some handicraft. . . . Fully one-third of those who have arrived thus far possess none of the requisite qualifications . . . not over one-third are really desirable emigrants. . . . [Many] are too old to learn any trade and not a few of them are burdened with large families. . . . Our charities [are considering] a proposition to refuse relief to persons who have not been at least two years in this country. . . . It has also been proposed by many, to take means to return to Europe all those who are paupers or likely to become such.[48]

They tried to pay the refugees to return to Russia, where the pogroms were continuing. They tried to send them to England, or even to Palestine, which—considering their own hostility to Zionism at the time—shows the desperation with which they sought to deflect their "coreligionists" from joining them in a " folk community" on North American shores.[49] In 1887, E. Kleinsmith, superintendent of the Young Men's Branch of the United Hebrew Charities of Philadelphia, complained to the U.S. secretaries of the Interior and Treasury that immigrants were entering illegally, and he tried to uncover the entry point of "these [undetected] paupers."[50]

The general response of the German Jewish bourgeoisie to the Eastern immigrants is often understood as snobbery, a snobbery intensified by embarrassment and a sense of threat. A deeper understanding may be obtained, however, by examining more closely the class position of the German Jewish bourgeoisie.

German Jewish businessmen varied from corner peddlers to garment factory owners, from petty contractors to meat syndicate owners, from department store families to stock speculators. But only a small, fairly well-defined group among them played a major role in philanthropy, institution building, and community leadership. At its core this group, linked by marriage, social ties, and business, was centered around the investment banking families such as the Seligmans, Schiffs, Speyers, Lehmans, and a few mercantile families such as Filene and Straus. Other nonbusinessmen such as Brandeis, Marshall, and Magnes were associated with them in policymaking and social life.[51]

As a group of finance and commercial capitalists they sought integration into the American business class. And although total social integration was denied them, they were quite influential, not only economically but also politically. Because of their links with German Jewish banking families in Germany, England, and France they were able "to benefit from the advanced [banking] practices across the Atlantic . . . [and] to profit from the contemporary need to import capital from Europe.[52] They floated government bonds after the Civil War, promoted railroads, served in diplomatic posts, particularly in Turkey, and arranged for the stock sales by means of which the major industrial capitalist families incorporated and "went public."

Jacob Schiff loomed at least as large in the Jewish community as did Andrew Carnegie nationally. He invested in and sat on the boards of directors of several major railroads in the United States, Canada and Mexico; floated loans to the government of Japan; assisted Edward Harriman in the struggle with James Hill (who was backed by no less a financial behemoth than J. P. Morgan himself) over control of the Northern Pacific railroad; sat on the boards of ATT and Western Union; invested in the New York subways; and extended loans to China. He also sat on the board of Governor Levi P. Morton's bank; was on close personal terms with the Japanese Minister of Finance; communicated with American generals on the military situation in China; and floated loans in Santo Domingo on condition that the Dominican legislature pass legislation permitting the U.S. government to take over its customs operation. He was used to thinking in systemic terms—communicating with President Cleveland on the gold reserve and on the "strengthening" of the currency system, and promoting the creation of the Federal Reserve System. His son-in-law and partner, Paul Warburg, became the Federal Reserve Bank's first governor.[53]

The German Jewish bourgeoisie maintained strong cultural links to Germany. They spoke German among themselves, vacationed there, and sent their children to be educated there, but they were highly imitative of the American bourgeoisie. They lived an upper-class life which faithfully mirrored the WASP upper class; they created a Jewish version of the settlement movement and a Jewish version of Progressivism. In the United States, as in Germany, they created, in their

Reform temples, "the social atmosphere . . . of a Protestant church of the upper and upper middle classes."[54] Some, like Schiff, were deeply devoted to Reform Judaism; others moved further away, to Unitarianism or Ethical Culture. The German Jewish leadership were not only hostile to the impoverished Orthodox Jews; they were hostile to Jewish orthodoxy. Although their rejection from white Protestant upper-class resorts reinforced their development as a somewhat separate sociocultural grouping, the very process of Americanizing the Eastern European Jews led them further to Americanize themselves.

But the German Jewish bourgeoisie were not merely imitative, they were also creative. Some of them were members of the National Civic Federation, the most important national organization of the Progressive movement. Formed in 1901 (the same year as the Socialist Party) to deal with the threats of socialism, populism, and labor militancy, the Federation sought to oppose business conservatism, to regularize labor relations by incorporating "respectable" (nonradical) labor leaders, and to promote a wide range of business-oriented social reforms. There, in conjunction with Andrew Carnegie, partners of J. P. Morgan, the heads of many of the largest corporations, Samuel Gompers, a few other labor leaders, and prominent academics, Jacob Schiff, Isaac Seligman, Oscar Straus, Louis Marshall, and Louis Brandeis helped develop the policies of co-optation which they had applied in (and later further adapted to) the Jewish ghetto. In creating the Hebrew Educational Alliance they were not merely imitating the Protestant settlement movement; they also provided many innovations which were later adopted nationally by the settlement movement and, through the settlement movement, by the public schools. They were architects of Progressivism in the nation and in the Jewish community.

Progressivism united social critics, muckrakers, academics, sundry radical reformers, and business liberals. From the point of view of the corporate liberals, the essence of Progressivism was the attempt to capture the forces of reaction, reform, and revolution, ride them, control them, and redirect them to businessmen's purposes, or, failing that, to deflect them from harming corporate interests. At the very least, by selectively extending legitimacy to some social movements and not to others, Progressives would render harmless the most severe challenges to the capitalist system while promoting those changes they needed in the new industrial society. Against radicalism and reaction they offered concessions, cooperation. and co-optation. They promoted "social harmony," with corporate leaders calling the tune.

Progressivism meant both the modernization of cultural and social forms which belonged to an earlier way of life, and the restraining of social and cultural forms reaching toward a new, more equal society. In a period of political, economic, and cultural ferment, Progressives strove to take into their custody both the past and the future.[55]

The Progressives remolded Jewish culture in the form of their philanthropy. Under traditional Jewish law and practice, charity, or *zedakah*, was part of the religiously mandated social obligation of every observant Jew. Optimally the donor should not know the identity of the recipient and the recipient should not know the identity of the donor. Such a conception of charity, however, precludes using philanthropy to control or influence the behavior of the poor. Consequently the German Jewish bourgeoisie generally adapted *zedakah* into philanthropy based on Andrew Carnegie's concept of the "stewardship of wealth."

Unlike *zedakah*, the stewardship of wealth presumes that the recipients must prove their worthiness to receive; in fact they must modify their behavior in ways deemed suitable by the donor. The stewardship of wealth insists that the control of wealth must remain in the ultimate hands of the wealthy; philanthropy must serve the purposes set by the wealthy. Thus, unlike *zedakah*, the stewardship of wealth was an instrument of social control. Here was the essence of Progressivism: controlled reform.[56]

In the Educational Alliance, the Breadwinners' College, and the New York *Kehillah* we see the interactive process by which the German Jewish bourgeoisie sought to reform Eastern Jewish culture. This process involved a cultural struggle in which the Eastern European Jews themselves changed these institutions of reform.

The Educational Alliance

The first social settlements in New York were Stanton Coit's in 1866 and the College Settlement in 1889, but in June 1889 a group of German Jews including Jacob Schiff, Isaac Seligman, and Isidor Straus began raising funds for a building for the Hebrew Educational Alliance on the Lower East Side. The organization was to be a merger of three organizations already in operation: the Hebrew Free School Association, the Aguilar Free Library, and the Young Men's Hebrew Association, which Oscar Straus had helped found in 1874 as "a copy of the Christian organization."[57]

The organization's 1893 constitution stated that its "scope . . . shall be of an Americanizing, educational, social, and humanizing character." The nature of the humanizing might be glimpsed from the comments of an "uptowner" in the *Jewish Messenger:* "They [the immigrants] must be Americanized in spite of themselves, in the mode to be prescribed by their friends and benefactors."[58]

Opening its doors in 1892, the same year as the founding of the Arbeiter Ring, the Hebrew Educational Alliance's program included the Free Library, reading and social rooms, lectures, entertainment, gymnasium, manual training instruction, "classes in American History, Civics, English Literature, Composition, Music, . . . Stenography, Biology . . . Applied Science," and sewing and other industrial work for girls.[59]

The goals of the founders of the Educational Alliance may be learned from the December 1, 1889 lecture of the Reverend Dr. J. Silverman at Temple Emanu-El, the religious organization founded, supported, and attended by the German Jewish bourgeoisie. Hence Rabbi Silverman's remarks were directed at the very group that was expected to support the Educational Alliance.[60]

The rabbi complained that the very existence of a large, noticeable Jewish population was "inconsiderate," "objectionable," and "a standing menace" to all Jews because it fostered anti-Semitism. The advertising signs in Hebrew letters, the Hebrew jargon (Yiddish), "those loud ways and awkward gesticulations are naturally repulsive and repugnant to the refined American sensibilities." A Jewish quarter with a population of 100,000 immigrants "in all stages and phases of civilization, largely tainted with Orientalism," generated four evils in addition to the immigrants' "clannishness and bigotry." The "*communal evil*," crowding, caused suffering, misery, disease, and poverty, some of which the immigrants had "brought with them." The second evil, "*the workingmen*," bred ill-feeling by crowding others out of work. Moreover the workers were "forced to join labor unions," becoming, "against their own inclinations, embroiled in the strife between labor and capital. The third evil is the *Socialist* [who] delights in creating dissension," and the fourth, the "*political*," was the tendency of political parties to cater to a distinctively Jewish vote.[61]

Silverman proposed an Americanization program:

[A] natural process of assimilation . . . will perhaps never take place, for . . . the jargon press, theatres and operas, the jargon homes and schools . . . tend to stifle every growth of Americanism and encourage the generation of Orientalism. We need strong forces to counteract these influences: our own schools, libraries and societies,

founded in those localities by men and women who have the true
interests of Judaism and Americanism at heart . . . . An American
education is the weapon with which to fight Orientalism. Let every
immigrant know how to read and write the English language and he
will not need the jargon press, the jargon theatres and the advertising signs in Hebrew letters. Let every immigrant learn to appreciate
American habits and tastes and he will soon discard the queer skull
cap, and the outlandish long-skirted kaftan of the Russian Jew. Let
him learn American history and the true spirit of American political
institutions and he will not be attracted by every political scheme to
wrest him from his vote.

The Hebrew Educational Alliance was to accomplish this transformation. Rabbi Silverman urged his listeners to contribute to a Hebrew
educational fair which was to raise the money needed "to build the
Educational Fortress where will be stationed the garrison of teachers
who are to make war upon ghetto-life." That the rabbi's pious wishes
expressed a bourgeois class's need for what Berger calls *class rap-
prochement* becomes clear from Silverman's vision of the future role
of the Jewish middle class as the professional Americanizers, the
Americanizers par excellence:

> And let us now, for a moment, indulge in a glance into the future,
> into the promised land itself. The Jewish quarter is gone. The
> Hebrew Institute, under the management of the Hebrew Educational
> Alliance, fulfilled its mission. It becomes in time a national institute,
> supported by the Government, and serves, in turn, to break up also
> the Irish, the German, the Italian and Chinese quarters. It becomes
> in foreign lands the American Institute for emigrants. Whoever
> wants to go to America, in whatever country he is, has first to under-
> go a course of study in that American Institute for emigrants. . . .
> The Immigrant Question is solved. No more paupers, idiots, or
> criminals, no more fools or adventurers, no more deluded immi-
> grants and self-seeking social reformers and anarchists, no more
> strikes and boycotts, no more strife between capital and labor.[62]

Americanization was inherently political, intimately involved with
"the strife between capital and labor," deeply concerned with "reformers and anarchists" and with influencing the immigrants' votes.

Rabbi Silverman's contempt for "self-seeking social reformers"
reveals the co-optative nature of the Alliance's efforts. Despite the

reputed American ideology of self-help and self-reliance, self-help and self-seeking social reform can be potentially dangerous to a social order. It is more orderly, and safer politically, to have "helpless paupers" than paupers who define how they might help themselves.[63] Nicholas Murray Butler believed in social reform "as long as 'the better sort' led the way."[64] Andrew Carnegie (as we shall see in Chapter 3) considered intricately orchestrated philanthropy preferable to both the redistribution of wealth through higher wages and simple charity. Carnegie opposed unguided charity on the grounds that the undeserving and profligate poor would receive money and use it at their own discretion.[65]

It was in this spirit that Rabbi Silverman promoted the Educational Alliance as an antidote to "self-seeking reform." The co-optative nature of the Alliance's activities can in part be gathered from the fact that these same German Jews who considered "signs in Hebrew letters" foreign and distasteful, who quickly dropped the word *Hebrew* from the name of the Educational Alliance because it sounded too sectarian to them, sponsored Hebrew classes "for boys and girls with an average daily attendance of 2,200." The Alliance's own annual report explains:

> The parents of these children are determined that they shall be taught Hebrew, and experience has demonstrated that if they have no opportunity of obtaining such instruction at our hands they are sent to private schools, called "Cheders" (in which the neighborhood abounds), where the general surroundings, considered from hygienic, moral and Americanizing standpoints, are of the very type which it is the chief aim of the Alliance to extirpate.[66]

Educating to "extirpate" alien ideologies, these Pied Pipers of the urban *shtetl* taught Hebrew, sponsored social and historical lectures, and bent their efforts at labor mediation. Years later, in the *Kehillah*, they were to take further steps to reform and reformulate Hebrew education and labor relations.

Americanization was simultaneously a class and an ethnic battle. The leaders were not only asserting the superiority of Western "civilization" against "Oriental" outlandishness; they were expressing the contempt of investment bankers, national civic figures and international merchants for petty traders, neighborhood customer peddlers, and tailors. They were helping to forge the association between foreignness and socialism, Americanism and respectable (nonradical) trade unionism.

Just as Schiff, Seligman, and their colleagues in the National Civic Federation aimed to promote "social harmony" to win restive workers away from their interest in independent politics on the national level, they encouraged and shaped the settlement movement to win Jewish workers away from independent politics and "anarchism" within the city slums. Just as the Federation fought small businessmen and the anachronistically anti-union National Association of Manufacturers on the national level, the Jewish upper middle class fought their Orthodox ghetto counterparts. Just as the Federation was the organizational effort to mute the "strife between capital and labor" on the national political front, the Educational Alliance waged that battle on the more purely cultural front in New York City's Jewish ghetto.

The analysis of the development of the Breadwinners' College will present further evidence that when Rabbi Silverman proposed that the Jews become the professional Americanizers, his purposes were simultaneously assimilationist and political.[67]

The Breadwinners' College: Education versus Socialism

The rise of the Breadwinners' College at the Educational Alliance exemplifies the interactive nature of co-optation as a process, the political nature of the educational program that the Alliance established, and the use of education to discourage socialist perspectives. In effect the College grew out of the Alliance's lecture program. It was eventually to inspire the Evening College of CCNY.

In 1898 Thomas Davidson, Scottish-born philosopher and historian of education, gave a series of four lectures at the Alliance. He had been forewarned that he would be confronted by "a very critical audience made up largely of socialists of the Marxian type, anarchists, single taxists, and the like who, at the close of each lecture, would subject me to a rigorous examination, and try to draw me into a dispute."[68] And he apparently *was* subjected to just such a response by, among others, his future disciple Morris Raphael Cohen, then an undergraduate at City College.

Cohen and his family had come to New York from Minsk and Neshwies, Russia, in 1892, when he was twelve years old. Partly because the schools were still decentralized, he was able to move through the public education system very quickly, entering the sub-freshman year of CCNY in 1895. Every time the family moved, Cohen would go to the new school and register himself. He would be asked what grade he had completed in his previous school, and he always permitted himself to skip a grade or two; in short, he lied. The teacher registering him would then quiz him on the work of the grade he claimed to have completed and, without sending for any records, would make her judgment with respect to assigning him to a grade on the spot. Once an examining teacher put him a year ahead of the grade he had actually claimed. In this manner he advanced seven school grades in two years, experiencing a flexibility that the school system was to lose dramatically when it was made more centralized and "efficient."[69]

As a youngster Cohen had participated in many of the informal and semiformal educational activities of the Lower East Side. In 1894 he joined a literary club which debated such relevant subjects as "Whether the Whipping Post Should Be Introduced in the State of Delaware," and "Whether General Hull was justified in surrendering Fort Dearborn to the British in the War of 1812." In 1897 he joined a Marx study club, and later a Comte Synthetic Circle. His informal reading was a potpourri of American history, English literature, Yiddish literature, socialist newspapers, and Marxism. He read Gibbon and Aristotle, *Das Kapital* and *Die Arbeiter Zeitung*. In 1896–1897, he helped run a young workingman's class in connection with his work in the Socialist Labor Party. In 1897, he worked in Daniel de Leon's socialist campaign for assemblyman.[70]

Cohen's socialist outlook was not only reinforced by the general political milieu of the times and the neighborhood; it was particularly fueled by his class position: his mother's floor scrubbing, his father's unemployment, and his father's work when he *was* employed:

> I had occasion to visit my father's "shop" and I was impressed with the tremendous drive which infiltrated and animated the whole establishment—nothing like the leisurely air of the tailor shop in Minsk where my Uncle Abraham had worked and where the men would sing occasionally. Sometimes my father and another presser would start a competitive drive to see who could press the largest number of jackets during the day. We all knew by his appearance that this had happened when he came home at seven o'clock in the evening. It was hard to dissuade my father from engaging in such drives, for he was paid according to the number of jackets pressed.
>
> I soon understood why the unions were fighting so hard for a weekly wage to take the place of payment for piece work. . . .
>
> When I later learned of the large profits that the manufacturers were making and how lavishly they spent their money, I could not

dismiss as mere rhetoric the complaint against the harsh injustice of the distribution of wealth under capitalism.[71]

Thomas Davidson's lecture was Cohen's first contact with the Educational Alliance, and it occurred because a member of his Marx Circle

> reported that a certain Professor Davidson was giving a course of lectures at the Educational Alliance in which he was defending the principle of individualism. . . . Such an approach implied a challenge to socialism and so, confident of the failure of the individualistic philosophy from the days of Martin Luther to those of Herbert Spencer, some of us thought it would be a good idea to go to heckle the professor. Accordingly, I went to hear him speak on "The Educational Problem which the Nineteenth Century Hands on to the Twentieth." I was not favorably impressed with his gospel of salvation by education, which to me meant preaching. I was convinced that no substantial improvement of our human lot was possible without a radical change in our economic set up. It was apparent to me that the lecturer did not have any program of social action and was unsympathetic to any solution or procedure except that of ethical exhortation as a way of removing social evils. Completely convinced of my own premises, I took advantage of the question period following the lecture to heckle the speaker.[72]

Apparently Cohen and his Marx study club were not the only people in the audience who had reservations about education as the solution to "social evils," for another young man said that it was all very well "to solve all problems through the means of education, but how were people such as he, who had to work every day, to obtain this education?"[73]

Davidson stood behind his ideology; he offered to give a class at the Alliance one day per week. This weekly lecture was to develop into the Breadwinners' College.

But not without M. R. Cohen. Initially Cohen had neither interest in nor admiration for Davidson's course. When he returned to the lecture, it was again as an opponent.

> I was not interested. But I kept hearing . . . that this class was an unusually large and enthusiastic one, and that Davidson was constantly attacking socialism. I thought, therefore, that I ought to come around and try to upset some of his arguments.

In the end it was Cohen's arguments that were upset. Cohen was overwhelmed by Davidson's erudition, genuine kindness, and rather paternalistic flattery.

I found him to be very interesting because of the multitude of topics and personalities that he referred to. Some of his erudition opened up new fields to me . . . I remember my amazement when I heard him refer to "my friend, William James." . . . William James, whose *Will to Believe* I had read in part, was to me one of the Olympians, and it appeared almost unbelievable that an actual mortal should be on terms of familiarity with him.[74]

Partially disarmed even at the first lecture by Davidson's unexpectedly friendly response to his heckling, Cohen was taken aback entirely by his direct overture of friendship.

After one of the meetings, Davidson came over to me and said, putting his hand in a friendly way on my shoulder, "You have a fine mind. You ought to cultivate it." I was startled. It was years since anyone had paid me such a compliment. I asked, "What makes you think so?" And he said, "I am an old schoolmaster and I have never met anyone whose eyes are as far apart as yours who did not have a good mind.[75]

Apparently Cohen was too pleased to notice that Davidson's criterion of intelligence had nothing whatever to do with the content of Cohen's remarks. Davidson gave no evidence of being impressed with socialism.

But Davidson pursued Cohen, corresponded with him, and invited him to his summer home in the Adirondacks. Here Cohen met David Blaustein, superintendent of the Educational Alliance, and the three men planned to expand Davidson's class into an evening school for people who had to work during the daytime. The school began with Davidson's course, a series of thirty lectures given by Cohen, and three other courses. Less than a year after his first visit to the Alliance, Cohen was recommending to his fellow former hecklers in the Marx Circle that they take Davidson's course. Davidson also gave a course in general philosophy to Cohen and a group of his City College friends who were prevented by their pedagogic course from taking philosophy at CCNY.

Davidson died in 1900, and Cohen and Davidson's other "disciples"—this is Cohen's word, and it is rich in its implications—formed

the Thomas Davidson Society to make the half-started Breadwinners'
College

> an institution that would make no distinction of race or creed, would
> be open to rich and poor alike, and would be founded upon the
> principles that Thomas Davidson had sought to perpetuate. . . . The
> Educational Alliance building was our campus.[76]

Cohen and the other volunteers labored exhaustively at the college,
offering English grammar, composition, U.S. history, geography, and
arithmetic at the elementary and high school preparatory level; history, literature, civics, economics, science, and mathematics at the high
school level; and philosophy, cultural history, literature, and social
science at the college level. Attendance increased from about two
hundred to about six hundred students. The Breadwinners' College
continued until 1917, by which time CCNY and various other extension courses and adult institutes had adopted the innovation.[77]

Before we follow the implications of this development, it would be
well to explore further the relationship between Davidson and Cohen:
the meeting of two political gestalts.

Davidson was obviously an inspiring teacher and a charismatic
intellectual. Cohen states that he "had been the spiritual inspiration,
in England, of the Fellowship of the New Life and its more activist
offshoot, the Fabian Society. . . ." Rischin says that Davidson "crossed
and recrossed the Atlantic in search of knowledge, inspiration, and
above all, the ideal spiritual society."[78]

Davidson was a universalist of the most broadly generalizing sort.
It was characteristic that he encouraged Cohen, "then still an undergraduate and only four years out of public [elementary] school, to give
a course of thirty lectures on the history of civilization" at the
Educational Alliance.[79] Although Cohen attributes Davidson's act to
his "optimism and courage," one might be tempted to view it as
exemplary of his lack of respect for history. Barnard Bailyn character-
izes Davidson's *History of Education* as a "heady distillation of Social
Darwinism," a work of almost cowboy flamboyance:

> Davidson starts with "The Rise of Intelligence" when "man first
> rose above the brute." Then he trots briskly through "ancient
> Turanian," Semitic, and Aryan education, picks up speed on "civic
> education" in Judea, Greece and Rome, gallops swiftly across
> Hellenistic, Alexandrian, Patristic, and Muslim education; leaps
> magnificently over the thorny barriers of scholasticism, the medie-

val universities, the Renaissance, Reformation, and Counter-Reformation; and then plunges wildly through the remaining five centuries in sixty-four pages flat.[80]

Bailyn attributes the book's enormous influence to its function as a professional ideology for educators. And education certainly was Davidson's ideology. According to Cohen he taught his disciples that "we have no right to break away from the past until we have appropriated all its experience and wisdom . . . ." Moreover, Davidson

> was intent on diverting us from our concern with issues of social reform, for which he thought we lacked knowledge and understanding, and leading us to the more fundamental problem of mind and matter. In this he was at least temporarily successful.[81]

Davidson's success may be measured in part by the fact that Cohen did not find it curious that Davidson thought his disciple had sufficient "knowledge and understanding" to lecture on the history of civilization, but insufficient "knowledge and understanding" to change the circumstances of the life that he, his family, and his friends experienced daily.

Although Morris Raphael Cohen claimed to have maintained his own independence of mind—and he clearly differed with Davidson on many points—he appears to have been more deeply influenced than he himself realized. His spirited and energetic dedication to "an institution . . . open to rich and poor alike" is certainly a curiosity for a socialist who ought to have seen rich and poor as having at least some conflicting material and educational interests.[82] Thus, although Cohen rejected Davidson's individualism, he unquestioningly accepted his mentor's Progressivism in his own implicit assumptions of social harmony between rich and poor.

Cohen may have failed to appreciate this conflict because of his particular interpretation of Marxism. He began by seeing his "socialist activity, although cast in Marx's materialist terms, . . . directed primarily to the conquest and democratization of knowledge." Later, he saw Marx's "exaggerated materialism" as antithetical to an understanding of "injustice" or an appreciation of "the immaterial services of scientists, inventors, doctors, and other nonproletarian groups." He continued "to recognize the poverty of most non-economic interpretations of history," but because he had an overly economistic interpretation of Marx, he was vulnerable to Davidson's spirituality.[83]

The Educational Alliance's opposition to socialism was not subtle.

In 1899, the same year that the Alliance provided space and resources for the Breadwinners' College, Cohen's Marx Circle dissolved, in part because its members could not find a meeting room. Several of them joined Davidson's class at the Educational Alliance, a direct triumph of Progressive education over socialism. However, when the Alliance actually boasted of its role in fighting socialism, this open claim caused a temporary rift in the deep personal attachment of Cohen and Davidson. Cohen recalls:

> The Educational Alliance reported that Professor Davidson was fighting socialism, and the Yiddish socialist papers, the *Abendblatt* and the *Forward* took up the challenge. Those of us who had been in the Marx Circle felt that it was up to us to declare ourselves as socialists, and we revived that group. . . . Davidson thought that his whole class had turned Marxist, and became highly incensed.[84]

But the misunderstanding was breached and the relationship restored, and when two years after Davidson's death the Breadwinners' College was again criticized, both "for alienating Jewish young people from Judaism" and "for alienating young socialists from socialism," Cohen and his fellow members of the Thomas Davidson Society were unmoved by the criticisms. In four short years Cohen had moved from conducting workingmen's classes for the Socialist Labor Party to conducting a college for the Educational Alliance. He had moved from political education to abstract universal education, and, willy-nilly, he had helped to institutionalize exactly the program he had "heckled." "Salvation by education" had become a substitute for "a radical change in our economic set-up."

Just as Rabbi Silverman had hoped, the Educational Alliance did become the model Americanizer. In 1914, at its twenty-fifth anniversary celebration, Rabbi Z. H. Masliansky, a "famous European preacher," said that the Alliance was "a national institution . . . the father of all other institutions of the same sort," hundreds of which had appeared in cities throughout the United States. And the experiments of the Alliance, especially in adult education, left their mark on public education. As early as 1902 the superintendent of schools of New York City commended the Educational Alliance "for exerting a significant influence in the public adoption of programs such as vocational training, recreation centers, kindergartens and adult immigrant education."[85]

In 1909 City College adopted the Educational Alliance's innovation and established the Evening Session—the first free, public, full-matriculation, evening college in the country. There had been numerous university extension programs in the West and Midwest, but City College's Evening College was the first night school leading to a baccalaureate degree. Beginning with 200 students, the Evening College had 863 students only four years later.[86]

The establishment of the Evening College illustrates the role of the Educational Alliance in creating what would today be called "demonstration projects" for the public schools. For their part, CCNY's President, John Finley, and its Board of Trustees wished to show the school's "service to the City" and, in particular, to have City College play a role in the Americanization of New York's immigrant population.

The Kehillah: A Continuing Cultural Struggle

The story does not end here. Orthodoxy continued, fueled by fresh immigration from abroad. "Strife between Capital and Labor," as Rabbi Silverman put it, continued, sparked by continuation of the labor conditions that provoked rebellion, the maturing of the U.S. labor movement, and the growth of Jewish socialism, freshened by emigrés from the abortive 1905 Russian Revolution. More than that, the cultural reform efforts of the German Jewish bourgeoisie had their own disadvantages, causing new difficulties.

As a mode of social control the efforts of the Educational Alliance had two opposite flaws: it was both unsuccessful and too successful. Its Americanizing efforts alienated the older generation, which generally avoided its activities. Like the settlement movement elsewhere, the Educational Alliance mainly influenced children.[87] But insofar as the Alliance and the public schools succeeded in separating the child from the influence of its parents, they so accelerated the generaton gap that children were growing up without the restraints of family socialization. At least that is how the increasing incidence of juvenile delinquency and crime was explained. Jewish crime was to be the immediate catalyst of the formation of the *Kehillah*, another major effort at social harmony and cultural reform.

In 1905, Charles Bernheimer observed that

some Jewish children of this immigrant population are becoming street children, children with the roughness and brutality of the people of the street, copying their vicious language and habits, and

. . . they sometimes enter into lives of crime. Juvenile delinquency is a serious matter.

The solution was a new innovation: the probation officer who would watch over the juvenile delinquent, "educate" the parents "in the proper training of their children," or perhaps remove the child from its home. In their view, the famed Jewish family was a danger to its children; its culture was in need of reform.[88]

In 1908 Jewish criminality was turned into a major scandal when the Police Commissioner announced that Jews constituted 50 percent of "New York's criminal class." The German Jews treated the Commissioner's charge as true and a reflection of the degeneracy of the Lower East Side. The Eastern Jews treated the charge as false and an anti-Semitic slander. Some of the socialists said that crime was a natural outcome of poverty, requiring an attack on conditions in the Lower East Side rather than a defense of its honor.

In 1908, as in the 1880s, the German Jewish bourgeoisie tried to ignore the situation, and only acted when the Eastern Jews made it virtually impossible for them to remain silent. After a complex series of initiatives and negotiations, the Lower East Side's conservative newspapers and growing "downtown" bourgeoisie was able to provoke the German Jewish "uptowners" into becoming "community spokesmen" and forming the *Kehillah*, an organization that put new Progressive content into a traditional European institutional form.[89]

Although the *Kehillah* helped to mediate labor disputes, developed "scientific philanthropy," and conducted other activities, its major effort, in light of the problems of crime and delinquency, was to revive and reform Jewish education. The Jewish bourgeoisie came to define the problem of Jewish criminality, in true Durkheimian fashion, as caused by the decline in the influence of the family and other socializing institutions. The solution proposed was a reconstitution of some of the traditional institutions formerly attacked as "foreign," "Oriental," and necessary to "extirpate."[90]

A Jewish Bureau of Education was established. Its staff included eighteen Teachers College graduate students, who surveyed hundreds of *hedarim* and produced dissertations on subjects such as *Jewish Education* and *Theories of Americanization*.[91] On the basis of its surveys, the Jewish Education Bureau attempted to standardize, modernize, and Americanize the *hedarim*—to attract more students but ensure that Hebrew education would not interfere with public schooling. Parochial schooling was rejected as dangerously ethnic and un-

American. Jewish children must receive just enough religious education to keep them from becoming delinquents, but not so much as to make them "un-American." The truly Orthodox were not pleased.

The *Kehillah* also set up a Bureau of Industry to help create "orderly relations between Capital and Labor within the Jewish Community."[92] The fierce strikes of 1909-1910 had strong community support. "Widespread sympathy for the strikers and their unprecedented militancy compelled management to enter into industry-wide collective bargaining."[93] The German Jewish bourgeoisie helped to bring them to the bargaining table, and the *Kehillah* acted as mediator.

But although the labor community expressed gratitude for the *Kehillah*'s aid in getting recalcitrant manufacturers to bargain, it refused to join the *Kehillah*. The socialists also boycotted it, forswearing class collaboration. "No more ground exists today for bridging the deep distinctions of class interest, class consciousness, and origin than [existed] for the thousands of years until now," said Abraham Cahan, representing the *Forward*.[94] Like its late nineteenth-century European counterpart, the New York *Kehillah* was torn by conflicts of class, authority, and culture. In the 1920s, it folded.

Thus in the *Kehillah* and in other institutions, the German Jewish bourgeoisie were pushed to create a more pluralist form of Americanization, a form that in both name and content conceded more legitimacy to traditional religion, the Yiddish language, and the more respectable forms of union activity. Unable to discourage orthodoxy, they sponsored the Jewish Theological Seminary as a way of promoting a more professional, religiously Conservative rabbinate. Unable to influence the Yiddish speakers through Educational Alliance programs in Hebrew and English, they gradually permitted a limited amount of Yiddish (which they had scornfully dubbed "jargon") to creep into the Alliance's program. Faced with communal support for strikes and the growing radicalism of the Eastern Jews, they pressured clothing manufacturers to accept mediation and collective bargaining. And confronted with a crime problem defined as the result of the disintegration of traditional culture, they sought to strengthen traditional education while remolding it in Progressive directions.

Therein lay their dilemma. Had the German Jews who provided the financial support for the *Kehillah* permitted it to be democratically controlled by its Russian Jewish membership, the organization would have taken cultural and political forms which were anathema to the bourgeoisie. Yet their effort to determine those forms, to remold orthodoxy and to contain socialism, once again alienated the very people they sought to influence.[95]

This is not to say that either Jewish socialism or Jewish orthodoxy remained untouched. The students at the Rabbi Isaac Elchanan Theological Seminary staged a major strike in 1906 demanding that secular subjects be taught in addition to the teaching of the Talmud.[96] And according to all accounts, the Yiddish press and the *Forward* in particular were major Americanizing forces on their own, although the content of *their* Americanism was certainly not anti-socialist.[97]

But the same World War that exacerbated conflicts within the *Kehillah* beyond any possibility of containment increased the popularity and strength of the Socialist Party, both nationally and in New York City.[98] James Weinstein reports, "After the Russian Revolution in November 1917, thousands of immigrants flocked to the Socialist Party." Eugene V. Debs (for whom New York City's Yiddish radio station, WEVD, is named) polled almost twice as many votes in 1920 as he had in 1916, and New York voters accounted for 22 percent of that tally. The New York socialist vote jumped from 45,000 in 1916 to 203,000 in 1920.[99] And although the Party and the organized socialist movement later declined under the combined impact of the Palmer raids, coercive Americanization, immigration restriction, and the schisms within the organization between Socialists and Communists, the socialist spirit revived very shortly afterward in the late twenties and the thirties.[100] Then it made a strong enough impact on City College to give the school the uncomfortable reputation of being both Jewish and Red.[101]

Far from being the set of unchanging integrated values which people think caused Jewish social mobility, Jewish culture was fundamentally divided in the 1880s and remained fundamentally divided through the 1920s. There were major cultural differences between and among German Jews and Eastern European Jews. The three separate Jewish cultural tendencies on which we have focused generally expressed the world views of different classes: the small businessmen, the working class, and the big businessmen. No simple one-to-one correspondence should be drawn between class position and cultural attitude, but the relationship could scarcely be denied.

Proponents of each of these separate Jewish cultural traditions attempted to create educational institutions that would develop, preserve, and propagate their tradition. The Orthodox and the socialist

Eastern Jews also created social institutions that would fill their material needs in an atmosphere in which they felt comfortable.

Continued waves of immigration strengthened both orthodoxy and socialism. Each was further affected, often in contradictory ways, by developments in the political economy. Some of these developments will be explored in Chapters 3, 4, and 5.

But Jewish culture was not only separately ramified, institutionally selected, and affected by changing socioeconomic conditions, it was also consciously molded by the efforts of the German Jewish *haute bourgeoisie.* The leadership of that group attempted to create, shape, and use educational institutions, particularly the Educational Alliance and the Education Bureau of the *Kehillah,* to replace orthodoxy and socialism with a new Jewish cultural unity—assimilationist, politically Progressive, and thus oriented to social harmony in explicit opposition to socialism. Insofar as the Jewish socialists were also assimilationist, they were assimilationist into a *working-class* political framework differing in many important respects from the one into which the German Jews wished to assimilate them.

Perhaps it was because many German Jewish leaders were primarily commercial capitalists, rather than industrialists, that they were initially reluctant to become leaders and innovators of the Jewish community. As finance capitalists, they did not make their profit out of direct control over the labor of a proletariat. The Eastern Jews did not work in their factories, thus the Eastern Jews were an embarrassment. They were claimants to a commonality the German Jews did not wish to acknowledge, claimants to even greater dedication to a culture which the German Jews were shedding as fast as possible. But because "it became impossible after a while for Jewish leaders to avoid the question of the public image of the American Jews,"[102] they began to mirror the involvement of such non-Jewish Progressives as Hutchins Hapgood, Jane Addams, and Jacob Riis.[103] Thus their initial behavior lends itself to the explanation common in the literature—that their initial revulsion was based on snobbery.

Yet once they understood that they would have to play (as Jews were uniquely equipped to play) a special role within the capitalist class in transforming Eastern Jewish culture and institutions in defense of both their class interests and their own prestige, men like Schiff were free to innovate precisely because they were not industrial capitalists. Just as, in the National Civic Federation, bankers like Morgan, Seligman, and Schiff could espouse harmony between capital and labor and recognition of "responsible" unions as against revolutionary ones, bankers like Schiff and Seligman could espouse harmony between capital and labor in the Jewish community.[104] It is undoubtedly these bankers' role as Progressives that permits authors such as Glazer and Handlin to perceive the Jewish leadership as being moved by compassion, and indeed as the partners of labor in the Jewish labor movement.[105]

As Progressives, many of the active members of the German Jewish business class sought to mold the diverse Jewish cultures into a single, reformed, Jewish culture—an effort at social control and political socialization. That effort reflected the Progressive movement's emphases on social harmony, its attack on socialism, its support for the recognition of labor unions as against labor radicalism, and its methods of implementing policy through the "stewardship of wealth."

Although the German Jewish bourgeoisie's emphasis on education was self-consciously motivated, it was not a conspiracy. Like the rest of the Progressive movement, it reflected a complex result of multiple interactions among individuals and between classes. As in most co-optative efforts, the original energy came from the efforts of dissident groups—the educational efforts of the *Talmud Torahs*, the *Arbeiter Ring*, and the various self-education circles, the strikes and demonstrations that provided the middle class with the need to promote social harmony. And as with most co-optative efforts, articulate members of the dominated group—in this case M. R. Cohen and his friends—were able to supply the energy and the insight into their own group's conditions in order to mold institutional innovation into forms most attractive to the group members and most suitable to their needs. They helped to change Progressivism, and Progressivism changed them.

Progressives within the Jewish community, dedicated to institutional innovation, contributed to the expansion and development of educational institutions. In so doing, these Jewish leaders stressed particular *forms* of education, as opposed to changes supported by the educational efforts of socialist and Orthodox Jews. By developing kindergartens and the Evening College, and by contributing to the development of manual training, the German Jewish business class helped to ramify the educational institutions Jewish children were to enter.

Garment workers' strike c. 1910. *Amalgamated Clothing and Textile Workers Union*

CCNY dedication ceremonies for the new campus, 1908. *Culver Pictures*

3

The Creation of Educational Opportunity

The problem with cultural theories that explain Jewish success in terms of Jewish values is not that they are incorrect, but rather that they are superficial. They are correct in the sense that Jews did have the benefit of a rich intellectual tradition and did place unusually high value on education and intellectual achievement. But cultural theories are trivial unless they go on to examine the broad structural factors that buttressed this value system [and] . . . permitted values to become realities.

—Stephen Steinberg,
Academic Melting Pot

In order for the Jewish passion for education to result in upward mobility, there had to be an educational system that was organized to provide an avenue of mobility, and educational achievements had to be relevant to occupational success. Before the end of the nineteenth century neither of those two conditions obtained. College education was not relevant to most occupations. Higher education was not linked to lower education in such a way as to provide a system of advancement available to students educated in public schools.

In the 1880s, when the first wave of Eastern European Jews arrived in the United States, education was scarcely a channel of social mobility. The poor sent their children to the Common School, whose graduates went directly to work. In the absence of child labor laws, the children of the poor often went to work with very little elementary school education. The wealthy generally educated their children privately and prepared the few who were to go to college in private preparatory schools. Where high schools existed—there were none in New York City—they generally did not prepare youngsters for college. And colleges generally did not prepare their students for occupations other than law, medicine, and the Christian ministry.

College did not offer much more inducement to the families in the capitalist class. Most of their sons went directly into business, although these families generally sent one son to college to become a lawyer, both law and politics being useful occupations to a business family. The German Jewish business families followed suit. Most of their sons went into the family business or into that of an associated family. One son—or perhaps a grandson—might go into law and from there into diplomacy.

Take, for example, the Straus family. Isidore and the other sons went into the family business (crockery merchandise, and then general retailing in partnerships in R. H. Macy and Abraham & Straus). Only Oscar went to college, to law school, then into diplomacy and Republican politics.[1]

The Seligman family history was similar. All of the Seligman sons went into the banking business. A grandson, Edwin R. A. Seligman, became the famed Columbia economist, but that was much later, after the transformation of higher education. Jacob Schiff prohibited his strongly academically inclined son, Morti, from going to Harvard, compelling him instead to enter his investment firm, Kuhn, Loeb. In short, before the turn of the century, education was not a major consideration in occupational placement, either for the working class or for the business class.

Underlying both the educational and the occupational changes was the transformation of an entire social system: the world-shaking spread of the capitalist economy, uprooting millions of peasants and artisans and sucking them across the ocean to feed American machines; the creation of new classes; the clash of cultures; and the creation of new social and organizational forms. This change in the social order transformed higher education, the nature of work, the relationship between work and education, and the possibilities and forms of mobility through higher education. The socialist and labor movements in which Eastern Jews participated helped to create the social crisis which made educational reform possible.

The Limits of Early Educational Reform

Throughout the nineteenth century businessmen and educational reformers had been trying to change higher education. When the century began, the primary function of higher education was the training of an elite in classical refinement and gentlemanly virtues. The colleges were run primarily by the president and faculty, who were generally clergymen rather than scholars, and financed by Christian denominations and state legislatures with periodic gifts from local merchants. Even the public state universities were headed by clergymen.[2]

The curriculum was prescribed; all students took the same classical course of study in the same order at the same rate. Although religious instruction was beginning to decline by the early nineteenth century, the theological influence remained. The curriculum stressed rote learning of Latin and Greek languages, Latin and Greek literatures, rhetoric, oratory, and through these classics a version of natural philosophy which deduced nature from "truths" known since Aristotle, rather than examining real things in the real world.[3]

But this curriculum, while well-suited to the transmission and preservation of a tradition, was an impediment to invention. Therefore, from the very first it incurred the impatience of a rising mercantile and manufacturing class. That class was interested in science and invention, the engines of technological progress.

A reform movement began with considerable initial impact, but it ran into setbacks and limitations. Reformers were only to succeed in fundamentally transforming the *system* of higher education at the turn of the century, around the time that the Eastern European Jews arrived.

The early reform period foreshadowed the later. The beginning of industrialization around the War of 1812 drew forth a working class from the peasantry of Ireland and the farms of the United States. Class conscious workingmen's parties formed, attacking aristocratic privilege. Businessmen began to see the colleges as a potential place to train personnel in mechanical arts and commercial subjects. They wanted the colleges to conduct research—on geology and minerals (for mining), chemistry (for dyes and other industrial processes), geography, mathematics, and engineering.

Industrialists' interest in science stems primarily from the need, particularly strong in competitive capitalism, to increase profits by employing technological innovations that permit increasing the productivity of labor at prevailing rates of pay. Moreover, all sorts of engineers and architects are needed to design the public works which provide the infrastructure for industry, and to plan and execute the building of railroads and factories. Control of employees within industrial firms and control of accounts within all capitalist enterprises requires a highly duplicative clerical system, implemented at this earlier stage by skilled clerks, bookkeepers, and accountants.

Consequently, educational reformers and business leaders—often the same persons—sought to introduce scientific research and scientific training, engineering, the languages of commerce (Spanish, French, English), and other practical subjects as curricula parallel to classical studies. They sought to introduce the German university model, which stressed research and graduate scholarship, rather than the teaching of undergraduates in traditional "truths." They sought to introduce an elective system, so that students could select those courses which would further their future occupational specialization.

As in the later period, educational reformers were concerned with the social control problems caused by the proletarianization and urbanization of labor. They couched their proposals as a democratic attack on privilege. Classical learning was the luxury of the wealthy; the poor would only be induced and enabled to attend college if college could prepare them for useful occupations in "engineering, merchandising, manufacturing, the merchant marine, canals, railroads."[4]

In the pre-Civil War period there was a general expansion of the sciences and recruitment of poorer students. The colleges began to hire a few professors for their scientific knowledge rather than simply for their Christian piety, and to permit faculty specialization in subjects rather than requiring them to teach in all fields of a memorized and unchanging culture. Some of these professors began to embrace the European scientific discoveries which had been ignored in the United States, and to prize invention and research rather than revealed truth. They began to hire themselves out to business firms for practical inquiry.

New institutions formed that were more geared to the new learning, among them the University of New York (NYU) and the Free Academy of New York, later renamed the College of the City of New York. Even elite colleges such as Yale and Harvard set up parallel courses or even whole schools in the more mercantile and professional pursuits.[5]

But reform reached a limit. The new sciences began to squeeze the classics. As early as 1828 Yale issued its famous *Report*, asserting that professional, scientific, and vocational learning was all very well for the masses but a classical education, including science but stressing Latin, Greek, and rhetoric, was indispensable in preparing the new men of wealth "to move in the more intelligent circles with dignity," and to rule "in our public councils."[6] As Frederick Rudolph has summed up the meaning of the *Report*, "Some advocates of the free elementary public school movement argued that the schools would tame the masses. Yale now proposed to use the classical curriculum and the colleges for taming the millionaires."[7]

Science continued to progress within the colleges, including Yale, well beyond 1828 and on into the 1850s. A number of colleges competed with Yale for students by dropping the "dead" languages (which Yale insisted on retaining). But the Yale *Report* was highly influential in preventing more fundamental changes in the college system. After the Darwinian revolution there was a religious reaction to the findings of science and a hardening of conservative educational thought. The German university model languished, as college trustees resisted further reform, rescinded some changes, expanded the classics, and reintroduced Bible study.[8]

The program of the reformers was very expensive and the money sufficient to carry it out did not become available anywhere until much later in the century. The Yale *Report* rejected the "ludicrous attempt to imitate . . . [the German universities] while it is unprovided with the resources necessary to execute the purpose." In 1838 NYU became "just another American college." In 1846 Columbia College rejected the introduction of an elective system. And in 1848 the Free Academy instituted, just one year after its founding, a Greek and Latin curriculum which was to remain rigidly in the classical mold even after Yale itself had changed.[9]

In the academies, and in particular in the new public high schools, the reformers had more success. Commercial subjects were introduced: bookkeeping, the sciences, and drawing, because drawing was useful to "engineers, professionals, architects, machinists and mechanics." Reformers wanted secondary education to assure social control over the children of alienated workers, to train these children in the capitalist work ethic, and to reassert a social harmony presumably destroyed by industrialization and foreign labor. Although the reformers had greater success in securing administrative control on the secondary level than on the college level, there too the "modern" subjects and modern conceptions of pedagogy had to compete with the rigors of Greek and Latin discipline espoused by educational conservatives. The reformers' effort to impose social harmony also met the opposition and recalcitrance of the working class.[10]

Most important, although the academies afforded some college preparation, they were private. The few public high schools did not offer a college preparatory curriculum. Before the Civil War, "no single articulated educational ladder existed, nor any clear concept of secondary education."[11] New York City's Free Academy was to remain one of the very few public educational ladders in the United States for many years to come.

In sum, as long as college did not prepare students for worldly occupations, for the jobs which business and the expanding economy had to offer, college remained the luxury of a leisure class and the status ornament of a governing class; it could not be a tool of an active business class or a vehicle of mobility for the children of the working class. Even for the three years in which NYU was prepared to offer an M.A. degree, "there was not a job in the United States for which an M.A. was required or desired."[12] Educational reform would have to await the maturing of certain developments which we have examined in the earlier period: the expansion of industry, the greater accumulation and concentration of capital, the acceleration of technology, the expansion of commerce and of the clerical work force in both commerce and industry, the greater expansion of the work force in general, the influx of immigrant labor, and the intensification of the social movements that all these socioeconomic changes brought forth. Reform would not become possible until after the accumulation of the Civil War, the depression of the 1870s, and all the contradictory and complementary forces which later social and economic development unleashed.[13] Without these reforms, social mobility through education would have been even more of a minority phenomenon than it was.[14] That reform was made possible by the social developments—and social crisis—of the turn of the century.

Social Conflict at the Turn of the Century

The turn of the century represented more than the maturing of certain tendencies observable before the Civil War. The increasing size and scale of industrial production involved and produced qualitative changes in the U.S. economy and social structure, and in higher education as well. The Civil War, continued westward expansion, and the building of the railroads not only contributed to accumulation of greater and greater fortunes but also to the creation of a national economy. Industry expanded in size, scope, and organization through accumulation, diversification, and merger. The incorporation movement diffused the ownership of industrial enterprise, formerly held by individual (extended) families, among the families of the business class. Based on the expansion of industry on a nationwide scale and the incorporation movement, a national business class formed, creating social and political organizations that promoted its social, economic, political, and cultural coherence as a class. Its members drew a boundary around themselves, excluding the Jewish bourgeoisie, and thus defining the ruling class. They created the *Social Register* to list the elect.

Among the diverse organizational forms created (including exclu-

sive resorts, clubs, and restricted communities), of particular significance is the network of elite prep schools and colleges. The geographic
spread of business and the decline of single-family ownership created
the need for a method of selecting trustworthy managers from among
the top corporate families. Heredity through individual family lines
would no longer do; what was needed was heredity of *class* property
through the family lines of a whole class. Just as dispersal of stock
ownership was the economic form of class property, recruitment of
managers from elite schools and social clubs was the social form of its
stewardship.

But elite schools became more than mills for arranging marriages
and sorting managers. With corporate firms no longer inherited in
individual families, industry undergoing continual technical revolution, and society in ferment, a genuine change in elite education
became necessary. To steer their property in interlocking director-
ships, the children of the wealthy now needed more expert knowledge,
if only to better select the experts they employed.[15] Neither classical
education nor informal apprenticeship to one's father was now sufficient training for the collective progeny of the propertied.

The development of monopoly capitalism undermined the position
of small businessmen and farmers, proletarianized many of them, and
pushed others to organize politically in various populist political
movements and organizations. Simultaneously, the expansion of industry recruited thirty million European immigrants. Each wave of
immigrant workers created the wealth that promoted further expansion and the importation of more workers.

The recruitment of that European work force wrought enormous
changes in the American working class, and created in the United
States, as it had in Europe, the need on the part of management to
mold those ex-peasants and ex-artisans into a factory-disciplined work
force. Encountering resistance, employers sought to frighten each
wave of new workers into sobriety and obedience by importing fresh
waves of immigrants, only to encounter the same problem anew.[16]

Members of the newly recruited work force reacted to machinery
and modern industry as had other ex-peasants and ex-artisans before
them in Europe and the United States: they drank, celebrated holidays
that interfered with factory work schedules, and formed nationwide
labor organizations. The Knights of Labor reached its peak in 1885;
the AFL formed in 1886; the IWW organized in 1905. Labor fought
numerous strikes, often with strong popular backing. In 1877 the
nationwide railroad strike aroused the sympathies of working-class

communities across the country, where crowds defended workers against the militia. In East St. Louis Black and white workers united for a higher minimum wage. Governors tried to rally troops of shaky loyalty against general insurrection. Class warfare, of words and arms, broke out in pitched battles, as at the Carnegie steel mills in the 1890s, and in "guerrilla warfare," as in Colorado in 1913.[17]

Between 1900 and 1918 a growing minority supported the Socialist Party, which had strong roots in some trade unions, a thriving press, and strong electoral support. By 1912 roughly 1,200 socialists were elected in 340 municipalities from coast to coast, among them 79 mayors in 24 states.[18] The turn of the century was one of the two periods in U. S. history of serious political challenge to capitalism as a system. Although only a minority of workers may have participated in each of these struggles, they contributed to an atmosphere of turmoil which was of great concern to corporate leaders and politicans at the time. They created the social crisis that made social reform possible.

As a social entity the capitalist class was born of conflict: conflict with Southern planters over control of political institutions; conflict with each other over control of railroads, markets, and pipelines; conflict with workers over wages, control of work, and the nature of the political and economic system. But they learned to mix force with order and organization. A segment of that class, the "corporate liberals," to borrow a phrase from James Weinstein, organized to do battle with business conservatives and labor radicals, and to create and shape the institutions which a changing economic order required.

Progressivism and Educational Reform

In the thirty-five years after the Civil War, accelerated capital accumulation made the reform of higher education simultaneously financially possible and socially and economically necessary. And as in Progressivism in general, the corporate liberals were able to use the socialist threat to win out over the conservatives in order to rationalize higher education according to business needs.

Even before the Civil War was over, higher education began, in effect, to be treated as part of the "infrastructure" which government provides under free enterprise. The Morrill Act, which gave "free" land to some small farmers, to the railroads, and to the states for the purpose of setting up land-grant colleges, was soon used to support vocationalism and the university movement.[19]

The stockholders of the railroads began to use part of their vastly increased wealth for direct sponsorship of universities on the German model. In 1867, Johns Hopkins "pledged his fortune in Baltimore and Ohio Railway stock to the creation of what would become the first substantial American effort to support pure scholarship." Captains of industries other than railroads contributed portions of their "surplus capital" to other new universities.[20] Thus the land grants fostered the universities in three ways: through direct federal government grants, through government grants to the states for building universities, and through gifts from private owners who had accumulated wealth through land grants. In effect, universities were more easily introduced *outside* of the established collegiate system.

But a transformation of the whole system, particularly the reform of the existing undergraduate colleges, required more complicated interventions and a more organized form of philanthropy. The organization of philanthropy, and its use in the form of contingent grants for essentially bureaucratic purposes, became possible only when dissident groups began, in the 1870s and 1880s, to demand the redistribution of wealth through socialism. Their attack on wealth called forth a legitimizing ideology.

Andrew Carnegie, along with fellow National Civic Federation members Charles Eliot and Nicholas Murray Butler, perhaps the three most influential men in the overhaul of education, realized that the Horatio Alger myth no longer carried conviction or inspired belief. He devised the Gospel of Wealth as a legitimizing theme. According to Carnegie,

> The problem of our age is the proper administration of wealth, so that the ties of brotherhood may still bind together the rich and poor in harmonious relationship. . . . The Socialist or Anarchist who seeks to overturn present conditions is to be regarded as attacking the foundation on which civilization itself rests: . . . Individualism, Private Property, the Law of Accumulation of Wealth, and the Law of Competition.[21]

Preferable to Communist collectivism was capitalist individualism; preferable to the redistribution of wealth (which, under capitalism, Carnegie admitted, accumulates in the hands of the few) was the administration of wealth by the wealthy in the interests of all. Since the opportunity to rise in business through work, luck, and grit was now limited, as Carnegie was forced to admit, businessmen could best serve civilization by creating opportunity for mobility through education. Opportunity could be created by investing a portion of surplus wealth in universities and libraries, to create "ladders upon which the aspiring can rise."[22]

Carnegie's message was designed not only for disenchanted workers; his words were also directed at entrenched clergy and educational conservatives who fought educational "modernization." Carnegie set the example for the stewardship of wealth by creating the Carnegie Foundation for the Advancement of Teaching, which gave grants to colleges for pensions for older professors. The requirements for the receipt of that grant were so carefully and ingeniously orchestrated that they provided the means by which the merely *advisory* recommendations of Butler and Eliot's Committee of Ten (of the National Education Association) on standardizing high school subject areas and college entrance requirements, and the recommendations of Butler and Eliot's equally *voluntary* creation, the College Entrance Examination Board, could be implemented with enormous impact. That single gift of pension funds achieved, or significantly helped to achieve, four major objectives: the establishment of elective systems at numerous colleges; the weakening of religious control; the redefinition of college entrance requirements; and the reorganization of high school curricula to prepare youngsters for college, effectively making the high schools an intermediate link in a "ladder of success."

Pension funds in themselves fostered reform, since they were used to retire the older, more conservative, more classics-oriented professors. Into their places moved younger, more reform-minded faculty who were amenable to the elective system. But more important than the effect of the money in pensioning off recalcitrants was the effect of the requirements for *getting* the money. Pension funds were given directly to colleges, and the Board of Trustees administering the Carnegie Foundation[23] defined as "colleges" only those institutions which would: give up their denominational affiliations; have at least eight departments, each headed by a Ph.D.; have at least a $200,000 endowment or, in the case of state universities, at least an income of $100,000; have a four-year liberal arts course; and require a high school course of applicants for admission.[24] A "high school course" was defined as consisting of 16 "Carnegie units" of 120 classroom clock hours for each subject. "Subjects" were defined according to the list which the College Entrance Examination Board had made of permissible subjects for admission.[25]

The requirement that the colleges give up their denominational affiliations was important in undermining the control of the local clergy who served as trustees and faculty of the hundreds of religiously affiliated colleges. At a time of economic depression in higher education, the Carnegie "gift" (and those of other "robber barons" funding similar foundations following similar policies) could scarcely be refused. Philanthropy set the conditions for institutional survival.[26]

The pension fund's insistence on at least a $200,000 endowment (it was later changed to $500,000) dovetailed with the foundation's decision to create a "lead system" of colleges "which by virtue of their overwhelming prestige would set the standards for, and in effect dominate, the rest of the educational scene."[27] The Carnegie Foundation concentrated its funds in about twenty colleges and universities, and these major institutions were generally the ones that produced (and still produce) a major proportion of the Ph.D's who taught at the rest of the colleges and universities across the country. Influence on the character of higher education would henceforth trickle down. The foundations thus provide the material underpinnings for the academic prestige hierarchy, at the bottom of which schools such as the College of the City of New York—serving poor and minority students—customarily get short shrift. The "lead system" ensured the continuance of a structure of institutional inequality.[28]

Probably the most far-reaching element in the program was the requirement that to be eligible for Carnegie money, a college had to require applicants to have passed a high school course made up of Carnegie units. That specification was of singular importance in transforming education into a nationwide system of educational ladders, preparing educated people for the changing occupational structure. By the ingenious use of philanthropy, Carnegie, Butler, and Eliot standardized both the chaotic anarchy of diverse high school curricula, and the rigid arbitrariness of college admissions requirements, into the interconnected, graded, cradle-to-grave, kindergarten-to-Ph.d. system that seems so logical and natural today.[29]

In understanding the development of this system, it is important to note that although the workers' militancy helped the liberals to convince conservatives of the need for reform and philanthropy, there is little evidence that the working class sought the reform of colleges in the interest of educational opportunity, and there is considerable evidence that they did not.[30] Although organized labor demanded elementary education, it was hostile to the foundations, and frequently saw college professors as hostile to labor.[31] The striking workers, whose militancy had converted Carnegie from the celebration of opportunity through competitive enterprise to the creation of opportunity through education, were not striking in favor of more opportunity for individual mobility; they were striking because of wage cuts administered in the face of widely published accounts of the increasing wealth of the owning class.[32] The response of Carnegie to the effort of "his" steelworkers to prevent a 25 percent wage cut and destruction of the steelworkers' union was to call out the Pinkerton guards, precipitating the "Homestead massacre." The response of Rockefeller to a copper workers' strike was to have the tents of strikers' families burnt to the ground—"the Ludlow massacre." The issue in the railroad strike, the Homestead strike, the Ludlow strike, and many others, was not the decline of opportunity for mobility out of the working class, but control over the labor process and the division of the surplus between workers and owners of the companies.

It is, therefore, at least arguable that the conditions that made possible the philanthropists' possession of sufficient surplus to sponsor educational opportunity was their ability to restrain workers' wage demands at Homestead, Ludlow, and on the railroads. At the same time, this labor militancy gave Progressive businessmen added incentive to push educational reforms and provided the threat with which they could disarm educational conservatives. Reform, they said, "the creation of educational opportunity," was needed to save the system. "Educate, and save ourselves and our families and our money from mobs," said Henry Lee Higginson, Harvard's benefactor.[33]

Education provided a channel of mobility at the turn of the century as a result of reforms initiated by businessmen and the educational leaders supported by them. These reforms included the substitution of the elective system for a prescribed curriculum, the introduction of scientific and commercial subjects in place of stress on classics and religion, the expansion of high schools and the creation of a hierarchical career ladder, and the establishment of linkages among colleges and universities based on a financially organized prestige hierarchy. Educational reform followed in the wake of both economic and political changes. Economically, changes in industry required a change in the character of knowledge, a change in the organization of knowledge-mining, and a change in personnel training. Politically, popular unrest required institutions of co-optation, such as mobility through education. The political changes not only made the institutional changes necessary; they facilitated their acceptance.

The socialists and the labor movement helped to create the social crisis that made reform possible. In this crisis businessmen were able to make the reforms which had been stymied by conservative reaction and religious opposition for years. Jewish socialists and labor militants contributed to this atmosphere of social crisis. The opportunity afforded to a select few to be upwardly mobile through higher education was much more than a coincidence.

Stephen Steinberg correctly asserts that it was by "historical accident" that the tide of Jewish immigration from Eastern Europe coincided with the emergence of the modern university.[34] The reform of U.S. higher education would have happened with or without the Jewish migration. Yet the two sets of events were not totally separate. Both Jewish migration and the reform of higher education were products of U.S. capitalist development, and both were agents of that development. The Jewish immigrants, few though they were, played their part, directly and indirectly, in the reform of higher education.

Laying the cornerstone, Sept. 29, 1903. *Archives, The City College, City University of New York*

4

The Rise and Reform of City College

As the children of the immigrants reached college age, the great channel for their educational passion became the City College of New York, CCNY.

—James Yaffe, *The American Jews*

The College of the City of New York was established in the first of the nineteenth-century higher-education reform movements and transformed during the second wave of reform. It was the first tuition-free municipal college and provided the first public educational ladder. These features were to make higher education possible for numbers of poor Jewish boys who would otherwise have been unable to attend college. (Girls were not admitted as full CCNY undergraduates until a century later.)[1] Throughout the second half of the nineteenth century CCNY exhibited the same struggle between educational conservatives and educational reformers that occurred in colleges across the country. Located in a city of intense class conflict, ethnic diversity, and political organization, the College of the City of New York was "modernized" and expanded threefold at the turn of the century, when business-oriented reformers finally gained control, and Russian Jewish boys came to predominate among City College students. Russian Jewish students changed the school's social and cultural atmosphere and helped, at least indirectly, to transform it into an instrument for the assimilation of the immigrant poor. The reformed City College—its free tuition, changed curriculum, and expanded size—made much of Jewish mobility through education possible and set the framework for that mobility.

The Free Academy

In 1848, Karl Marx and Friedrich Engels, in the Old World, issued their "Communist Manifesto," calling upon the workers of the world to unite in establishing socialism. Here, in the largest city of the New World a democratically-inclined merchant named Townsend Harris preceded them by a few months in issuing another kind of manifesto—a manifesto calling for a democratic and free system of higher education for the working masses, in order to perfect and strengthen American republican institutions.

—S. Willis Rudy,
The College of the City of New York: A History[2]

Harris's manifesto establishing the College of the City of New York really began as a counterfoil to two others—the manifestos of the laboring population, and the Yale *Report* of 1828. In 1829 the Working Men's Party of New York had advocated the ten-hour day, the periodic redistribution of property, and the education of all young citizens until age eighteen.[3] The good merchants found educational reform more acceptable than restrictions on property; they proposed the creation of the Free Academy in the name of the creation of a business-relevant curriculum and the democratization of access to education. In the words of the report proposing the establishment of the first institution of higher education supported entirely by public funds, the College would enable "the laboring class of our fellow citizens [to] have the opportunity of giving to their children an education that will more effectively fit them for the various departments of labor and toil by which they will earn their bread."[4] Accordingly, they created the Free Academy, using the Literature Fund set up by the State Legislature to aid *private* academies. The Free Academy admitted, on examination, male graduates of all New York public elementary schools to a five-year program consisting of a sub-freshman preparatory year, and four years of college. In 1854 provision was made for a female academy, but it was not put into effect until sixteen years later.

Although the college was called an "Academy" for purely technical and financial reasons, it was established at the crest of the private academy movement, and its characteristics were typical of the academies, the vast majority of which were established just before 1850. The academies were a transitional institution between the aristocratic private Latin grammar school and the public high school. Their main purpose was to introduce a curriculum that included subjects which would prepare students for business and the professions.[5] Also typical of the academies (often called "colleges") was the Free Academy's immediate adoption of two parallel courses, "a classical course, intended for preparation for college, and an English course, intended to prepare for the ordinary business of life."

City College, which tried "to perform the functions of High School Academy, Polytechnic School and College" until the beginning of the twentieth century, went the ordinary academy one better and combined the practical studies and college preparation of the academies with the classical studies of the colleges.[6] As late as 1903, City College students spent seventeen hours per week on Latin and twelve hours per week on Greek. As early as 1851 the course of study included "Mathematics, History, Languages and Literatures, Drawing, Natural and Experimental Philosophy, Chemistry and Physics, Civil Engineering, Moral and Intellectual Philosophy, and Law and Political Economy."[7]

In New York, unlike Massachusetts, the establishment of the Free Academy was supported by working-class demands. Those demands were not only expressed by a faction of the Working Men's Party, they were also overwhelmingly supported in a public referendum. Yet in New York, as in Massachusetts, secondary education founded in the name of "the laboring class" was primarily attended by the children of the middle class. Mike Walsh, a working-class leader opposed to the Free Academy, had predicted that it would be controlled and attended by the middle class. In fact, working-class youngsters were not to use City College in significant numbers until the turn of the century.

Even among the middle-class youngsters who attended the Free Academy, social distinctions mattered. The establishment of a parallel course of study created a dual system of education implicitly based on social origins, a fact which is obvious from the "Address Delivered at the First Anniversary of the Free Academy" given by Erastus Benedict, then president of the Board of Education:

> Will you say to the community that at the Free Academy, they are entitled to free education for the lower and middle classes, but that those who would shine in the dress circles of society, must go to the college and the university? Will the ends of public education be answered by declaring, if your son is to go to a counting room or a trade, you may send him to the Free Academy where, in a short period they will give him French, Spanish and German, a few colloquial phrases in each, enough to make a bargain, with bookkeeping and the practical branches, and these are enough to make money, but if you intend him for a profession, or have a fortune to leave him—if you would make him a cultivated gentleman, send him to college and teach him Greek and Latin and Polite Learning? If public seminaries do not exclude the poor who cannot pay, they surely should not practically exclude the rich who do pay.[8]

This stirring defense of the democratic rights of the idle rich to an elite "gentleman's" track, to match the more pragmatic education suitable to the more plebian citizens, expresses the particular definition of democracy which ran throughout public education. Since the only condition which would have "practically excluded" the sons of the rich would have been the absence of an elite channel which would maintain their advantages, it is apparent that democratic education was defined as that form of education in which rich and poor attend the same school, and in which their common attendance does not fundamentally tamper with their inequality. Just as the National Civic Federation was to applaud a condition in which corporate leaders and labor leaders, presumably locked in a zero-sum struggle over the distribution of wealth, could sit harmoniously at the same table, so Benedict's statement fifty years earlier asserted the same ideal for the Free Academy. It was of the essence of liberal democracy that formal equalities must not *substantially* undermine substantive inequalities. The sons of "gentlemen" would inherit wealth and remain "gentlemen"; the sons of merchants would learn "enough to make a bargain."[9]

Benedict's statement, coming only one year after the establishment of the Free Academy as an alternative institution, indicates that, for the time being at least, the Yale *Report* was to be not so much overthrown by the merchants' "republican manifesto" as restricted in its domain, and that its domain was to be subtly, voluntarily, but definitely determined by social class.

Led by two West Point-trained presidents, the school quickly developed a conservative, classics-oriented majority on both its faculty and the governing Executive Committee of the Board of Trustees, and this group fought curricular reforms for the rest of the century. An effort to introduce a pedagogy program failed in 1870. A one-year commercial course, introduced in 1871 as an alternative to the classical course, particularly oriented to the many students who did not remain for the full five-year curriculum, was abolished in 1881. Courses such as a post-graduate civil engineering program were sanctioned in the late 1870s only when offered by zealous professors on their free time, in addition to their ordinary instructional responsibilities.[10] Even manual training, which was the only reform having the support of President Alexander S. Webb (he was also president, from 1885–1886, of the Industrial Education Association, the private group fostering manual training), was initially introduced as an optional, after-hours course. And even then the two-year manual training course, involving "wood-working, turning, metal-working and vise-work"—not in the interest of learning a trade, but of furnishing "a good general knowledge of the workshop crafts"—was only rescued when, in 1886, the F. W. Devoe Co. established a series of commencement prizes for the best wood and metal work. But until the late eighties and nineties, the continual struggle between classicists and reformers was generally won by the classicists. The classicists even won expansion of the requirements in Latin and Greek at the expense of calculus, mechanics, architecture and aesthetics. As late as 1881 the chairman of the Executive Committee of the Board of Trustees reiterated the dogmas of the Yale *Report* of 1828 virtually word for word (although without attribution), and the commercial course disintegrated.

In 1907, in honor of CCNY's move to its new campus at St. Nicholas Terrace, and during the period of the real Progressive takeover of the College, the Alumni Association published a memorial volume, commemorating sixty years of City College history in the old building.[11] Its subsections are titled in Latin, and the individual essays contributed by alumni endlessly repeat the same anecdotes about the chemistry lab, the German professor, and the French professor. Among the 112 photographs in the volume are six pictures of the workshops, showing the carpentering room, the forge room, the engine room, and the molding shop. Not a single nostalgic alumnus so much as mentioned the existence of manual training or the commerical course. Some alumni confess to boredom in history, others to disliking memorization in Latin or French, but the commercial and manual courses exist neither positively nor negatively in their collective and individual memories. Instead the volume is filled with the silly pranks and superficialities of college youth—the type of silliness which reflects a definite class attitude toward college. The poorer Russian Jewish students, who were coming to predominate at CCNY at the time that these earlier alumni were memorializing an earlier era, presented a contrasting attitude toward school.[12]

Although the reminiscences are undoubtedly unrepresentative, reflecting a particular selection of alumni, that very unrepresentative selection is significant, indicating the type of student constituting the earlier elite of the school. Many of the authors had become lawyers, others had joined the faculty of the school from which they had graduated, and some, like Richard Bowker, Everett P. Wheeler, and Edward M. Shepard, were very influential in shaping the subsequent reforms of the College. In portraying or expressing the tone of the school, they gave little evidence of being concerned with learning either carpentry or bookkeeping as "the departments of labor and toil by which they will earn their bread." Although many of them were vigorous advocates, within the faculty and the Associate Alumni, of the business-oriented reforms, and they often expressed great frustration at the traditionalism of the conservatives, their fond memories of their *own* schooling at CCNY held no place at all for bookkeeping, ironwork, or woodworking.

In the 1880s student newspapers began to advocate reform of college admissions, curriculum, and student disciplinary rules. They supported introduction of the elective system and protested censorship of free speech. The papers were suppressed and the offending editors suspended. In 1887 faculty regulations prohibited student chapel speakers from discussing " 'questions of a local character on which there is heated discussion in the community,' issues of party politics, 'irritating subjects' such as Nihilism, Anarchism, and Socialism, denominational views on Religion, and all questions of College discipline or College curriculum."[13] Student impetus toward social concern and college reform was throttled, and would be until the new century began.

Yet despite the conservative hold on the faculty and the Executive Committee, in its actual functioning the College did produce graduates and dropouts whose subsequent careers more nearly reflected developing business needs for bookkeeping, commerce, modern languages and education.

> In 1863 . . . ten years after the graduation of [the Free Academy's] first class . . . the greatest number [of alumni] had gone into the teaching profession. In addition to 52 in this category, there were 42 clerks, 33 lawyers, 19 clergymen and physicians, 7 merchants, 7 engineers, 6 bookkeepers and 5 architects.[14]

A comparison of the career destinations of graduates of City College with those of Columbia College shows the more modern cast of CCNY's character, especially in the period preceding 1885 (see figure on the following pages). For example, in both schools the number of alumni in engineering was small but increasing, while the proportion becoming clergymen showed a secular decline. But the differences are as illuminating as the similarities. Especially during the first two decades of its existence, CCNY produced relatively fewer clergymen, roughly half the proportion of lawyers, around twice the percentage of businessmen, and ten times the proportion of educators as did Columbia College. Although the turn of the century shows a general convergence between the two schools in the proportion of graduates entering each field, in the early period it is precisely in the newer fields, such as education and business, that City College differed most from Columbia.[15]

These differences in the careers of their alumni undoubtedly reflect not only differences in the nature of the two institutions, but also in the social origins of their students. For despite its tenacious embrace of the classics and its aura of gentlemanly irrelevance, City College never really served the *haute bourgeoisie,* which sent its sons to elite schools such as Columbia and Harvard. Until the turn of the century, when it began to serve the Russian Jewish poor, City College was mainly a school for the sons of prosperous but not really wealthy and well-established families. Among the parents of CCNY students, the largest group were merchants. If the classics at Columbia, as at Yale, were to tame the millionaires, the classics at CCNY would tame the merchants.

The commercial orientation was selectively used, most often by students who did not attend for the full five-year course. The school served as a sort of revolving door; as of 1902, 30,000 students had been admitted, but only 2,730 graduated. Many had been screened out—a reflection of severe examination standards often made even more rigorous to alleviate the lack of space in the available building.[16] By and large, however, the high dropout rate reflected both the nature of the student body and the weakness of the occupational-educational nexus in this earlier period. Most of the students dropped out because their parents could no longer afford to keep them in school; others left because a business career did not *require* four years of college, nor did a career in teaching, medicine, or law.

Before the Progressive reforms, CCNY reflected mid-nineteenth century higher education in several respects: its classical curriculum was typical of the pre-Progressive colleges; its sub-freshman curriculum was typical of the private academies; and its clientele was typical of small, local, non-aristocratic colleges.

Although the establishment of the Free Academy was clearly part of the early reform movement, City College's contribution to the reform of education was probably less in curricular reform than in the development of mass education above the elementary level. By combining academy and college in a public, tax-supported tuition-free institution, and by opening entrance examinations to persons who had attended the public elementary schools, the founders of the Free Academy created, in effect, the first public educational "ladder." They accomplished this more than a generation before the high school-college nexus was constructed on a national scale by reforms of the

**Comparison of Professional Distribution of Graduates
of City College and Columbia College (1853–1928)***

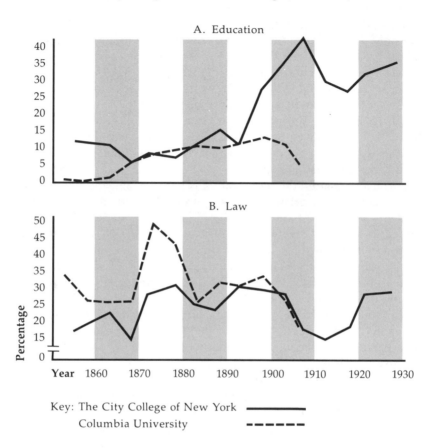

A. Education

B. Law

Key: The City College of New York ──────────
     Columbia University   ── ── ──

*SOURCES: Mortimer Karpp, "Vocations of College Men, 1849–1934," *The Personnel Journal* (October 1934), pp. 158–168, and Bailey B. Burritt, "Professional Distribution of College and University Graduates," *U.S. Bureau of Education Bulletin* 19 (1912), pp. 9–144.

Both Karpp and Burritt base their data primarily on alumni records. Karpp's study rests particularly on a special Register published by the Alumni in 1932, covering about two-thirds of all students in attendance between 1849 and 1930, and on the records of

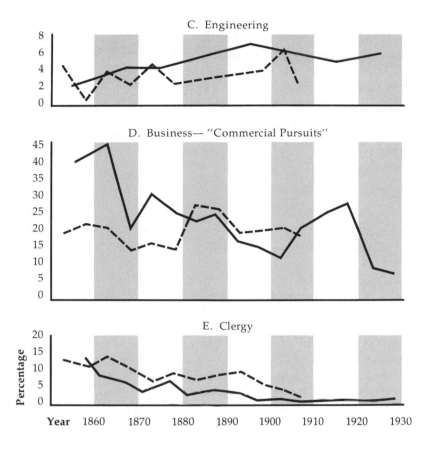

C. Engineering

D. Business— "Commercial Pursuits"

E. Clergy

Year 1860 1870 1880 1890 1900 1910 1920 1930

the CCNY Personnel Bureau. Burritt's study covered 37 institutions and, in addition to alumni records, used various special studies generally done by the institutions themselves. Although such data present certain methodological problems, Burritt's study falls within the period of measurement fetishism of the first two decades of this century, and thus would have been done with extreme regard for scientific standards. Karpp's study was undoubtedly aided by the fact that most CCNY graduates stayed within New York City, and were thus easier to trace by means of other sources.

Unfortunately Karpp's data are presented entirely in graph form (as shown). Burritt's data also appear as tables, and I have superimposed these data on the graph.

Carnegie foundation, National Education Association, and College Entrance Examination Board.

Half a century before the first high school was established in New York City, the Free Academy made it possible for a New York boy, whose family was not immediately dependent on the income from his wages, to obtain free public schooling from "common school" through the sub-freshman year of the Free Academy, and on through the remaining four years of a City College baccalaureate. As we will see in Chapter 6, as late as 1911 that possibility became a reality for an extremely small proportion of the population and an even smaller proportion of the working class. But its significance, especially in the earlier period, lies not in its mass effect, but in its institutional innovation.

The Restraints on Reform

Despite its early start in educational reform, CCNY remained in the prescribed classical mold for a number of years after the elite colleges had begun to introduce more "modern" subjects, a more modern pedagogical method, and the elective principle. "While American Higher Education was being transformed by a notable group of academic reformers," Rudy says, "the College of the City of New York . . . remained what she had always been, a liberal arts college with a number of prescribed curricula." But Rudy seems to exaggerate the backwardness of CCNY; judging by a 1901 survey on the prevalence of the elective principle in "97 representative colleges" City College was about average in the timing of its reforms.[17] It had, however, lost the vanguard to Harvard, Johns Hopkins, Cornell, and Columbia.

Adolph Werner, one of the members of the faculty who pushed hard and long for the modernization of City College, attributed the slowness of reform to "the lack of able leadership, the conservatism and inertia of the faculty, and the apathy and lack of imagination of Trustees and Alumni."[18] But Harvard and Yale had certainly not lacked conservatives, and if the classical faculty had not developed *everywhere* an entrenched interest in the virtues of tradition, Carnegie's pension funds would scarcely have been as essential as they were for the introduction of the elective system. The conservatism of the faculty is thus of minor explanatory value in understanding the failure of the educational reformers to triumph. Indeed when funds did become available in 1900, exactly the same measure as in the nationwide reforms—the establishment of a pension fund for President Webb and the recalcitrant faculty—quickly removed conservative faculty and incapable leadership as impediments to reform.

City College was not considered a "lead institution"; it did not receive foundation grants, and it was subject to municipal politics. The lack of financial resources on a scale large enough to finance the expensive elective system was of fundamental importance at CCNY as it was throughout higher education. Like the trustees of Yale in 1828, the trustees and faculty of City College could regard as "ludicrous [the] attempt to imitate . . . [the German universities] while it [was] unprovided with the resources necessary to execute the purpose."[19]

City College's position in the stratified system of higher education played a role in slowing reform that went beyond lack of finances, although the stratification was increasingly economically based. There is at least one indication that the College was supposed to keep its place. According to Rudy,

> As late as 1901 a City College trustee, J. F. Mulqueen, advised his fellow trustee, Edward M. Shepard, not to carry through a plan for a postgraduate course leading to the Master's degree at the College. The reason given was that the plan might offend President Low of Columbia and thus in the long run injure the larger interests of the College. Shepard and the other trustees seem to have heeded this cautionary advice, for no Master's degree was established at this time.[20]

This diffidence is especially noteworthy since Low was considered a friend of City College, and its backers supported him for mayor. Apparently his friendship was conditioned on CCNY's inferiority.

Finally, the nature of prestige in a stratified system would explain how an innovative institution like the Free Academy became relatively conservative. The more that higher education ceased being local, and became nationally hierarchically organized, the more institutions such as Columbia set the definitions of prestige and educational legitimacy. Less established institutions may take the risk of experimentation, but it is only when their "demonstration projects" are adopted by the established institutions that these innovations acquire real legitimacy.[21] The fact that Columbia served the children of wealthier parents, and was run by more prestigious trustees, would have reinforced its ability to define educational legitimacy more readily than CCNY (although Columbia President Frederick A. P. Barnard had great difficulty with conservatism among Columbia trustees as well). Thus we may conjecture that CCNY's position as a "poor cousin's" college would have encouraged segments of its faculty and some of its students to insist on the prescribed, classical curriculum until *after* the elective principle and the more pragmatic studies had been securely sanctified at the leading institutions.

Social Conflict and Social Change in New York

In New York City, as in the nation, the reform of higher education had to await the transformation of economy and society. The reform of CCNY did not become possible until the very turn of the century, when immigration to New York was surging to its peak, the labor movement was growing stronger, and New York City experienced the social conflicts and social changes which made educational reform necessary and possible on a national scale.

Except for agrarian populists, the whole dramatis personae of the Progressive drama were in New York at the end of the nineteenth century. New York housed the polar opposites of capitalism: the captains of industry and finance, and a foreign-born proletariat.

In New York City, the most populous city in North America, the European immigrants' most important port of entry by 1900, 76 percent of the population consisted of either the foreign-born or children of the foreign-born. Thousands marched on May Day. Cloak-makers struck yearly. Socialist factions struggled, wrote newspapers, and organized unions. In New York City the industrial giants, fresh from their victorous battles in the social Darwinian struggle, located their headquarters near the largest and most powerful financial institutions.[22] New York City either spawned or housed many of the nationally important Progressive leaders, men such as Nicholas Murray Butler, Bernard Baruch, August Belmont, Louis D. Brandeis, Seth Low, Theodore Roosevelt, Jacob Schiff, Isaac Seligman, and Oscar Straus. New York City was also the base of the Jewish *haute bourgeoisie*, of part of the Jewish *petit bourgeoisie*, and of most of the Jewish proletariat. In New York City the Jewish bourgeoisie waged educational war in Jewish culture.

In the 1890s, the business class in New York City mobilized to gain control of municipal government, much as the smaller municipalities were to do beginning in 1900.[23] Turning the efforts of muckrakers into a condemnation of Tammany rule, wrapping themselves simultaneously in robes of "non-partisanship" and "reform," forming such neutral-sounding political groups as the "Committee of Seventy," the Progressives captured City government in 1894, winning the election of Republican William L. Strong as Mayor. In 1897 their victory in centralizing the schools sufficiently antagonized the local ethnic communities to result in the defeat of their mayoralty candidate to Tammany's Robert C. Van Wyck. But once again they were able to use muckraking against him, and in 1901 a "Fusion of Independents" won the mayoralty for Seth Low.[24] Meanwhile, the Progressives captured the governorship under Levi P. Morton in 1894 and Teddy Roosevelt in 1900.

The Committee's "non-partisan drive to secure a non-political city administration"[25] mobilized such national civic figures as Butler and Low, backed by bankers and corporate lawyers; national and international businessmen such as Vanderbilt and Olin; big real estate interests concerned with the development of "model tenements," and such local notables as City College alumni Edward M. Shepard, Everett P. Wheeler, and R. R. Bowker, all prominent lawyers active in city politics. As David Hammack has put it, these big businessmen had been for fiscal restraint as long as they mistrusted government, "but when they gained power for themselves, they discovered that an active government could be a good thing."[26]

The Progressive Transformation of CCNY

The main difference between CCNY and the prestige institutions was that City College was a public institution, which from a Progressive point of view had economic advantages and political disadvantages. Financially, the fact that CCNY was publicly supported meant that tax money could be spent for educational innovation without drawing on private philanthropy. In 1896, with the backing of the changed New York City administration, CCNY was able to induce the state legislature to pass a bill raising the College's annual budget from $150,000 to $175,000. The increase was used to raise salaries and expand the faculty, a measure that facilitated internal changes within City College.

Although public education was a relatively inexpensive way of implementing educational reform, public monies could be used for that purpose only if the reformers secured political control. Whereas private philanthropy could be both direct and swift in its results, action through government required either mobilizing public support or neutralizing public antagonism, or both. Given the divided nature of the public, reform in fact involved another set of alternatives. The reformers either had to meet each political and educational issue head-on, by simultaneously mobilizing a "respectable" public and discrediting the mere masses, or they had to remove educational decision making from the open political arena entirely. The latter is the course that they in fact took, but its achievement required several years of vicious political battle in order to wrest control of educational decision making from public election and vest it in appointed and virtually self-perpetuating boards. Not until control of public education was taken out of the public's hands could New York business and educational liberals remold public education—in the interest of business—in the public's name.

Although New York City had two educational "ladders"—the preparatory schools of City College and its female counterpart, the Normal College—those ladders were too narrow for the developments of the late nineteenth century.[27] The absence of separate high schools meant that New York youngsters could not be prepared in public institutions for any college other than the two City colleges, a fact which impeded their integration into the developing national system of higher education.

The creation of the middle rungs of the career ladders—the high schools—required fighting a battle on several fronts. The Regents, who favored the private academies and were generally hostile to public education, had to be reorganized and prodded into pursuing their statutory responsibility for the development of high schools throughout the state. The hostility of the private colleges, City College, and the Normal College, had to be overcome.[28] And the local boards of trustees, which controlled lower education in New York City, had to be divested of their power.

THE CENTRALIZATION OF NEW YORK CITY SCHOOLS

Until 1900 CCNY's basic educational policy was made by a Board of Trustees selected by the New York Board of Education. Before 1896 most educational policy for the grammar schools was made by local school boards elected within electoral wards; the central Board of Education for Manhattan and the Bronx, which was also popularly elected, was not very powerful. Local control over public education was not very conducive to the development of high schools, and it was not very conducive to control by big businessmen and major educational leaders.

In 1896 the Progressives took over New York City schools administratively by removing control over the public schools from the elected local school boards and centering it in an appointed central School Board for Greater New York. Centralization was a successful attempt by big business white Protestant Progressive Republicans to wrest control of the public schools from local ethnic communities, from Democratic politicians, and from local, primarily ethnic, business-men.[29]

The main figure in the seven-year struggle was Nicholas Murray Butler, who was in these same years helping to standardize high school curricula and college admissions through the National Education Association and the College Entrance Examination Board. (Butler was elected President of the NEA in 1894.) The organizational force in centralization was supplied by a Committee of Five of the Committee of Seventy, which had ousted Tammany in 1894, a Public Education Association under Butler's virtual control, and finally a Committee of One Hundred.

The Committee of One Hundred stood for "efficiency, Republican control and Americanization," for forced assimilation as against plu-ralism and "the melting pot." School Commissioner Joseph Little called its members "Anglomaniacs."[30] Several belonged to the anti-Catholic National League for the Protection of American Institutions, notably Abram S. Hewitt, ex-Mayor of New York and industrialist, who had backed Butler for U. S. Commissioner of Education in 1889. They were generally big businessmen with direct business interests in the projects involved in "municipal reform," as well as class interests in supporting that education "which would inculcate respect for private property and individual liberty."[31] Later, many of these same men would be involved in reforming CCNY.[32]

Virtually all of the members of the Committee of One Hundred were listed in the *Social Register*, with the exeption of Jacob Schiff and Isaac Seligman, who as Jews were of course excluded from it, but who as bankers and Progressives were similarly dedicated to "converting the Russian Jews and Italian Catholics" to Americanism and anti-socialism.[33] They wanted to establish mayoral appointment of a small, strong, centralized board under their control. As they saw the problem, the schools could not be left to local influences because "the American middle class had left the city, delivering the schools in immigrant neighborhoods into the hands of political hacks."[34] School board positions had to be "sanitized" by making them subject to appoint-ment by the mayor. Mayoral appointment of a central board would put education in Progressive hands; it would make education "nonpoliti-cal"; it would "substitute intelligent men and women"—persons like themselves—for foreigners. As Hammack says, the reformers "wished to select men for positions on both lay boards and the professional staff by a process similar to that with which a man gained entrance to and advanced within their private clubs."[35]

Butler, who had accomplished the same feat of political accumulation in New Jersey on both the state level and locally in Paterson, Trenton, Vineland, and Camden, expressed the political meaning of such reform when he boasted that in New Jersey, by the end of 1893, "there has been no partisan legislation on educational subjects during the past five years. Every important act that has been passed during that time has been either drawn or suggested by myself and those who are associated with me in the oversight of the system."[36] He had eliminated "partisanship" by monopolizing power.

Butler's own career illustrates perfectly the meaning of non-partisan, non-political reform. Rejecting any and all offers to run for public office, even an 1883 New Jersey Assembly nomination which would have virtually guaranteed election, Butler preferred "non-political" power—that is, power conferred by appointment—to what he termed "political jobbery"—that is, popular election. A year after he rejected the nomination to run for the New Jersey Assembly, he accepted appointment to the New Jersey State Board of Education. In 1892 Butler and many of these same Progressive leaders began a ten-year campaign to remove supervision of the New York Common School from the *elected* State Superintendent of Public Instruction and place it in the hands of the *appointed* Regents of the University of New York. Until then the Regents had had control only over secondary schools, colleges, and universities, although they had considerable indirect influence on the lower schools.

But Butler and his associates met strong opposition in their effort to "sanitize" public education. Arrayed against them in the New York school centralization fight were business and community leaders from Yorkville, Harlem, and the Bronx whose base would be destroyed by centralization, some county Republican leaders (particularly the Jewish and German ones), the entire Democratic organization, and "spokesmen for a variety of Protestant communities, for some Jews and for the Catholics, and nearly everyone connected with the public schools."[37] Virtually *all* the teachers opposed centralization vigorously and actively (with the possible exception of Julia Richman, who was a prominent Progressive).

The battle was fierce. It took the Progressives seven years to win. In 1895, when they attempted to legislate centralization in Albany, four thousand teachers attended a mass meeting sponsored by the New York City Teachers' Association. They accused Butler's "Committee of Five" of "trying to introduce politics into the schools," and lobbied successfully against the bill. The audience at a meeting held by the Women's Association for the Improvement of the Public Schools was so hostile that Thomas Hunter, president of the Normal School, "abandoned the attempt to speak [at this meeting] and [reformer Payson] Merril retired under a barrage of catcalls. . . ."[38]

Despite this opposition, the reformers eventually prevailed. In 1896 they succeeded in getting the state legislature to pass the Pavey bill, centralizing control in an appointed Board of Education and empowering that board to establish high schools.

The centralization of control in the hands of an appointed and centralized Board of Education had many implications. With the abolition of the local school trustees, one of the teachers observed that parental interest, participation, and pride in the schools declined. Workers, who had had very little say in educational policy making in the old system, had even less in the new.[39] Pluralism, as the mode of integration of ethnic groups favored by the local trustees, suffered a severe blow. The social position of teachers and principals declined. For educational system-building, and for City College, the impact was immediate. The establishment of high schools permitted the State Board of Regents to require modifications in CCNY's curriculum and admissions requirements, beyond the changes the board had already begun to set in motion.

LEGISLATING THE LADDERS

Even before they were able to make internal administrative changes within CCNY and other institutions within the state, Butler and his associates used their influence with the legislature and the State Board of Regents to transform the colleges from without.[40] Over the years, the Regents had been given control over licensing and certification of physicians, dentists, veterinarians, and lawyers. For years they had used their control over the Literature Fund to specify the kind of pre-professional training acceptable for certification.

In 1893 the State Board of Regents ruled that it would grant certification for admission to law school only to those candidates who had had a full four-year high school course, and they refused to accept as an equivalent City College's sub-freshman year, which until then had substituted for all of high school. The Regents insisted on three preparatory years at the College for certification. In 1896, the year of the passage of the Pavey Bill centralizing the school board and mandating it to establish high schools, the Regents introduced what might be called the Carnegie contingency. They required that "for an institution to be ranked as a college in New York it must not only have a course of four full years of college grade in liberal arts and sciences, but must also require for admission four years of high school in addition to pre-academic or grammar school studies."[41] Under the threat that it could not grant degrees after 1901, the City College faculty expanded the preparatory course to a three-year, multi-curriculum program, and restricted admission to the College to graduates of that program or of the new four-year municipal high schools.[42] The increase in preparatory training lengthened the course of study at CCNY from five years to seven (three preparatory years plus four years of college). The "ladder of opportunity" had added a few more rungs, which meant, of course, that it was accessible to more people but involved a steeper and longer climb.

In 1897 New York State changed its certification requirements for teachers in the common schools, stipulating that they had to have passed a course in pedagogy. Since City College had been, from the very beginning, mainly engaged in producing teachers, the change in state certification requirements necessitated an immediate change in curriculum, a change which William Wood had previously been unable to get the CCNY trustees to pass. As Graph A on page 68 shows, the proportion of CCNY graduates entering the field of education increased markedly at this point.

Thus by means of its administrative control over certification, the State Board of Regents, prodded by a legislature pushed by the Progressives, was able to force the City College trustees and faculty to substantially revise the College's curriculum even before internal administrative changes made reform from within possible. Their influence was facilitated, however, by the simultaneous changes in the politics of education within New York City, by the availability, after 1897, of funds for the hiring of new faculty, and, beginning in 1900, by changes in CCNY's own administration.

REORGANIZATION AND REFORM

The administrative reorganization of CCNY was brought about by means similar to those used on a national level. Pension funds were created to entice conservatives to retire, and the faculty (restricted, as at all unreformed colleges, to professors) was expanded and "democratized" to increase the proportion of liberals. Echoing the Dartmouth College case (although under far different circumstances), the role of the trustees was strengthened at the expense of public authorities.[43] Finally, General Alexander Webb, a college president in the old-fashioned tradition of the moral leader, was replaced in 1903 by a modern young Progressive, John H. Finley.

The strong force behind all these changes was a group of "militant members of the Associate Alumni," led principally by Edward M. Shepard, Everett P. Wheeler, R. R. Bowker, Alexander P. Ketchum, and Edward Lauterbach. The group had organized around 1890, initially in the interest of securing municipal funds for new buildings, the old building having become inadequate as early as the 1850s.[44]

Encountering the opposition of state and city authorities to greater investment in higher education (at the presumed expense of the improvement of elementary education), these alumni found in their goals for CCNY added reason to promote the election of Progressive government on the city and state levels. The 1894 victories made possible authorization for funds for a new site and new buildings from the state legislature, and an expanded budget for the city. Furthermore, the new mayor, William L. Strong, appointed his close personal friend, Alexander P. Ketchum, chairman of the Executive Committee on City College of the Board of Education. Ketchum, a leading Republican lawyer and banker, had been president of the Alumni Association in 1879 and was elected president of the City College Club when it was organized in 1890.

The new Executive Committee immediately took advantage of a protest made by the tutors and supported the creation of the ranks of instructor and assistant professor. Significantly, they did not accede to the tutors' demand that promotion be automatic after seven years; instead they maintained a structure of power by vesting authority over promotions to the new ranks in the existing faculty. When, after three years, the twelve professors who constituted the existing faculty had failed to promote anyone to the rank of assistant professor, however, the trustees promoted eight instructors, some of whom had served in the College for twenty-five years or more, to assistant professors. In addition, they appointed two new assistant professors from Yale and Cornell. The new appointments "made it possible to inject new blood into the Faculty for the first time in almost three decades. This strengthened the younger, more liberal contingent in that body, creating [a] progressive majority. . . ."[45] The Progressive majority was further strengthened in 1908 by means of promotion and appointment, and again when funds became available for altering the political composition of the faculty by the same means.

If ultimate power over CCNY rested with the Board of Trustees, the remodeling of the faculty along Progressive lines would be effective only if the Board of Trustees remained securely in Progressive hands. Therefore the next major administrative reorganization involved the Board itself. The 1897 Progressive defeat in the municipal elections (caused in part by public anger at the centralization of the schools) no doubt increased the desire of the Progressives to "sanitize" the Board of Trustees of City College, even from the influence of the newly "sanitized" Board of Education.

In the eyes of the Associate Alumni, the larger Board was preoccupied with the problems of setting up new high schools, too large and unwieldy, and "made up of overworked men who were not always in sympathy with the College or conversant with its needs."[46] They proposed a small Board of Trustees for the college, independent of the Board of Education.

Apparently the overworked men on the Board of Education were not grateful for their deliverance from the chores of overseeing the governance of City College. They fought the reorganization. The Board of Education was joined, in opposition, by the majority of the College faculty.

The opponents argued that the creation of a separate Board of Trustees would separate CCNY from the elementary school system, from the high schools that "had been constituted as the future feeders of the college" and from "our sister college" (Hunter). Furthermore, the separation would alienate popular support.[47] But Edward M. Shepard, Everett P. Wheeler, and Alexander P. Ketchum, "had a great deal of influence in the politics of the State, and their opinions carried weight with both parties." With the support of the mayor and the governor, the reorganization passed the legislature. Thenceforth, "full and complete power to govern the College" was vested in nine men appointed by the mayor for nine years, with the president of the Board of Education serving ex officio.[48] The staggering of the initial appointments further insured that the composition of the Board of Trustees would not be influenced by the vicissitudes of popular election. Only a few of the subsequent vacancies would fall open to appointment by any particular future mayor. The new, reorganized Board of Trustees contained Shepard, Lauterbach, and several other "militant alumni." In the reorganization of the Board, they had moved from a position of informal influence to direct control. They had institutionalized their power.

The new Board members moved immediately to make the final changes in administration necessary for the implementation of curricular and pedagogical reform. They established a pension fund, which finally induced Webb to leave a post in which he had long been under attack, and they began the search for a new Progressive president.

The man they selected, John Huston Finley, was the very model of a modern educational executive. A student of history and political economy at Johns Hopkins, the youngest college present in the country when installed as president of Knox College in 1892, Professor of Politics at Princeton, he was a total contrast to Webb. He represented scholarship rather than theology, reform rather than tradition, national political links rather than local political links. At Johns Hopkins he had aided Richard T. Ely in the preparation of *Taxation in American States and Cities;* in 1908 he was to co-author *The American Executive and Executive Methods*, and later published numerous other works.[49] Finley's status as a Progressive is indicated by the list of his friends and supporters: Woodrow Wilson, his classmate at Hopkins, had brought him to Princeton, where Grover Cleveland was his close friend; Nicholas Murray Butler urged him to take the position in New York; and his appointment was hailed by the major Progressive magazines of the day—*The Outlook, Harper's Weekly,* and the New York *Commercial Advertiser.* In 1907 Finley was elected to the Board of Directors of the New York Peace Society, where he befriended Andrew Carnegie. He was also acquainted with Taft and Roosevelt.

Finley's Progressive connections were important, both in assuring that New York City provided the money necessary for the implementation of further reforms at City College and in linking City College into the national educational system. His friends of national repute— Felix Adler, Franklin Giddings, Helen Keller, Andrew Carnegie—spoke at the College. International figures visited the new campus. As a result of all these linkages, the College began to recruit faculty nationally rather than locally, partly through Finley's own connections and partly through the reputation which his national and international efforts gave to the College.

Marvin Gettleman argues that Finley was more a traditional than a modern college president, on the grounds that he was still personally related to his students and served as a charismatic and moral leader. Gettleman also shows that unlike Harvard's Charles Eliot, Finley was not an educational innovator.[50] But Finley did not need to be an innovator like Eliot in order to be a Progressive force at CCNY. Eliot already existed; his reforms had already been introduced at Harvard and elsewhere; a group of alumni/businessmen/trustees already knew which reforms they wished to implement, and Finley was enough of a Progressive modern president to help them implement those reforms. Thus, in the particular social context, his personal dynamism, charisma, and general Progressive philosophy were sufficient for the role he was to play.

At the heart of the Progressive reforms, it will be remembered, were original research, particularly in the sciences, rather than received "truths"; a professional faculty based on scholarship rather than on Christian piety and traditional knowledge; and individualized, "meritocratic," career-oriented instruction, based on the elective system in the place of a prescribed and uniform curriculum that failed to differentiate sufficiently among students. With the Progressive reorganization of the trustees, faculty, and presidency, this trinity of interrelated reforms became more attainable at City College.

In 1904 the trustees made the Ph.D. a prerequisite to future instructorships, thereby further linking CCNY to the higher education hierarchy in which only a minority of elite institutions train Ph.D.s for the rest. In 1905 a thorough reconsideration of CCNY's arts and sciences curriculum resulted in the creation, a year later, of six alternative prescribed courses of study. Within each of these increased scope was given to elective studies in the junior and senior years. In 1907 several new departments were formed, among them political science; and, in response to further state efforts to professionalize teaching by raising certification requirements, a department of education was established. After 1907 the curriculum expanded continually, introducing more and more of the "modern" courses in the new disciplines.[51]

The expansion of the curriculum facilitated expansion of the faculty, which in turn bolstered attempts to change its political composition. Attempts were made to fill several vacancies by recruiting persons of national scholarly repute. In 1908 the democratization of the faculty was carried a few steps further. The right to vote within the faculty was extended to assistant professors, and numerous promotions were made. The democratization of the faculty, at City College as elsewhere, was inextricably linked with the creation of a faculty hierarchy, the increase of credentialism, the organization of national professional disciplines and national scholarly reputations, and the politics of curricular reforms.[52]

The development of "meritocratic," career-oriented individualized instruction of students was also dependent on administrative, political, and curricular changes. Increased Progressive control brought reforms in student life. Hitherto suppressed student complaints were honored. The student status was transformed from the traditional pedagogy of uniform promotion by class and closely regimented discipline based on compulsory attendance and a minute merit and demerit system, to the "modern" pedagogy suitable to the elective principle—promotion by subject, greater differentiation of degrees and honors, and more indirect and subtle supervision. For example, in 1904 Finley substituted public speaking for required daily attendance at chapel, a change which must have reflected the fact that the majority of the student body was now Jewish at least as much as it reflected the liberal thinking of its devoutly Presbyterian president.

The atmosphere of reform was in turn facilitated by the questioning spirit and greater seriousness of the working-class Russian Jewish students who were just starting to predominate among the student body. To these students school was not a mere extension of adolescence; they took their schooling seriously and, in turn, demanded to be taken seriously. In part, the reforms of both faculty structure and student governance were responses to protests by tutors and students. The Progressives were able to take advantage of these protests to transform the balance of political forces on the faculty and to introduce the type of student governance suitable to the elective principle. Each of their reforms involved democratization. Democratization meant greater differentiation, the ramification of hierarchy, and the creation of career ladders for both faculty and students. Democratization meant both greater individual freedom and greater centralized control.

Democracy and the Progressive Reform of CCNY

The reform of education, and the reform of City College in particular, illustrates the definition of democracy promulgated by the Progressives as against the definition of democracy promulgated by the socialists. To the Progressives *democracy* meant the philanthropic administration of wealth by the capitalist class as opposed to redistribution of wealth between the classes. *Democracy* meant individual opportunity for mobility as opposed to working class organization; democracy thus required the removal of policymaking from the public and its centralization in Progressive hands. *Democracy* meant a college education for rich and poor in which opportunity for the poor would not undermine advantage for the rich. Finally, *democracy* meant closer articulation between education and industry, to provide individual choice among alternative career paths within a *given* structure.

The battles between educational liberals and conservatives were serious and far-reaching, but they had their own limitations. None of the protagonists on either side was representative of the toiling masses. The Progressives who waged the school centralization fight included the heads of international banks, international law firms, and other major corporations. The old Board of Education and local school boards included local bankers and other local businessmen and lawyers. The Associate Alumni who created the new, separate Board of Trustees for City College were, with a few exceptions, much the same folk who centralized the schools. Their opponents on the Board of Education were local businessmen and lawyers. No workers were on the Boards of either side.

Workers may very well have been on the reformers' minds, however. City College's Progressive faculty, alumni, and trustees consciously modeled their reforms on the national reforms, and many of the New York reformers were Carnegie's associates in various Progressive organizations. The CCNY policymakers were very aware that CCNY was located in a city filled with political turmoil and radical sympathies, "at the place where Europe [was] stepping up to America," as Finley put it.[53] Many of the Progressives believed that City College had an obligation not only to provide opportunities for social advancement for children of immigrants but also to teach these offspring to assist in the political socialization of the immigrant community. But none of the protagonists in the higher educational battles—neither the classicists nor the pragmatists, neither conservatives nor Progressives—proposed to make the College of the City of New York a place that would fulfill the aims of workers' education as various Working Men's Parties of the 1830s had articulated them: "not only to enlighten the mind upon general subjects, but to teach that class, who supply the fountain of existence, whence their evils spring and how to remedy them."[54]

At the end of the nineteenth century, precisely when the Russian Jewish immigrants were arriving in New York City in great numbers, CCNY and the New York educational institutions as a whole were transformed into a hierarchical system—an educational career ladder—that had only partially existed before. Whereas in 1880 no public high schools existed in New York beyond the sub-freshman year of the

Normal College and the City College, by 1911 there were nineteen high schools, and despite the fact that very few youngsters graduated from them, 60 percent of elementary school graduates did enter their freshman year. In these years the educational career ladder became wider, steeper, more bureaucratically organized, and more definitely under the control of the Progressives.

In 1900, precisely when the children of Russian Jewish immigrants were entering CCNY in great numbers, it was tripling in size and was being transformed from a place primarily oriented to the consumption of cultural tradition to a modern college primarily oriented to the production of knowledge and educated manpower—a college more suited to widespread use as a channel of mobility.

By 1918–1919 nine institutions of higher learning served the New York metropolitan area. With the exception of the College of Dental and Oral Surgery, which enrolled only 589 students, City College had the largest proportion of Jewish students. With only 18 percent of New York City students, CCNY had 29 percent of New York Jewish students. Undoubtedly these were the students from poorer homes, CCNY and Hunter College being the only schools among the nine to be tuition-free.[55] These two city colleges soon became even more important for the education of Jewish students when the elite schools, including Columbia University, abruptly began a quota system to exclude Jews, preferring to preserve elite institutions in white Protestant purity.

In a system based on class and ethnic inequality, exclusiveness is a class privilege and becomes mythologized into a mark of superiority. A democratic institution in such a society must suffer, by definition, the mark of inferiority. City College, college of the Jewish poor, bore that mark. It was stigmatized as the "Jewish University of America." It was "taken over" by too many "dirty and tactless Jews." It was, like the University of Pennsylvania, lowered to "the democracy of the street car."[56]

But a democratic institution often comes to take on a culture of its own. While Harvard, Princeton, and Columbia were cultivating the "gentleman's C," students at the City College were making CCNY into a unique institution, with a scholarly, ethnic, and political character all its own.

Manual training class c. 1890. *Jacob A. Riis/Jacob A. Riis Collection, Museum of the City of New York*

Public school classroom, c. 1910. *Lewis Hine*

5

The Creation of Occupational Opportunity

Every school-house may be made a stronghold of defense against the spread of socialistic and un-American ideas.
—Governor Roswell P. Flower

It will certainly be a revelation to many an American to learn how many Russian Jewish young men and girls are doing this work of "Americanization," not only of Jewish, but of Irish, German and Italian children.
—Isaac Rubinow, in Bernheimer,
The Russian Jew in America

Schoolteachers, especially those in grammar and high schools, are the economic proletarians of the professions.
—C. Wright Mills, *White Collar*

Scholars celebrate not only Jewish success, but the American opportunities which, they say, made that success possible. What were those opportunities? How did they happen? And what was their meaning?

Jewish immigrants and their children went into business, clerical work, and sales. They became dentists, doctors, and lawyers. But of the professions, the most prevalent was education. Education was the largest profession at the turn of the century. It was the occupation that showed the greatest numerical increase and the second largest proportional increase between 1870 and 1930. Education claimed the largest number and percent of all college graduates in 1900, and the largest number and percent of City College graduates from 1895 until at least the 1930s. By 1935, education was second only to business as the most common occupation of Jewish college graduates.[1]

Because the development of the teaching profession sheds light on the manner in which the occupational structure changed at the turn of the century and because the teaching profession was one of the major occupational destinations of college-educated Jews, in this chapter I will focus on the social forces that led to the expansion and transformation of education as a career. I shall argue: 1. that the Jewish immigrants and the movements in which they participated contributed, directly and indirectly, to the expansion of schooling and thereby to the expansion of teaching; 2. that the professionalization of teaching endowed it with an ideology antithetical to the aims of Jewish and non-Jewish labor; 3. that just when Jews were moving into the teaching profession, it was being transformed into an administrative structure that diminished the power of teachers while professionalizing them; and 4. that these forces are evident in the development of the Education Department at the College of the City of New York, where the children of immigrants became professional Americanizers as teachers and principals, while Columbia University was developing top administrators. Jews in the teaching profession were subject to the conflicting social forces that brought that profession into being.

Class Conflict and the Growth of Education

Social conflicts at the turn of the century were major factors in the expansion of public elementary and high schools. For over a century, from the 1820s well into the twentieth century, organizations of labor fought for the restriction of child labor, the shortening of the working day, and compulsory schooling. Without the shortening of the working day, they said, workers lacked time for education and cultural development; without child labor laws, children were not free to learn or develop.

In the early nineteenth century, Working Men's Parties demanded free public elementary schooling, and some local workers' groups set up schools of their own. Like some other organizations before them, the Knights of Labor in the 1880s supported free elementary schooling in the context of their demand for the abolition of child labor. They stressed compulsory attendance because they understood the ineffectual nature of voluntary education when parents were underpaid and industrialists had the option of voluntarily hiring their children for even lower pay. The AFL took a similar stance, becoming more and more adamant in favor of compulsory attendance and prohibition of child labor as the decades wore on.[2]

In this struggle, business groups sought to prevent, limit, or weaken all laws that tampered with child labor. In times of social crisis, however, when faced with an active and radical working-class movement, or in economic depressions when unemployed youth roamed the streets, capitalists were more apt to become enraptured by the civic need to inculcate moral discipline by means of expansion of the common school. They espoused truancy laws that stipulated that children had to be "either at work or at school."[3] In the 1870s and 1880s, with the rise of labor militancy, organized labor secured the support of middle-class social reformers in curtailing or modifying child labor by some form of enforced schooling. At the same time, employers developed an interest in the use of the schools for manual training.

Radicalism among foreign-born workers led to a zealous—sometimes frantic—effort to Americanize the immigrants. "These people form, as a whole, an unassimilable element wherever they congregate," John Buchanan declared in a Progressive magazine.

> The only way in which they can be reached is through their children, by means of the new ideas that the children have conceived and carried home. . . .
>
> Education will solve every problem of our national life, even that of assimilating our foreign element. . . . The nation has a right to demand intelligence and virtue of every citizen, and to obtain these by force if necessary. Compulsory education we must have as a safeguard for our institutions.[4]

Buchanan was principal of one of New York City's new high schools at the time.

Large-scale immigration; socialist and labor movements; the struggles over compulsory schooling, an end to child labor, and manual training; the conflicts over the creation of high schools—all of these social struggles led to an enormous expansion of schooling, and therefore of teaching.

Given the level of conflict and capitalist development in New York City, it is no surprise that New York led in labor legislation and compulsory education. New York State's 1853 truancy law was the third compulsory education law in the nation. The truancy law did not restrict child labor, however; it restricted child vagrancy, encouraging the children of the poor to work.[5]

After the Civil War, workers' organizations and philanthropic organizations again pressed for passage of child labor and compulsory schooling laws, and in 1874 such a law was passed in New York State. Enacted against manufacturers' pressures and lacking enforcement, the state law was strengthened in the 1880s as a result of consistent pressure by organized labor and social reformers. The law was finally made more effective in 1903, under the cooperative pressure of organized labor and settlement Progressives. These later measures restricted child labor in addition to compelling school attendance. Enforcement of the child labor laws was more thorough in New York City, thanks to "a more aroused public" outraged by the killing of 146 workers, mostly women and children, in the Triangle Shirt Waist fire.[6]

Americanization was also more fierce in New York with its strong socialist movement. Buchanan exclaimed, "Without its free public schools New York would be helpless in dealing with its hundreds of thousands of foreign population." New York had a disproportion of those particularly dangerous aliens, the Southern and Eastern European immigrants. Although they formed 37.4 percent of immigrants to the United States, Southern and Eastern Europeans formed 59.1 percent of the immigrants residing in New York City in 1910.[8] Almost 58 percent of the children in the nation's thirty-seven largest cities were of foreign-born parentage in 1909; in New York the figure was 71.5 percent.

In addition to the socialist and labor activities that frightened policymakers into expanding education, immigrants made direct demands on the school beyond their sheer numbers. Jewish parents rioted when overcrowded schools excluded their children.[9] And responding to the same constituency, the Jewish bourgeoisie expanded the *forms* of public schooling through their experimentation at the Educational Alliance.

Between 1860 and 1896, the number of pupils taught in New York public schools jumped from 145,870 to 318,545. The number of teachers almost tripled, from 1,548 to 4,484. By 1903, with the former cities of Brooklyn, Queens, and Richmond consolidated into Greater New York, 622,201 pupils were taught by 13,131 teachers. By 1925, 848,596 students were taught by 22,497 teachers.[10]

National figures show similar leaps. Between 1870 and 1930 the U.S. population doubled: the number of persons engaged in teaching multiplied eight-fold, increasing from 126,882 in 1870, to 1,062,615 in 1930. Bailey B. Burritt's 1912 study of the professions of the graduates of thirty-seven representative colleges and universities revealed that "within [the last] 100 years the profession of teaching has grown from about one-twentieth to about one-fourth of the graduates." Teaching surpassed the ministry in 1880, and law in 1890. "Thus at the close of the century it is the dominant profession, with business as its closest competitor."[11]

This expanded teaching profession was responsible for the giant share of the opportunity for Jewish mobility into the professions. And the expansion of this opportunity had its roots, in part, in the conflicts between capital and labor, and the social movements of immigrant labor.

The Transformation of Teaching

Teaching was a modest vocation in the mid-nineteenth century. Many teachers came from poor families and had little more schooling than their students. In rural areas boarding and meals, rotated among the families of their students, comprised part of the wage. In cities the salary was so low as to require odd-jobbing to provide enough for subsistence. As late as 1911, when L. D. Coffman published *The Social Composition of the Teaching Population,* he found to his professional dismay that "most teachers become so out of economic motive," having come from families whose income "can be but little more than a bare minimum. . . ."[12]

Before the 1860s teachers taught by rote, cookbook style, hearing recitations of prescribed materials. As late as 1910, the nation's teachers had, on average, four years of schooling beyond elementary school. Twenty-one percent of Coffman's sample had had less than a year's schooling beyond grammar school; almost half had less than four years of high school.[13]

Although the years of training were sufficiently short to make teaching a possible profession for youngsters whose families could not dream of sustaining the expense involved in the even longer preparation for medicine or law, it was in itself a severe struggle. Even Coffman, who feared the influence of teachers from the uncultured lower classes, expressed his admiration that such families would "give their children the advantage of four years of school beyond the elementary school."[14]

The degree to which becoming a teacher was economically difficult for the children of the poor is illustrated in Joseph Van Denburg's data on New York City high school students (1911), which refers to the same period as Coffman's study. The students were generally working class or lower middle class. Professionals and big businessmen tended to send their children to private schools. Van Denburg collected data on the students' occupational choice, the occupations of their parents, and of their siblings. Since there is no reason to believe that this particular set of high school students would fare very differently than their older siblings, it is possible to use the occupations of those siblings as an indication of their probable fate.[15]

Most boys wished to become engineers, lawyers, and businessmen. Five percent chose teaching but only 0.8 percent of their brothers were teachers. Sixty-four percent of the girls wished to become teachers, although only between 6 and 13 percent of their sisters taught. (Teaching was 78 percent female at the time.) Instead the probable destiny of New York girls was to become clerks, stenographers, and dressmakers. The boys would become clerks, workers, and tradesmen. Those who did succeed in becoming teachers must have done so with great difficulty indeed!

The expansion of schooling fostered changes in teacher training. At the very least the development of the high school meant that some teachers had to be trained to at least the high school level, and some college training began to seem necessary to keep the teacher at least a little ahead of the students. The training of teachers began to involve not only the lengthening of their training but also a change in its nature. Beginning in the 1860s, teaching began to be seen as more than drumming a prescribed set of facts into children's memories; it came to be a matter of eliciting understanding. As Ellwood Cubberly, a major force in the professionalization of teaching and the managerialization of educational administration put it in his extremely influential text:

> [A] real "technique of instruction" was now called for, . . . Class lessons must be thought out in advance, and teacher-preparation in itself meant a great change in teaching procedure. Emancipated from dependence on the words of a text, and able to stand before a class full of a subject and able to question freely, teachers became conscious of a new strength and a professional skill unknown in the days of textbook reciting.[16]

The various Progressives who created this newly professional teacher were most concerned about the nature of the person who would "stand before the class." Coffman, writing from the heart of administrative influence, Teachers College, felt that "certainly the lower the class from which teachers come in social position the more inadequate their rational basis and insight for determining the values of the materials and techniques of education."[17] He feared that they might be "insufficiently Americanized."

There are two obvious solutions to the perceived problem of the cultural inadequacies of the poor: increased training and increased administrative control. Progressivism produced both.

The number of public normal schools in the United States rose from less than 25 in 1860 to over 150 in 1900, and close to 300 by 1930.[18] But the normal school was to be a relatively transitory phenomenon. First developed to extend the training of teachers in ordinary school subjects beyond the level of the students they were themselves teaching, the normal schools were transformed into schools for the professional study of the art and science of teaching. Later they were either supplanted by college departments of education, or retained as a lower level of instruction for teachers when administrators were receiving B.A.'s in education or graduate degrees. More recently, they have been transformed once again into general educational institutions, offering the B.A. in liberal arts.[19]

The class nature of teacher training went through a similar development. Originally, the less impoverished prospective teachers went to the normal schools, the poorest getting by with a few years of public school. But with the development of college and university departments of education, it was the poorer teaching recruits who went to normal school and the more privileged who were trained in the public college departments of education. They, in turn, were overshadowed by those still more privileged—the graduates of Columbia University's Teachers College, an institution unique in the nation.[20] The creation and development of Teachers College in New York City made that school a focal point for educational change from 1870 to 1902. During this period the institutionalization of training was integrally linked to the creation of professional ideology.

The Class Content of Pedagogy

The conflicts that expanded the schools and the teaching work force underlay the creation of professional pedagogy. It was the Progressives who defined professionalism. They endowed it with an ideology favorable to business, hostile to socialism, and scornful of immigrant cultures. Perhaps more than anyone else it was Nicholas Murray Butler who defined professionalism.[21] In creating Teachers College of Columbia University, Butler and his associates institutionalized a professional ideology that favored management's side of the dispute with labor over manual training.

THE MANUAL TRAINING CONFLICT
AND THE CREATION OF TEACHERS COLLEGE

Since 1881 F. A. P. Barnard, President of Columbia College, had been trying to implement his plan for "a Columbia University school of education that would provide leadership for the whole of American public education,"[22] but he had been thwarted by educationally conservative trustees. In 1887 Barnard and several of the more modern trustees who were members of the Industrial Education Association secured the Presidency of that Association for Nicholas Murry Butler, replacing CCNY's President Webb. The Executive Vice-President of the IEA, Grace Hoadley Dodge, daughter of "one of New York's wealthiest merchants," had built the IEA from the Kitchen Garden Association into a powerful force for manual training. She had just secured a $10,000 gift from George W. Vanderbilt in order to set up a training school for teachers of manual training.

Butler and Dodge immediately set up the New York College for the Training of Teachers, later named Teachers College of Columbia University, an institution Butler was to dominate as president for thirty-two years. Butler outlined the meaning of professionalism in innumerable articles and speeches. Professionalism required high admissions standards, supervised teaching, and educational theory. "On these principles, and on the further one that manual training should be an integral part of the common school course, the New York College for the Training of Teachers has been founded."[23]

Manual training was a subject of great controversy between capital and labor. Insofar as it represented the forces for technological change and the tendency of businessmen to look to the schools to meet some of the technologically relevant needs of industry, the manual training movement was the counterpart, on the elementary and high school level, of the movement for a scientific and technically relevant college curriculum. The colleges and the new universities would produce the research and the scientific personnel to revolutionize the machine processes of industry; manual training in elementary and high school would train workers in the constantly changing skills needed to run those machines. But changes in industrial technology are complex. They are the result of competition among businessmen and of conflict between management and labor over productivity. The continual problem of socializing new waves of ex-peasants and ex-artisans also encouraged manufacturers to mechanize.[24]

Mechanization undermined apprenticeship; manufacturers proposed to replace apprenticeship with manual training. Workers charged them with using public schools to break union control over apprenticeship and the size of the skilled work force.[25]

In 1887 the Knights of Labor supported manual training as an effort to give due dignity to labor and to prepare boys "to become good mechanics, of wider mental horizon than heretofore. . .," but the AFL opposed manual training in the 1890s as an attempt "to turn out botch mechanics who can be used as 'dummies' in time of strikes." They called it "scab training." With the development and expansion of the high school, the controversy continued, the National Association of Manufacturers advocating "giving dignity to labor" through trade training beginning at age nine, and the AFL asserting that "general education is more important than industrial education.[26] (Notice that it was primarily the businessmen who spoke of giving dignity to labor and the unions that espoused general cultural education.)

When Butler and Dodge based their Teachers College on the Industrial Education Association, they were, in effect, integrating the corporate side of a management-labor conflict into the training and professional ideology of teachers. As Butler explained it to the business/trustees:

> The cause of manual training [can] be promoted in a permanent way only by thoroughly trained teachers; and . . . these teachers must be trained so as to view manual training in the light of the history and principles of all education, and not as a special—and more or less accidental and temporary—addition to the course of study.[27]

Thus, manual training, a most controversial political issue, could best be slipped into the schools if it lost its special character and became politically neutralized into a professional ideology.

The organizations representing capital and labor struggled for thirty years over the content, direction, meaning, and control of manual training. When Butler brought the manual training-centered New York College for the Training of Teachers into Columbia University as Teachers College, he built business interests into the structure of the leading institution in U.S. education, which was to produce top administrators for the nation.

Meanwhile City College had taught manual training for years. In the 1890s CCNY produced *all* of the manual training teachers for the New York City public schools. Thus at CCNY too, management's side of a labor dispute had become part of the assumed training of New York City teachers.[28]

TEACHERS AS PROFESSIONAL AMERICANIZERS

When "every schoolhouse [was to] be made a stronghold of defense against the spread of socialistic and un-American ideas," teachers became professional Americanizers. Progressivism had at least two divergent thrusts with regard to the immigrants. As immigration increased and radicalism of the foreign work force mounted, and as that radicalism came to be expressed in anti-war sentiment around the First World War, the more business-oriented Progressives came to favor 100 percent Americanism. The slogan of the National Americanization Day Committee, "Many Peoples, But One Nation," was replaced with a new one, "American First." Americanization, in the

Committee's hands, increasingly meant "Anglo-conformity," and was increasingly reinforced by active coercion, including the threat of deportation for those reluctant to become citizens.[29] The more sympathetic Progressives, however, were impressed by the cultural contributions of the immigrants and favored a more pluralistic approach emphasizing "immigrant gifts." The National Conference on Immigration and Americanization, in which "philanthropic, business, civic and educational organizations" met for the first time "to discuss the problem of Americanization," even expressed a rhetoric of two-way influence:

> The immigrant's standards would certainly have to be changed, . . . his grasp of political structure and ideals strengthened, and his standards of living altered. But just as surely would the newcomer modify and change the native American's point of view, enlarge . . . his industrial organizations, and cause changes in his nation's economic values and political organization.[30]

But even those Progressives most enamored of "immigrant gifts" made no effort to have the schools teach native Americans to comprehend Italian or Yiddish. On the contrary, it took enormous pressure to get the New York Board of Education to give Leonard Covello permission to teach his Italian students Italian.[31] Horace J. Bridges observed that although it should have been natural for Americans to learn many more languages than Europeans, given the mixture of immigrant peoples in the United States, Americans learned only English.[32]

Under the circumstances, the fact that the melting pot was not polyglot is an amazing social fact, a tribute to the ability of a dominant social class to exterminate, via Americanization, the creative potential of a natural learning situation. Civics lessons in the elementary schools were to emphasize American institutions and love of country. Teachers were urged to encourage children to be kind to immigrant newcomers, to help them to adjust and "learn our ways." But they were not instructed to teach children appreciation (or knowledge) of the immigrants' "ways." And they were not expected to criticize "American institutions."[33] In truth, although the less coercive Progressives developed a democratic ideology of mutual influence reflective, perhaps, of the immigrant's real impact on U.S. institutions, they were able to institutionalize only educational programs aimed exclusively at changing the behavior and attitudes of the immigrants.

Teachers were expected (regardless of origin) to be "American, 100 percent pure."[34] In a 1918 article Isaac Rosengarten decried Jewish teachers' internalization of dominant ideology. Jewish teachers, he said, had been so thoroughly Americanized and Christianized in the public schools that they perpetuated dominant ideology almost without realizing it. "The Jewish teacher in the New York Public School is the one on whom the responsibility and reproach for this disastrous assimilation rests," he said. The school system was permeated with anti-Semitism and hostility toward Jewish culture, and Jewish teachers were agents of apostasy.[35]

In 1917 seventeen teachers of De Witt Clinton High School were questioned by the superintendent on their loyalty. Eleven of the seventeen were Jews. Three of the teachers, all Jews, were fired for radicalism. Observers stated that the firings were based on the Board's "opposition to the socialistic views of the teachers, and possibly to some extent by racial considerations also." One of the Board members explained that "all of the [dismissed teachers] . . . were Russian Jews. . . . They try to practice the things they couldn't do in Russia." He thus wrapped Americanism, anti-socialism, and anti-Semitism into one.[36]

The purge at De Witt Clinton shows that anti-Semitism and anti-socialism were easily wed in the minds of many professional Americanizers. It also shows that some teachers had quite a different model of education, of loyalty, and of professional pedagogy; these teachers were Jewish socialists.

Hierarchy and Conflict

Just as Eastern European Jewish men and women were moving into the teaching profession, it was being transformed in multiple contradictory ways. Teaching had been professionalized, emancipated from rote learning, endowed with a lengthened, professionalized training and a professional ideology. Yet at the same time the teaching profession was differentiated into an administrative hierarchy that lessened teachers' control over their work, lowered their salaries, and reduced even principals to closely managed employees. In effect, teachers and lower-level administrators were simultaneously professionalized and semi-proletarianized. In response they began to unionize.

TAYLORING TEACHERS

As the teaching work force expanded, business and educational leaders developed an interest in controlling and cheapening it. They allowed inflation to overtake teachers' salaries, and replaced the one-room schoolhouse with the graded school, with a graded pay scale to match.

Increasingly they hired women for the lower, more numerous, and lower-paid grades. Women moved from being 30 percent of the teaching work force in 1870, to over 78 percent in 1911. Said Coffman:

> [The low salary] partly explains why young men are increasingly dissuaded from entering teaching. It is claimed . . . that the male recruits in teaching come from a lower social stratum than they did a half century ago.[37]

A 1914 national survey showed teachers' annual salary to be considerably lower than that of "other skilled workers" such as plumbers, bricklayers, plasterers, painters, and, in some cities, molders and machinists. In each year between 1890 and 1926, farm laborers and domestic servants were the only categories of workers earning less than teachers. Meanwhile, the feminization of teaching led more girls to stay in school through high school, thereby adding to the expansion of schooling and jobs for (usually male) high school teachers.[38]

As the sexual division of labor became the main form of control of the working teacher in the lower grades, school centralization put top decision making in the hands of the Progressive bourgeoisie. According to David Hammack, besides wresting decision making from local, primarily ethnic, school boards, the aim of school centralization was "to reduce the principal to a mere record keeper, [and] to subject [teachers] . . . to the discipline of a streamlined bureaucracy."[39] The middle levels of that bureaucracy were created by the school management movement, which reduced even further the power of principals and ordinary teachers, male and female.

Between 1913 and 1925, under relentless attack by business and newspapers for the high cost and high failure rate in the schools, school administrators became obsessed by school efficiency. In Gary, Indiana, a platoon system was devised, in which students were rotated among classrooms so that no teacher and no portion of the "school plant"—shops, laboratories, playground, classrooms—would remain idle for a moment. The platoon system was also known as "the Gary plan." Attempts were made to introduce it in school systems all across the country.

In 1913 Franklin Bobbitt developed principles of management for the schools closely patterned after Frederick Taylor's general principles. Raymond Callahan explains:

> Just as Taylor had said that the development of the science of the job was too difficult for the worker in the machine shop, so Bobbitt took

the position that "The burden of finding the best methods is too large and too complicated to be laid on the shoulders of the teachers."[40]

The school management movement aimed to turn, not teaching, but school administration into a "profession." It centered power in school superintendents, who minutely specified the operation of the schools aided by scorecards, manuals, checklists and record-books produced by the center of professional administration, Teachers College.[41]

Taylorism in education, like Taylorism in industry and Taylorism in the office, was fundamentally an effort at labor control and at reduction of the wage bill. In education, as in industry, scientific management involved measurement fetishism and increased work loads for each employee. In education the efficiency movement was motivated by the desire to cope with school overcrowding, continually aggravated by burgeoning immigration, while simultaneously reducing the amount of money spent on school buildings and teachers' salaries. Moreover, scientific management in education reflected the desire to control the rapidly expanding teaching force, including the recruitment of women, lower-class men, and the children of immigrants—that is, people who were culturally suspect, an especially serious matter when their job was the transmission of culture.[42]

In New York City the *Journal of the Board of Education* listed charges and reprimands against individual teachers. It noted each teacher's absence, stating whether or not the absence was "excused," and if so, whether it was excused with or without pay. Teachers had to have a doctor's note even when absent for a single day.[43] These rather demeaning regulations cast a rather strange light on Cubberly's grand portrait of the professional teacher who "stood before the class." Rather, the rules express the age of the professional administrator, concerned with gaining control over the activities of immigrant Jewish teachers. Yet New York City was also a center of opposition to the Gary plan and scientific management in the public schools.

TEACHERS FIGHT BACK

Coinciding with the school management movement was the movement to unionize teachers, which was well under way by 1906. In 1916 the New York Teachers Union formed, and the American Federation of Teachers became the first group of professional public servants to affiliate with the AFL.

Teachers' unions were very much professional unions; they demanded the right to organize but eschewed the right to strike. (It was undignified; and besides, they were servants of the whole public.) And yet they reacted by no means gullibly or gratefully to Butler's efforts, within the National Education Association and the cities, to reduce their power while increasing their prestige. Teachers' required years of training had been lengthened, and their control over curriculum had been weakened. Their work had been dignified into a profession, but the meaning of that profession was carefully circumscribed. They were to do manual training; they practiced a non-manual trade. In 1921 the trustees of CCNY called the professional pedagogy program "vocational training."[44]

So teachers did organize. The New York centralization fight, and the movement to introduce business efficiency, scientific management, Taylorism, and the factory model into the schools can only have fueled the teachers' union movement. After all, if, as scientific managers claimed, the school was a factory with children as the raw materials and products, the administrators as the managers, and the teachers as the employees, then the teachers were, indeed, not free professionals but employees.

And since they were employees, it was not so extraordinary that they thought of forming unions to defend their rights as employees. In fact, where they were organized they were better able to fight not only for better salaries, but against the very introduction of the factory model which overtook the school system of less organized cities.[45]

The structure of the teaching profession changed at the turn of the century. Through Teachers College, the Progressive bourgeoisie was able to create and train a network of male administrators to organize hierarchies of management in school systems throughout the country. In these managerial hierarchies they attempted to control their line supervisors—the (largely male) principals—and through them, a work force of female and lower-class male teachers. These efforts provoked the organization of teachers. Jews who entered the various ranks of the education profession at the turn of the century experienced these conflicting forces and were especially conspicuous in the unionization movement.

CCNY: Teachers for the New York Public Schools

Just as the origins and existence of Teachers College were bound up with producing higher administrators and a professional ideology for the U.S. school system, the origins and existence of CCNY were bound up with producing teachers and curricula for the New York public schools. Until the 1890s, City College graduates had an absolute advantage in access to teaching and administrative positions in the New York City school system, but beginning about 1900 they began to experience competition from graduates of the new high schools and of Teachers College. As an institution setting the course for the City schools, the City College's position was undermined by Teachers College. Both institutions were committed to manual training, and both promoted the ideology that only the suitably degreed could make educational policy: educational decisions were beyond the ken of the ordinary working people who sent their children to public schools.

TEACHER TRAINING

In the 1850s a New York City teacher had a minuscule salary and no guarantee of tenure. His or her job was secured through appointment by the Ward trustee, who was often a local politician. But a person could become a teacher with no more training than a common school education, and the teacher often had considerable discretion over school content. Palmer notes that "in some schools the Trustees selected the textbooks, in others the Inspectors . . . [did], while in still others the teachers were vested with discretionary power over the books." Attendance at the normal schools run by the Board of Education—the Male Normal School (ten hours per week in the evenings), the Female Normal School (five hours per week on Saturdays) and the Colored Normal School (hours not specified), was voluntary until 1853, when attendance was required for "all teachers below the grade of principal, unless duly excused." The very blanket nature of that requirement indicates the virtual absence of secondary education among teachers. The Annual Report of the Board of Education notes that "the term normal, which early attached to these institutions was not well chosen, as no normal instruction was given. They were really supplementary schools for teachers who did not hold the highest grade of certificates as to scholarship."[46] That is, these "normal schools" offered no pedagogy; they simply kept the teacher a few grades ahead of his or her students.

The only other source of teacher training in the mid-1800s was the Free Academy. Like the private academies after which it was initially modeled, the Free Academy was strongly oriented to producing teachers long before a formal pedagogy program was developed. The first four Board of Education presidents who presided over the Free Academy held that there was an intimate connection between the general education of the whole people and the diffusion, throughout society, of a higher and more extended culture. They believed that the Free Academy would aid the common schools, enhancing their prestige, stimulating competitive improvement in their methods, and raising up from among them a body of teachers.[47]

In "raising up . . . a body of teachers" and in exerting influence on the common schools, the Free Academy played a role typical of the private academies in whose image it was founded. According to Ellwood Cubberly, the academies "offered no instruction in pedagogy, except in rare instances, but because of their advanced instruction in subjects related to the work of the common school they served as the forerunners of the normal schools."[48]

It was not until the 1870s, when immigration increased, labor became more organized and in parts more radical, and the first compulsory education law passed the New York legislature, that further steps were taken to upgrade teacher training. In 1870 the Board of Education, which had been authorized in 1854 to organize a Free Academy for females similar to the one organized in 1847 for males, picked up its dormant option for educating women, and established the Female Normal and High School. Renamed the Normal College the following year, it began with the three-year course common in normal schools at that time.[49] The school was later named Hunter College after Thomas Hunter, its first principal. (Hunter and Payson Merril were the men who were booed when they attempted to speak in favor of school centralization.) In 1879, "in spite of much opposition on the part of parents and others," the course of study was extended to four years, three years of academic work and one of practice.

Parental opposition was quite understandable. For working-class families, each additional year of schooling meant another year of hardship. It was partly for this reason that organized labor resisted the extension of schooling. However, parental opposition notwithstanding, in 1888 the course was extended to five years, and in 1902 a seven-year "collegiate course" leading to a bachelor's degree was established.[50]

Thus in thirty years the Normal School moved from post-grammar training to high school to college. The Normal College gave maximal training. The legal requirement remained somewhat lower, however, and a high school diploma was not required for teacher certification until after the administrative reorganization of the nineties.

The 1870s also saw the first abortive attempts to introduce pedagogy in the male Free Academy. In 1870, and again in 1876, the Board of Trustees, under Chairman William Wood, tried to get the faculty of City College to institute a course on the Art of Teaching. Wood was a member of the Board of Education's Committee on Normal, Evening, and Colored Schools, and was, with Hunter, most instrumental in the establishment of the Normal College. A Glasgow and Liverpool businessman who emigrated to the United States in 1844 and became the head of the British and American Bank, Wood retired from business in 1867, became Commissioner of Docks and a member of the Commission on the widening of Broadway, and was instrumental in securing the 68th Street building for the Normal College. His biography resembles strongly those Progressives who were active in municipal reform and who sought to centralize the school board. But in the 1870s he was unable to move the City College faculty to teach pedagogy. It took the state certification law of 1897 to do that. At the same time, the Progressive victory in the centralization fight subjected teachers to appointment by a new Board of Examiners. In 1904, the central Board of Education took over the selection of texts, and even the construction of syllabi.[51]

The development of an explicit pedagogy program at CCNY in the late nineties coincided with vastly increased immigration of Southern and Eastern European immigrants, rising labor organization and radicalization, the further expansion of the manual training movement, the establishment of high schools, the centralization of power in Progressive hands, and the rise of the New York College for the Training of Teachers. At the same time that teacher training was being raised to the college level, poorer boys were going to CCNY and girls to the Normal College. At the same time that Russian Jewish youths were entering teaching, teaching became even more poorly paid and even more closely supervised. At the same time that City College developed an undergraduate program in pedagogy, Teachers College developed a graduate program in school administration.

There is evidence that some of its most influential graduates came to see City College as threatened from both above and below. In the lead article of the very first issue of the *City College Alumni Quarterly* (December 30, 1904), Magnus Gross, Class of 1878, president of the New York City Teacher's Association, discussed the conflict between the College and the recently developed high schools, "among whose warmest advocates at the time were many who were inimical to the College, and who would have witnessed its abolition without regret."

However, Gross decided that the development of the public high schools was "a distinct advantage" and advocated "a closer articulation with the schools":

> For many years prior to consolidation, the City College supplied the bulk of the male members of the teaching force as the Normal College supplied most of the women teachers. No one has yet come forth to prove that they, as a class, are in any way inferior to the foreign product that has been grafted upon our system. There are many who hold the reverse opinion. They give many reasons for this opinion. The holder of a college graduate diploma, other things being equal, stands higher in most professions, than one holding a certificate from a secondary institution, of whatever title. The training received by the graduates of the City College in academic branches, has long been recognized as thorough and efficient. So much so, that it is a matter of record, that wherever graduates of this College have entered competitive tests with the graduates of other institutions (not excepting Yale and Harvard) they have commonly carried off the honors.
>
> An institution with a record like that should continue to supply a liberal proportion of the teaching force.[52]

Gross lauded the special qualifications of New York City-born teachers, and asked, "In view of all these facts, the usual arguments in favor of introducing 'new blood,' new ideas, into our teaching staff, are insignificant." Clearly the high schools were not the only source of competition for teaching positions. The New York College for the Training of Teachers, later to become Teachers College, posed an even graver threat:

> The longer one thinks of this subject, the more he is apt to conclude that it was not at all necessary to establish a distinct Training School for teachers. It might easily and less expensively have been subordinated to, or co-ordinated with, the two colleges that are legitimate fountain-heads for the supply of teachers.[53]

Fueling the sense of injured pride was Gross's belief that City College had a special advantage—the familiarity, trust, and experience that would make City College's new immigrant student population especially able to assimilate their younger siblings, and to diffuse general education throughout society:

> The great majority of the students of the College are graduates of the public schools, born and bred within the limits of the city. Who,

better than they, are calculated to appreciate, as teachers, the practical as well as the professional needs of the schools? Who will be more likely to assimilate the diversified moral and mental habits, the foreign customs and prejudices of a mixed population, of which they themselves have formed a part from childhood? Who in short, are better fitted to accomplish the highest purpose of our local school system—the welding of the population of this most cosmopolitan city into a common American citizenship?[54]

The children of immigrants were best suited for Americanizing the children of immigrants.

The importance of teaching at City College is suggested by the fact that Gross's article, which is almost exclusively about teaching, is entitled "The College of the City of New York: Some of Its Real Functions." Gross urged that the pedagogy program be enlarged, and that "preference . . . be given the graduates in assignments to the schools."[55]

SERVICE TO THE CITY: THE DIFFUSION OF CULTURE

Two years after Gross's article, in 1906, City College joined the large number of colleges and universities that had established Departments of Education. Stephen Duggan, head of the new Department, later cited the same "service to the city" theme as among the special reasons for its founding:

The majority, not only of the male teachers, but of the male principals of the elementary schools, are graduates of our institution. An increasing number of our graduates annually enter as teachers into the city high schools. A considerable number are found among the superintendents. It was felt that this strong bond between the schools and the City College should not only be maintained, but strengthened, and that one of the best ways for the College to make a return to the city was to increase the efficiency of those who left its portals to go into the schools as teachers and administrators.[56]

The Department of Education was as much a child of its time as the Free Academy had been a child of the 1850s; the department was formed when university education departments were springing up everywhere. Duggan noted, "More than 25 percent of the taxes levied in all the states of the Union are expended for educational purposes, and the school tax is the largest single tax in every budget."[57] One hundred and seventy-one Departments of Education had already been established when Duggan's Department began.

Not only the timing of the Department's establishment, but also the mode of discourse with which it was established and the curriculum with which it began, reflect the educational campaigns of the early twentieth century. The use by both Gross and Duggan of the magic word *efficiency* reflects the prevalence of the efficiency movement. And Duggan's explanation of the need for college-level pedagogy reflects the elitist suspicion of popular decision making that served as motive and rationale for school centralization:

> The conviction has become general that the problems involved in the administration of school systems are difficult and complex, and require the attention of the most intelligent and public-spirited persons in each community. These persons should be and usually are the college graduates, and it is in college that they ought to have the opportunity to obtain a true insight into educational problems which will enable them in later life to advocate real reforms and prevent the school system from falling into the control of the venal, the ignorant or the ill-balanced.[58]

The Department's original five courses also reveal something of the ethics of the age:

1. History of Education, taught by Professor Duggan
2. Principles of Education
3. School Management and Administration
4. Methods of Teaching and Class Management
5. Secondary Teaching

The use of the word *management*—even with respect to teaching methods in a single classroom—again reflects the growing new dogma—the school management/school efficiency campaign.

But S. P. Duggan was not an efficiency man. He was a man most concerned with social control. Like a great many members of the City College faculty he was trained at CCNY and Columbia University. He received his training in political science, not education, and came to establish the pedagogy program at CCNY only because his advancement within his own field was blocked. Faced with the need to develop a program quickly to meet the new state certification requirements, President Finley prevailed upon Duggan to reject a faculty appointment elsewhere and to use his historical training as the intellectual basis of the new department.

The Department of Education that Duggan founded was more oriented to the cultural aspects of education than to the technicalities of administration. As he explained in 1911, "those in charge of the organization of the Department determined to emphasize the general and cultural aspect of the subject so that it would make its appeal to every student as a man, a citizen and a probable parent."[59]

Perhaps it was Duggan's background in liberal culture, rather than administration, which led to this emphasis on the cultural aspects of education. In part his remarks were also a justification for the upgrading of teacher training to the college level:

> The conviction has steadily grown among educators that, as the work of men engaged in education is becoming more and more confined to the tasks of a supervisory and administrative character, such as principalships and superintendencies or to teaching special subjects in the high schools, men teachers should receive their preparation in colleges where they will obtain a broad culture and see their professional work in its true relations to the other activities of life. *It cannot be well from a social standpoint that school systems should be under the control of men whose training has been narrow and devoted chiefly to the technique of teaching.*[60]

Finally, Duggan's emphasis on the cultural rather than the financial and actuarial aspects of education may have derived from his great concern for the role of education in social control and the political realities of the city in which his students were to work.

According to its preface, Duggan's text for his course in History of Education

> has for its primary purpose the explanation of the way in which each people has worked out the solution of the great problem that has confronted every people at all times, in all places, and in all stages of development, namely the reconciliation of individual liberty with social stability; and of the way in which each has organized its education to prepare the individual to live in accordance with that solution. . . . [E]very great thinker who has written upon education has emphasized either social control . . . or individual freedom.[61]

In the United States, Duggan explained, the social control functions were of even greater moment because the country was a democracy.

> The State, which is the institution that represents all classes and interests of society and that represents society as a whole . . . [must

educate its citizens for citizenship]. . . . Even in England the gradual extension of the suffrage to all males has made the upper classes conscious of the need "to educate our masters."[62]

(That is, the extension of the vote required the socialization of the voters, lest they seek to become "masters.")

The catalogue description of the course in Principles of Education carried through the social control theme:

> In this course an attempt is made to discover the best ways in which the great contributions of the sciences, Biology, Psychology and Sociology, can be so correlated and formulated as to fit the individual for his proper place in society and enable him to contribute to its advancement.[63]

Although later courses in the Department—and then School—of Education did include a good deal of vocational guidance, class management and use of testing mechanisms such as the Stanford-Binet, the curriculum continued to emphasize the cultural and social control aspects of education, and the importance of adapting individuals to the social order. Child study and educational psychology and philosophy were stressed. Manual training, which had preceded pedagogy in the curriculum by ten years, continued to be of interest. And the School of Education's emphasis on the cultural and social aspects of education easily lent itself to training teachers for the Americanization programs that were pursued with such vigor in the late teens and early twenties.[64]

City College had produced educators from its inception as the Free Academy. R. R. Bowker said in 1907 that the college had been "virtually a normal college for men." Although its curriculum was wedded to the classics long after other schools had embraced the more modern subjects, it was in the forefront of the manual training movement, partly by virtue of President Webb's participation in the Industrial Education Association. "In 1892 two members of the Board of Education (and many ex-members), the Superintendent of Schools, 16 out of the 62 male principals and 10 vice-principals, the complete roster of instructors in manual training—in all 86 out of the 280 male teachers in the public schools—were City College men."[65]

The College continued to graduate male teachers for the high schools and for special subjects in the elementary schools. A handful of City College boys even taught in the elementary schools, where, by the turn of the century, almost all teachers were women. The Board of Trustees noted in 1921 that "over 90 percent of all the men who go into the elementary school system come from the College."[66] And from its inception in 1904 through the 1920s, the *Alumni Quarterly* was filled with notices of graduates who reported that they were teaching in the public schools of the city, or that they had attained various administrative posts in its growing bureaucracy.[67]

The school sought to influence the curriculum of the lower schools by means of its admissions requirements; later it sought to influence the immigrant community through the immigrant sons who went to CCNY.

In its pedagogy program, however, the school was not innovative. It generally responded to outside pressures and influences, revising its curriculum in response to Regents mandates and to pedagogical movements that were initiated elsewhere. In general, Teachers College of Columbia University took the lead. Despite that lead, CCNY's claim to pedagogical preeminence became the special advantage that its students, the children of immigrants, provided in influencing the immigrant community.

Teaching as a Career

Jewish youngsters became teachers, principals, and college professors in the first quarter of the twentieth century, when both teaching and educational administration expanded enormously. The social forces in the expansion of schooling included: the sheer increase in the number of students brought by continuing waves of immigration; the demand by organized labor and social reformers for laws restricting child labor and for the expansion of elementary education; the demand by businessmen that the schools teach manual skills; the interest of the business class in the use of the schools for social control; the development of high schools as, in part, a career ladder promising social mobility as an alternative to the redistribution of wealth; and the focus on the schools as agents of Americanization, both of adults, in school-center evening classes, and of children in public schools. Most of these developments and forces expressed, directly or indirectly, conflicts between business and labor. Schooling was to deal with these conflicts by serving as a means of socialization and social control.

Although the content of pedagogy underwent innumerable fads and reflected the changing and conflicting definitions of educational Progressivism, in general the content of pedagogy reflected the social functions of the school—Americanization and social control.

Both teachers and principals were subject to somewhat contradictory forces. On the one hand professionalization meant greater prestige. Teachers' training was lengthened to the B.A. College faculty were required to earn Ph.D.'s, and educational administrators were expected to do college and perhaps even graduate work. The ideology of professional pedagogy emphasized the teacher's discretion by stressing child development and pedagogical principles instead of rote memorization. Similarly, academic disciplines and the elective principle replaced rote memorization of the classics on the college level. All of these forces bolstered the prestige and independence of the educator.

On the other hand, the development of administration in the specific form of scientific management instituted the business model in the schools, embodying an ideology which turned the professionally trained teacher into an employee and the principal into a record-keeper. A similar model was applied to colleges and universities.[68] The continual efforts to minimize or cut the school budget kept the salaries of these new professionals very low.

Progressives professionalized education by centralizing control over public education, by creating Teachers College as the leading institution dominating the U.S. educational scene through the production of top administrators, and by defining pedagogy as manual training, scientific management, social control, and Americanization. Professionalization of education meant a greater regimentation of teachers and a greater bureaucratization of administrators. City College men, who became high school teachers, principals and superintendents, participated in both processes.

In the absence of direct evidence it is difficult to know how these structural and institutional forces affected those who experienced them. Jewish students who became teachers and school principals went through a double socialization: once as students, a second time as teachers. Particularly as teachers they undoubtedly experienced the self-socialization that taking the role of a parent or teacher generally involves. Van Denburg pointed out that teachers often instill contempt for manual labor by warning students that those who do not do well in school will be relegated to mere manual work. Considering the severe struggle that staying in school involved, one may conjecture that it would be common for those who made that struggle to internalize such a view.[69]

It was partly to counteract such a view that the other AFL unions supported salary increases for teachers. Although they gave that support on general principles, they were also well aware of the anti-union biases in social studies texts, particularly in high schools and colleges, and they hoped that unionizing teachers might help keep teachers in touch with the viewpoint of manual labor.[70] Coffman's data on the social origins of teachers indicates that they may have been more in touch with manual labor than they wished to be. As Coffman put it:

> *The tastes of the teachers might be those of people in refined economic leisure, but the salaries, being those of mechanics and day-laborers or even less, prevent the enjoyment of these higher things.* Between what they ought to do and what they can do there is a wide gulf.[71]

Besides the pejorative conception of manual labor, another aspect of the self-socialization of Jewish educators was the Americanization movement. It is through teaching that the Jews entered Rabbi Silverman's "promised land," where the Jews were to be the professional Americanizers.[72]

But educators were also subject to conflicting everyday forces other than those of their previous training and their current administrative superiors. Particularly important was the community itself, even when teachers and principals no longer lived in the community in which they taught. Recall that Leonard Covello had petitioned for permission to teach Italian under the determined prodding of his Italian high school students. The Gary plan was defeated by the opposition of the teaching and administrative staff and the rioting of the Lower East Side and (largely Jewish) Harlem communities, including some vandalism on the part of high school students.[73] Some of those marching against the Gary plan carried posters boosting Morris Hillquit, Socialist candidate for mayor (though the Socialist Party claimed it had no role in the matter). And no matter what went on inside of the schools, the labor movement and political conflict continued to help create the milieu ouside of them.

Insofar as becoming a teacher or a school principal may have meant internalizing the conceptions of professional pedagogy, that process contained a certain irony. For the rise of the Jewish teacher was made possible by the militancy of Jewish labor, which, with other immigrant and immigrant-descended labor, created the problems of worker control and political strife, which in turn inspired the business class to solve those training and social control problems by expanding the schools and hiring the sons and daughters of immigrants to socialize the sons and daughters of immigrants. The class consciousness of immigrant labor became the condition for the upward mobility—and *embourgeoisement*—of immigrant children. The rise of the Jewish teacher was stitched by the Jewish tailor in more ways than one.

City College at Lexington Ave. and 23rd St. *Picture Collection, The Branch Libraries, The New York Public Library*

6

Jobs and Schooling of the Jewish Poor

David Levinsky anticipated his move upward through higher education with a mixture of religious incantation and inspired discovery.
Levinsky planned to go to City College "with a heart full of quiet
ecstasy":

> More than once I went a considerable distance out of my way to
> pass the corner of Lexington Avenue and Twenty-Third Street,
> where that edifice stood. I would . . . gaze at its red, ivy-clad walls,
> mysterious high windows, humble spires; I would stand watching
> the students on the campus . . . and go my way, with a heart full of
> reverence, envy, and hope. . . .
>
> It was not merely a place in which I was to fit myself for the battle
> of life, nor merely one in which I was going to acquire knowledge. It
> was a symbol of spiritual promotion as well. University-bred people
> were the real nobility of the world. . . . The red, church-like struc-
> ture . . . was the synagogue of my new life.[1]

But David Levinsky never went to City College. Instead he became a
garment manufacturer, and thereby a millionaire.

Abraham Cahan's *Rise of David Levinsky* (1917) subtly captured a
truth about Jewish mobility: education was honored; business brought
mobility. For the first half century even that mobility was modest, and
affected only a small proportion of Russian Jews. Although Jews took
to formal schooling and the professions more than those other ethnic
groups with which they are customarily compared, the vast majority
were wage workers; most dropped out of school early; those who were
upwardly mobile took paths other than schooling; and only a tiny
minority graduated college or entered the professions. The extent,
process, and meaning of Jewish mobility requires a much more careful
assessment than it has generally been given.

The Occupations of Russian Jewish Immigrants and Their Children

Systematic studies of the occupations of New York Jews are not plentiful. They include Thomas Kessner's analysis of the 1880 and 1905 census manuscripts, Herbert Gutman's examination of the 1905 census manuscripts, the Baron de Hirsch Fund study of Jews in three districts of the Lower East Side in 1890, and Ben Seligman's study of a random sample of New York City Jews in 1952. We may also use the 1900 New York State census, detailing occupations of "Russians," the vast majority of whom were Jews. All other data on New York City are either fragmentary or impressionistic. Studies of Jews outside of New York City give a distorted picture because the most complete data concerns small communities, where economic conditions and the initial Jewish migrations were very different. No U.S. city had as substantial a Jewish proletariat to begin with as New York. So we must keep our eye on New York.[2]

In reading these data we will speak as though we are following trends, but to do so is to grossly oversimplify. The different dates do not refer strictly to the same population, not only because the data came from very different studies with different sampling methods and different categories but also because migration continually altered the population and economic forces unevenly affected it.

WAGE LABOR

Poor Jews did not arrive in North America in substantial numbers until the 1880s. Some were downwardly mobile from businesses and professions in Russia.[3] For the first fifty years, the vast majority of Jewish immigrants remained proletarians. So did a large proportion of their children.

As late as 1952, the majority of Jewish men and women in New York City were wage workers, clerks, or salespeople;[4] for the early immigrant generations, the proportion was much larger. In 1880, 56 percent of Russian Jewish household heads were manual workers, as were 77 percent of their offspring (see table). In 1890, three-quarters of the Jews on the Lower East Side were wage workers. According to the 1900 census, 61 percent of male immigrants from Russia, and 72 percent of female Russian immigrants, were employed in manufacturing and mechanical pursuits. By 1905, 54 percent of Jewish household heads were still doing manual labor.

According to conventional wisdom, the second generation did not follow the first into the shops.[5] There is little statistical support for this

Occupations of New York City Russian Jews, 1880–1933
(Percentages of Total)

	Manual workers	Domestic service	Peddlers, clerks, sales	Big business	Pro-fessional	Total Number
1880[a]						
Household heads	56		39	3	2	(524)
Offspring	77		22	1	0	(318)
Sons	62		37	1	0	(174)
Daughters	97		3	0	0	(144)
1890[b]						
All Jews in 3 districts, Lower East Side	75		24	1		(26.1)[e]
1900[c]						
First generation						
Males	61	6	30		3	(73.2)[e]
Females	72	14	12		1	(18.6)[e]
Second generation						
Males	33	5	58		4	(4.5)[e]
Females	57	5	34		4	(2.5)[e]
1905[a]						
Household heads	54		31	12	3	(963)
Offspring	62		33	4	1	(724)
Sons	55		39	5	1	(430)
Daughters	73		24	2	1	(294)
1933[d]						
All Jews	38	5	49		8	

NOTE: These data are taken from diverse sources using different classification schemes and different sampling methods. Because of rounding of percentages, rows may not add to exactly 100%.

[a]SOURCE: Thomas Kessner, *The Golden Door,* pp. 60, 79, 90. Categories: "skilled," semi-skilled, and unskilled workers" (which I have aggregated into "manual workers"); "lower white collar" (including peddlers, clerks, salespeople); "higher white collar" (including professionals, major proprietors, managers, and officials). In private communication, Kessner gave me the raw data on professionals, which I have subtracted from "higher white collar" and presented separately. Data are based on every fifth household in selected census tracts.

[b]SOURCE: Simon Kuznets, "Economic Structure and Life of the Jews," p. 1636. This was apparently taken from the Baron de Hirsch Fund Study, and was also reported by Lloyd Gartner, "The Jews of New York's East Side, 1880–1893," pp. 267–275. Categories: "needle workers," and "other industrial workers" (which I have aggregated into "manual workers"); "peddlers," and "retail dealers" (which I have grouped into "peddlers, clerks, sales"). I have listed the remaining 1 percent as "all others," which includes all professionals.

[c]SOURCE: *Reports of the Immigration Commission,* U.S. Senate, as reported by Kuznets, p. 1639. Categories: "manufacturing and mechanical," shown here as "manual"; "trade and transportation" (including clerks, hucksters and peddlers, retail dealers, and salesmen); "professionals"; and "domestic and personal," which includes "laborers unspecified" for men, and "servants and waitresses" for women. It is possible that "manufacturing" includes employers as well as workers.

[d]SOURCE: Jacob Lestchinsky, "The Economic and Social Development of American Jewry," p. 93. Categories are the same as for 1900. Kuznets presents the same data, citing Lestchinsky, but groups them differently, putting 56 percent in trade and transport and only 31 percent in manufacturing. See Kuznets, p. 1640.

[e]Rows for 1890 and 1900 are in thousands.

assertion. In 1880, shopwork held 62 percent of Jewish sons and 97 percent of Jewish daughters. Many of these offspring might later leave factory work for other occupations but the census found them in manual work.[6] In 1900 only a third of second-generation Russian men but more than half of second-generation women were in manufacturing and mechanical trades. In 1905 more than half of Jewish sons, and almost three-quarters of Jewish daughters, were manual workers. There was apparently even a considerable amount of downward mobility toward and within manual work. Although a large proportion of Jewish immigrants entered the United States as skilled workers, and a majority were employed as skilled workers in 1880, mechanization and the task system relegated many more Jews to semi-skilled work by 1905.[7]

PETTY TRADE

The largest category of non-manual work among early Jewish immigrants was peddling and petty trade. In 1880 peddling and small business occupied 39 percent of Jewish household heads and slightly fewer of their sons. (Daughters were overwhelmingly in manual work.) In 1890 a quarter of gainfully employed Lower East Side Jews were either peddlers or retail dealers. In 1900 hucksters, peddlers, retail dealers, and salesmen made up around 30 percent of Russian immigrants and twice as many of their sons, although the sons were most likely to be employed salesmen rather than owners. In 1905 about a third of Jewish household heads and their sons were in lower white collar occupations. The parents tended to be in small businesses, the sons were small businessmen and clerks.

The economic level of these businesses varied. Some of the business was on so pathetic a scale that to call it evidence of mobility is ludicrous. Some immigrants turned to peddling out of unemployment's desperation. Because the garment industry was seasonal, many workers were forced to survive by peddling in slack periods.[8] Yet for conventional sociologists, this refuge of despair was a move upward in prestige, since workers forced to peddle have moved out of the manual class and become small entrepreneurs.[9]

Not all people who experienced this form of impoverished mobility reacted with great pride. In Michael Gold's autobiographical novel, *Jews Without Money*, his father considers suicide preferable to the shame of peddling, and the family suffers near-starvation because of his unsought-for rise from unemployed house painter to "small entrepreneur" of the banana wagon. A Boston study in 1900 showed that 20 percent of Jewish traders were peddlers, while only 2 percent of German traders and less than 1 percent of British traders were peddlers. In New York State in the same year, one out of every four Russian Jews engaged in trade were peddlers, over half were retailers, and 20 percent were wholesalers.[10]

When entrepreneurship required little capital, family pooling of resources and family labor and a combination of grueling exploitation and self-exploitation made the slow accumulation of wealth possible. The nature of the garment industry was such that with fifty dollars one could obtain the means of production (a sewing machine) and become an entrepreneur (employ one's children and boarders). All in all, in an era when retail trade was not yet monopolized by corporate giants, small business did afford about a third of Jewish men with a livelihood, and some of them with prosperity.

BUSINESS

The major avenue of substantial mobility was through business: garment, fur, shoes, retail trades, real estate, and entertainment.[11] In 1880 about 3 percent of Jewish household heads were major entrepreneurs. By 1905 this group had grown to 12 percent. Business is the big story of upward mobility for the first quarter century of Eastern Jewish life in New York City. It required no formal education whatsoever, and most of the Russian Jewish men who made it big in business probably had very little schooling.[12]

Big as these big businessmen became, they did not approach the commanding heights of the U.S. political economy. As a *Fortune* magazine study showed, as late as the 1940s not even the German Jews had penetrated heavy industry or commercial banking. They were even a very small minority in investment banking, and certainly in government policymaking. The Jewish wealthy, Jacob Lestchinsky claimed, would never be as rich as Rockefeller. Nor would they be as powerful.[13]

Why did Jewish businessmen fail to penetrate the boardrooms of power in democratic America, land of opportunity? Scholars rarely ask this embarrassing question. Or they whisper "discrimination" and quickly dismiss it. But why did discrimination not prevent Jewish businessmen from getting as far as they did? Was the Protestant upper class more anti-Semitic than less fancy folk? (If so, why do sociologists look for prejudice almost exclusively in the working and middle classes?) Was the Protestant upper class simply more powerful? Was there something about the *kinds* of businesses which Jews entered that limited their rise? Was it in the relationship between a segment of finance capital (which was the German Jews' economic base) and industrial capital, which Protestants controlled? If so, that only begs the question: why were Jews unable to move out of a restrictive sphere of merchant capital and the most competitive corner of industry? Perhaps if scholars were not so infatuated with the rise of a handful of early second-generation immigrants to doctor and college professor, they might begin to explore the processes of capital formation and ethnic-class relations that formed the conditions, process, extent, and limits of Jewish success in business. As for the Eastern European Jews, the entrepreneurial rise went just so far.

CLERICAL WORK

In addition to petty trade and big business, the major non-manual occupations of second-generation Eastern European Jews were in clerical work and sales, both of which were just beginning their phenomenal growth.[14] Few of the immigrant generation went into clerical work, but in 1900 almost 17 percent of second-generation men of Russian descent were clerks and 12.5 percent were salesmen. More than 10 percent of second-generation women were clerks, stenographers, and typists. In 1905 about a quarter of the daughters were typists and bookkeepers.[15]

PROFESSIONALS

Now that we have counted manual workers, clerks, salespeople, peddlers, small shopkeepers, and bigger businessmen, we are left with the professionals, the prototypes of Jewish mobility through education. They were less than 3 percent of Jews in 1880. They were almost 3 percent of first generation immigrant males from Russia in New York State in 1900. They were 4 percent of the second generation, both male and female in New York State. And in 1905 they were less than 3 percent of household heads and only 1 percent of their sons and daughters.[16] Clergy and teachers made up the largest groups of professionals in these early years. In Kessner's 1880 sample there were ten religious teachers, three secular teachers, and an attorney. According to the 1900 New York State census, of 1,809 Jewish professionals, 36 percent were teachers, 29 percent were musicians, 17 percent were physicians, and 12 percent were lawyers. The remaining 6 percent were dentists and actors. Of the thirty-four Jewish household heads who were professionals in 1905, almost half were either clergy or religious teachers. In addition there were five physicians, six pharmacists, one dentist, two attorneys, a news editor, an engineer, and three artists. Their sons the doctors numbered only three, joined by three attorneys, two engineers, a pharmacist, a teacher, and two artists. Seven Jewish daughters were professionals in 1905: six of them were teachers and one was a dentist. (Remember that the 1880 and 1905 data are only samples of certain wards. The percentages are probably representative of all Russian Jews in New York, but there were clearly more than an *absolute* number of seven Jewish women professionals in the city.)[17]

We cannot trace these early migrants much farther. There are no extant studies of the Jewish occupational distribution for 1915, or 1920, or even 1925.[18] Piecing together various bits of data in 1955, Jacob Lestchinsky estimated that there were at least 350,000 Jewish manual workers in New York City in 1916, representing more than 50 percent of all "gainfully employed workers." He also stated that "in the 1920s Jewish manual workers constituted a majority of all the gainfully employed Jews in America."[19]

Several things changed after 1924. The discriminatory immigration restriction laws cut the supply of Jewish immigrants and the constant replenishment of the Jewish working class. Those Jewish immigrants who did enter the United States after 1924 included a much larger proportion of tradesmen and professionals. The 1930s migration included half as many wage workers, three times as many tradesmen, and ten times as many professionals as the pre-World War I migrations.[20]

These changes both revealed and concealed the true process of mobility among Jews. They revealed the continual shift of Jewish workers out of manual trades, a process often noticed but masked statistically by the continual influx of fresh Jewish proletarians from Europe. On the other hand they exaggerated the amount of apparent mobility by inflating the numbers of businessmen and professionals.[21]

By 1933 wage workers had decreased from over one-half of gainfully employed Jews in 1920 to around two-fifths. The Great Depression and discrimination once again threw Jews out of work and into peddling. The proportion of businessmen and clerical workers increased to 50 percent. Around 5 percent were domestic workers, and professionals expanded to 8 percent.[22]

For at least two decades thereafter, these trends continued. Most New York Jews went into clerical work and into business, large and small. Well over one-third were in manual work and domestic service. A growing minority became professionals.

History is not a straight line. In the course of five decades the Russian Jews changed, the laws and practices of immigration changed, and the economy changed. Every year fresh waves of immigrants infused the class distribution of Russian Jews. Economic forces hit them unevenly, buffeting them from prosperity to panic, so that in one year a small businessman became a major entrepreneur, and in another year depression turned workers into peddlers and business-men into wage laborers. Political forces altered economic relationships. And all of this flux is hidden between the columns of a statistical table which appears to mark the simple march of a people through time.

The number and proportion of Jewish professionals increased over these fifty years, but "no evidence can be found for the commonly held notion that there occurs a sudden and massive ascent of the children of immigrants to professional and middle-class status; the process, though it will occur over the subsequent decades, seems to be more gradual and difficult than has usually been supposed."[23]

Jews in School

Most of the children of Russian Jewish immigrants did not get very far in school. Like working-class and poor children of all races and ethnic groups, Russian Jewish children attended inferior, overcrowded schools and quit at or before the legal school-leaving age.

School buildings in immigrant areas were old, often poorly venti-lated, and overcrowded. From the 1890s through at least the First World War, classes of sixty to a hundred children were common. In Brooklyn seventy students per room was the norm; some classes reached 150. Children sat three to a seat. Sometimes they were crammed onto benches and, lacking desks, had to work on their laps. In the 1890s, while middle-class schools in upper Manhattan stood half empty, fifty to sixty thousand children were denied admission into ghetto schools because of lack of space.[24] As a result, six-year-olds were barred from first grade to make room for older children. As Selma Berrol reports, Jewish immigrants received

> much less schooling than is commonly assumed. Although the normal entry age was 7, the shortage of space meant that many children did not begin school until they were 8 or older. This, coupled with the fact that [until 1903] working papers could be

acquired at age 12, resulted in thousands of children leaving school with only minimum literacy. The non-English speaking child who was placed in first grade regardless of his age was even more likely to leave after only a few years. This was also true for the "holdover," the low achiever who, under the strict promotion policies of the day, could be left back indefinitely.[25]

The greatest number of non-promotions in Manhattan occurred on the Lower East Side. A 1903 study of Lower East Side youngsters applying for working papers showed that 1,719 were fourteen years old but had not finished the fifth grade. Cram remedial courses developed in most of the schools on the Lower East Side, as the School Superintendent voiced fears that students were leaving "totally unprepared for employment."[26]

Most contemporary social scientists and educators commented on the brightness and eagerness of Jewish students (usually as compared with other "races"). These comments have been quoted in loving detail and repeated in virtually every book on the Jews. But there were also studies of retardation and truancy, which were blamed on poverty, lack of English, and "slow mentality or emotionally disturbed background." These comments have been buried. District Superintendent Julia Richman, discovering that many Jewish children were in serious difficulty in school, found that disease, parental neglect and abuse, child labor, malnutrition, delinquency, and even rape by the boarders who shared their homes made attention to schoolwork difficult or impossible.[27] The Hanus Report of 1913 showed that New York City children scored below the national average in math accuracy and reasoning ability. The curriculum was simplified: much of history was expunged and sewing substituted. French and German were taken out of ghetto schools (but left in the more middle-class schools) on the grounds that ghetto youngsters did not need foreign languages because "for them English is a foreign language."[28] Some Lower East Side boys were expelled for rowdyism, and a special truant school was set up for tough Lower East Side boys.

"There is no doubt," says Berrol, "that teaching in the schools below 14th street was more difficult, and the number of teachers who requested transfers was high."[29] Reviewing much of the contemporary literature, Irving Howe said,

> The bulk of Jewish children . . . were not very different in their capacities or performance from the bulk of pupils from most other ethnic groups. . . . To read the reports of the school superintendents

is to grow impatient with later sentimentalists who would have us suppose that all or most Jewish children burned with zeal for the life of the mind.[30]

Even those with such zeal often had to drop out to help support their families. Like other poor people, Jews sometimes simply could not afford to keep their children in school.[31] Jewish girls especially were wrenched from school to help support the family, often to make it possible for a brother to go to college, in what might be called the Jewish oppression for education.[32] The fact that many more Jewish daughters than sons were in manual work, and many more sons than daughters were in professions (see table) may be an expression of this slaughter of the daughters to the glory of the sons.

Moses Rischin cites evidence that in 1891, "of some 60,000 East Side children, only 1,000 received no education and most of these would soon be in classrooms; on the Lower East Side, a school absenteeism rate of 8 percent was caused almost entirely by sickness." In 1897 Jewish parents "nearly rioted" when their children were turned away from an already overcrowded school. And Jewish children did stay in school longer than other groups.[33]

Nevertheless the dropout rate was very high. The children of Jewish immigrants were concentrated in the first three grades. In 1908 there were 25,534 Jewish children in first grade, less than half that number in seventh grade, and only 10 percent of that number in the first year of high school. The 488 Jewish high school seniors represented 1.9 percent of the number of first graders.[34]

A 1911 Teachers College dissertation shows just as drastic a dropout rate. In the study, a highly comprehensive and detailed examination of all New York City school children who entered high school in 1906, Joseph Van Denburg found that:

1. About 60 percent of New York City school children who graduated from elementary school entered the freshman year of high school.

2. Only one-eighth of a representative sample of those who entered high school in 1906 graduated. Seventy-four percent dropped out. (The other 13 1/2 percent were still in school at the end of this four year study.)

3. When comparisons by nationality of father were made, Russians (largely Hebrew) tended to drop out later in their high school career than Germans, Irish, Italians, Scots, and Austro-Hungarians, and had a very slightly smaller overall dropout rate than the group as a whole. The Russians had a larger proportion graduating than the children of

Americans, Irish, and English, but a smaller proportion of graduates than Germans and Austro-Hungarians. Of the ninety-one Russians in Van Denberg's special study sample, sixty-four dropped out, fifteen graduated on time, and twelve were "retarded" (still in school after four years).[35]

4. "Less than two percent of [high school entrants] . . . ever reach[ed] the freshman class of college." Thus around 1 percent of public elementary school graduates would have entered the freshman class of college. Even if the proportion of Russian Jews in this group maintained their very slight lead, they would still constitute less than 1 percent of Russian Jewish youngsters of college age. In sum, Jewish students achieved more school success than many other youngsters, but the successful were a selected few among a mass of Jewish and non-Jewish dropouts.[36]

By the turn of the century three-quarters of the students at CCNY were Eastern European Jews, although German Jewish names predominated among the graduates at least until the 1930s, the dropout rate being extremely high.[37] At Hunter College Eastern Jews were 8 percent of the graduates in 1906, and one-quarter of the graduates ten years later.[38] In 1918–1919 78 percent of CCNY students were Jewish, as were 38.7 percent of Hunter College students. In the same year Jews (Russian and German) comprised almost 40 percent of students in the nine institutions of higher learning serving the New York metropolitan area. Since Jews then formed only a quarter of the New York population, it is clear that, rich and poor, they did have a greater tendency than non-Jews to attend higher education.[39]

This increasing proportion of Jews among college students has nourished the widespread belief in the miraculous rise of the Jews through education. What is forgotten is that although more and more students were *Jews*, very few Jews were *students*. The entire graduating class of CCNY had only 209 students in 1913; if Eastern European Jews constituted less than 11 percent of the graduates, then they were fewer than 23 men. The 25 percent of Hunter College graduates who were Eastern Jews included only fifty-eight women! At the same time the Jewish population of New York was almost a million, at least 350,000 of whom were manual workers. For the vast majority of Eastern European Jews, college was more a matter of mythology than experience. The saga of such a small group cannot be the main story of the class experience of poor Jews in New York, nor even the main explanation of the movement of Jews out of manual trades.

Class, Education, and Occupation: What Little We Know

We have seen that the movement of Jews out of manual work and into the professions was much more limited in extent and gradual in process than has often been implied. Most East European Jews received very little schooling, at least in the first three or four decades since their mass migration began. The only occupations requiring formal schooling were clerical work, for which one needed an eighth grade education at first and a smattering of high school later, and the professions, which were the fate of the very few. Who then went to school and entered these occupations?

We don't really know. We have little data systematically linking the education and occupation (or class) of a parental generation with the education and occupations of their children. The only data we have for the proof or disproof of the famous "scholarship thesis" seems to suggest, first, that college students and professionals were not drawn from the poorest of the poor, and, second, that they tended especially in the earliest generation to be drawn more from the petty business class rather than from the working class. These conclusions are based on the slim evidence of two studies.

A study of the 1905 census suggests that only the families that could afford to forego the earnings of at least one child could send their children to college. Detailed comparison of households on three streets shows that on Cherry Street, the poorest, tenements were overcrowded; workers were in proletarian occupations; all teenage children were at work; and "most sons continue to work in trades like their fathers." There is little sign of upward mobility and some evidence of downward mobility. On relatively prosperous East Broadway, nine out of thirty-seven household heads were workers, eleven were businessmen, seven were professionals, and several others were white collar workers. Here the offspring include doctors, dentists, two daughters at normal schools, three CCNY students, and two other students. People surveyed on Rutgers, Rivington, Madison, and Henry Streets were only moderately prosperous and fell between the other two groups in the fate of their daughters and sons.[40]

In later years, as the number of Eastern European Jews in small business grew, and as the Jewish labor unions began to win higher wages for their members, the number of parents able to forego the labor of their children long enough to make their attendance at high school and college possible also increased. Stephen Steinberg's study of the social origins of college faculty throughout the United States shows that the largest proportion of these professionals were the children of small businessmen, not workers. Among those Jewish faculty born before 1914, over half were the children of the owners of small businesses. Another quarter were equally divided among the offspring of big businessmen and professionals. Only 19 percent were working class, despite the inclusion of clerical and sales workers in the working-class category.

It was only among the next generation, the academics born between 1914 and 1923, that almost a third (29 percent) were of working-class origin. Still, 45 percent of these college faculty came from small business families.[41] (The fact that more of the later group were from working-class families lends some credence to the suggestion that workers were able to send their children through higher education only after the labor movement had made some real gains.)

It now appears probable that at least outside of CCNY most Jewish students and professionals were the children or grandchildren of those workers who had moved into small business. There is mounting evidence that, despite numerous exceptions, for Jews as for other groups, educational achievement was more a result of economic advance than a cause of it.[42]

The most severe poverty did not foster college attainment, no matter how passionate the thirst for education. This does not mean, however, that students at a school like CCNY were wealthy; retrospective and contemporary accounts of City College refer to their poverty. In Morris Friedman's reminiscences, the fathers of City College students in the 1920s and 1930s "were concentrated in the garment and the unskilled trades."[43] Morris Raphael Cohen's father was a presser in the garment trade, who later had a soda-water stand in a poolroom. A study compiled for the state legislature in 1944 found that CCNY students of the 1920s and 1930s

> came largely from lower income groups, and had grown up in homes where there had been a continuous and severe struggle for existence. More than three-quarters of them were found to hold some outside employment during the summer vacation, and well over half were likewise obliged to work during the regular school year, despite the lack of a tuition charge at the college.[44]

Russian Jews studied under extremely adverse conditions and at great sacrifice, despite their relative economic advantage over even more impoverished neighbors.

Russian Jewish college graduates were a tiny minority of the Jewish population, but this fact does not take away from the immense cultural importance of those few Russian Jews who did move up via higher education. They reinforced a cultural conception of a path out of poverty. Their existence and gradual growth over several decades reinforced a cultural myth much larger than themselves—a Bunyan-esque story of Jewish success in which these few came to stand for all the rest.

The Great Ethnic Derby

The limits of Jewish mobility, and particularly the limits of Jewish mobility through education in the earlier years, have been masked by scholars' obsession with comparing various ethnic groups on the speed with which they scrambled out of the working class. This preoccupation with competitive de-proletarianization expresses two ideologies at once. The first is that to be working class is bad, and that any move out of it is good. To be a clerk, even at lower pay, is better, and to be a businessman, no matter how poor, is a blessing. So any seller of suspenders is higher in prestige than any sewer of shirts or shoveler of soil.

The second ideology is that it is legitimate and reasonable to compare races and ethnic groups on their achievements, intelligence, tractability, or any other dimension or cultural value on which invidious distinctions may be made. This ideology has provided academicians and pundits with livelihood and occupation for over a hundred years, even unto today. *If* the burning question is speed of movement out of the working class, then it does make sense to measure the relative speed with which various sub-categories of the working class succeed in becoming "non-manual," "white collar," or "in business." It might make as much sense, however, to compare the degree to which various industries, crafts, types of work, and institutions *lend themselves* to movement out of the working class.[45]

The demonstration that Jewish mobility through education was more modest than is usually believed is generally answered with statements of their relative success. Jews are said to have gone farther in schooling and status than certain other ethnic groups. Generally, Jews are not compared with Scandinavians and Germans but with Poles and Italians, and, more recently, Blacks.

It is true that Jewish immigrants moved out of manual work faster than Italian immigrants. A larger proportion of Italians than Jews were wage workers in 1880 and 1905. More Jews than Italians were in white collar (probably business) occupations.[46] Although a majority of Jewish children in the earlier migrations became, like their parents, proletarians, the proportion of the children of early Italians in manual work was even larger.

Despite the small number of Jewish professionals, they were still more numerous than Italian professionals. A larger proportion of Jews became college professors than either Catholics or Protestants. But a larger proportion of Catholic faculty came from working-class families, which prompted Stephen Steinberg to say that "if anything, the legendary image of the scholar rising out of the working class fits Catholics far more often than it does Jews."[47]

The majority of male Russian Jews were skilled workers when they arrived. Italians, Poles, and other ex-peasant groups generally became wage workers when they arrived. Most Southern Italian and Polish immigrants were rural people. A growing number of scholars have established that the greater tendency of Jews to enter business was probably due to the Jewish immigrants' greater urbanization, greater literacy, greater familiarity with capitalist social relations, possibly greater access to (small) amounts of capital, and orientation to permanent residence in the United States. In contrast, many Italian men were "birds of passage" until the beginning of the twentieth century. They did not learn the English language rapidly, nor take out citizenship, bring their families, or look for permanent economic improvements until they stopped trying to return with their wages to their real home in Italy.[48] These factors limited their entrance into business and handicapped their children at school.

In 1908 the U.S. Immigration Commission studied over two million school children, focusing on "the rate of retardation"—the proportion of children who were two or more years older than the average age for their grade. The measure is quite biased, since many children had to drop out periodically to help support their families, and since older children who could not speak English were often put in lower grades. Russian Jews were at about the average rate of retardation for non-English-speaking foreign-born: 42 percent. They ranked seventh out of twelve groups. Swedish immigrants were first, with only 16 percent "retarded," followed by English immigrants, native-born whites, Irish, Germans, and German Jews, in that order. Five groups had higher proportions of overage school children than the Russian Jews. These were the Northern Italians, Rumanian Jews, Poles, Southern Italians (with a 64 percent rate) and Polish Jews (with 67 percent).[49]

These are national statistics. In New York, Russian Jews had a slightly higher high school graduation rate and a slightly lower drop-out rate than the average. The opposite was true of the Italian children. Eleven of the thirteen Italian high school students in Van Denberg's study dropped out before graduation; none of them graduated on time. (Note the small size of the sample, however. If the two Italian students who had neither graduated nor dropped out of high school in their ninth semester had graduated on time, they would have changed the results by 15.5 percent.)[50]

Many Italian children came from poorer homes; their parents were more likely to need the contribution of their labor and less likely to speak English. Italian parents were less likely than Jewish parents to regard school as important, *in part* for historical/cultural reasons which have been emphasized to death. But this attitude was reinforced by the schools. Teachers generally expected Jewish children to do well and Italians to do poorly.[51]

I have conducted this brief excursion to the Ethnic Derby because experience has taught me that people feel that something essential is missing if Jews are discussed without comparison to someone else. Frankly I find such static comparisons sterile. If it takes this whole book to explore the causes and implications of Jewish mobility through education (only) for males (mainly), then a comparison of Jewish and Italian class experience as a whole requires a deeper study of both the Jewish and the Italian class experience than is usually given. It is simply not enough to count the number of Jewish workers and professors, count the number of Italian workers and professors, and plug in "cultural values" as the explanation. The process of class formation among and between ethnic groups requires specific historical study of each. What industries are they in? How does their specific kind of work keep them at work, or drive them to other ways of making a living? What are the chances for accumulating capital, and what are the barriers to its accumulation? How do the institutions they encounter treat them similarly or differently? What are the facilities for tuition-free collegiate education in their main centers of concentration? What knowledge do they bring with them, and how possible is it to use that old knowledge in the new situation? What networks absorb them, and what networks exclude them?

But why compare only Jews, Italians, Poles, and Blacks? What can we learn by looking at the historical experience of Swedish, German, and English immigrants and at white Protestants? It is curious that Swedes and Germans are not given greater attention, in view of their higher scores on various educational measures. I suspect that these groups are no longer even considered ethnic groups: they have disappeared into the mainstream. May it be possible that the celebration of Jewish success relative to other groups simultaneously expresses its opposite, the relative incompleteness of Jewish integration into the class structure? In short, a really serious comparison requires moving beyond the superficial scoring of a numbers rat race to creating a comparative analysis of the specific historical relations among class, race, and ethnicity in the changing U.S. economy.

As for those Eastern European Jews who moved through educational institutions and into professions, let us not forget how few they were, but let us now take them on their own terms. To change from worker to teacher, lawyer, or professional, is not simply to boost one's pay and prestige. It is to make a *qualitative* change in social relations. To call this change "success" is to make a value judgment based on conventional, dominant ideology. Scholars have been so busy calibrating professionals and celebrating their success that they often fail to consider the conditions that made the rise of Jews through education and into professions possible, the meaning of this rise, or the cultural price it exacted. In the previous chapters I have argued that the very possibility of using higher education for mobility was a result of class conflicts in which Jewish labor participated. But what did it all mean? In the rest of this book, I address this question of the cultural meaning of educational mobility.

Part II

Social Conflict and Culture

Herbert Spencer. *D. Appleton & Co.*

7

Dominant Culture

To our minds, this culture we were studying . . . was not the creation or the possession of a particular group of people; it was a repository of the universal.
—Norman Podhoretz, *Making It*

God forbid that Stanford University should ever favor socialism of any kind.
—Mrs. Leland Stanford, ordering the firing of Prof. E. A. Ross.

By the time we were leaving the university, we were no longer culturally Jews.
—Joseph Freeman, *An American Testament*

People have often been so preoccupied with who gets where that they have forgotten to ask what happens to them along the way. It all sounds so easy. Milton Gordon said, "The traditional stress and high evaluation placed upon Talmudic learning was easily transferred under new conditions to a desire for secular education, if not for the present generation, at least for the children."[1] S. Joseph Fauman added, "The group value oriented towards religious learning was transferred to the sphere of secular learning, without losing its hold upon the group."[2] Almost all scholars of ethnicity have played variations on this theme.

In 1969 Mariam Slater challenged this folk myth. She claimed that *shtetl* learning was ritualistic, scholastic, conservative, and "unrelated to technology, art or science." In contrast, she said, Western learning is pragmatic, humanistic, oriented to natural and social science, and innovative. "Western knowledge," she said, "facilitates entering the mainstream." Therefore, rather than involving an "easy transfer" of cultural patterns, Jewish upward mobility required a sharp *break* with *shtetl* values and Eastern European attitudes toward education.[3]

The academicians, normally known for taking scholarly disputation to Talmudic lengths, ignored her. Only Werner Cahnman replied, and he simply reiterated the Jewish scholarship theory without dealing with the issues which Slater had raised.[4]

Slater was half right. College was not simply the rainbow at the end of the Jewish quest through rainy days. College was also a beginning, a cultural process in itself. Western culture was far different from

Lower East Side culture. Embracing it would require some break with the past. But Slater was only *half* right: Western culture was not the rainbow she painted. Beneath its aura of rationalism, pragmatism, and democratic assimilation, it was also Christian, racist, and politically conservative.

This Western elite culture dominated the curriculum at CCNY. It permeated course content and faculty scholarship. It violated the realities of Jewish workers and ghetto life. It ignored the vibrant Yiddish socialist culture that was flowering among poets, journalists, artists, and workers at the turn of the century. Jewish students commuting between these two cultural worlds subjected themselves to a world of business assumptions and Anglo Saxon dominance. Social mobility through the institutions which promulgated such a culture was not simply a series of agile leaps up an abstract "social ladder." It required some form of confrontation with a dominant, alien, but seemingly all-embracing way of life.

Appearances

The colleges of the late nineteenth and early twentieth century seemed to many students to be golden temples of universalism. Immigrant boys commuting to courses in "Western Civilization" from ghetto homes expressed a sensation of expansion, enlightenment, and even conversion to a culture far broader and loftier than the seeming provincialism of the Jewish ghetto.

Joseph Freeman came to the United States from Russia as a small child. He participated in the socialist movement in his teens and much later was to become a leftist writer of some renown.[5] In 1916 he entered Columbia College and became enthralled by universal culture. Universal culture healed all divisions of race, class, and nationality:

> There was a line, we thought whenever the problems of the external world became too pressing or too confusing, which divided mankind into two parts, regardless of class, nation or race. There was that part which loved culture and that part which did not. On the campus the average student was interested in sports, women and money .... But there was another group, select without being exclusive, a group which anyone could enter if he deserved it, whatever his race, nation or social status, a group of Choice Spirits devoted to philosophy, science and the arts—to culture. We imagined that this culture embraced all mankind, all lands, all times.

This all-embracing culture left out the culture of women, Black people, and the immigrant working class. Jewish socialism was not included. Only years later did it occur to Freeman that there had been something particular about Universal Man:

> From this all-human culture we excluded, in practice, a large section of humanity. We knew nothing and cared less about the knowledge, thought and art of Asia, or of our neighbors in Latin America. Russia, too, was outside the cultural realm in which we moved, for Russia, the myth ran, was Asiatic and barbarous. . . . Not until the October Revolution did we become interested in Russian culture. . . .
>
> [O]ur myth of universal culture omitted from consideration three continents, most of Europe and nearly all of America, and concentrated on that narrow learning and art which, masked as the Hellenic spirit, glowed over the isolated circles of a few Western capitals.[6]

Not all North American colleges and universities could have been as successfully seductive in the deceptive mask of universalism, but all were confined within the narrow bounds of Christian ethnocentrism.

The Protestant Ethos

Before the Revolutionary War, colleges were established to "recreate a little bit of Old England in America." At the time, Florida was Spanish and Louisiana was French. Therefore, the establishment of explicitly *English* colleges was a matter of some political and cultural importance. The proliferation of colleges across the continent in the early nineteenth century was an explicit part of the colonization of the West. College founding was considered crucial to missionary work, aimed at saving settlers and "savages" alike. It prepared the conquest of more and more territory for the English Protestant world.[7]

The religious rivalry which led virtually every sect to found at least one college spread Protestantism in many varieties across the nation. The effect of the philanthropy of the Carnegie Foundation and of Rockefeller's General Education Board, however, was to homogenize Protestant education and to foster modernization within the framework of the major denominations.[8] Jencks and Riesman describe a tension

> between diversity and ecumenism . . . in Protestant higher education. Diversity led to the establishment of an inordinate number of

separate colleges, but ecumenism then led most of these colleges to emphasize their collegiate rather than their sectarian side, seeking faculty and students of all persuasions and becoming annually more like one another.[9]

Jencks and Riesman thought they saw in this late-nineteenth-century modernization "the Rise of Meritocracy"—the triumph of universalism over particularism, of professionalism, competence, and natural ability over narrow religious loyalties. But they also provide evidence that in the vaunted professional transformation (which continues today) the Catholic schools, the women's colleges, and the Negro colleges decline while the secularized Protestant schools remain. It is to the established and prestigious (state and secularized Protestant) schools that ambitious Catholics, women, and Blacks must apply if they wish to make a successful career in "the wider society."[10] Diversity remains, but the result of the earlier expansion and the late nineteenth-century reforms was a more uniform educational system led by New England upper-class male Protestant universities.

In short, the religious trustees of the private, sectarian colleges across the nation may have thought that the Progressive bourgeoisie was the Devil dealing, but the Progressives were very Christian gentlemen. True, they rationalized Protestant higher education by supporting the wealthy and powerful sects at the expense of the more plebian ones. And they promoted secularization by introducing sciences, vocational subjects, and the elective system. But consciously and unconsciously they presumed that the colleges and universities would remain Protestant institutions.

For themselves they created exclusive social clubs, resorts, summer colonies, and prep schools, based on the principle that national economic and political power was and of right ought to be white Protestant. At the same time that they were secularizing higher education, they were attacking Catholic political power in the cities and excluding German Jewish business families from the social settings in which intermarriage, informal sociability, and major business and political decisions were constructed; that is, they excluded Catholics from municipal power and Jews from integration into the ruling class.

Lacking aristocratic roots, some Protestant "robber barons" flattered themselves by having their English genealogy traced. The prep schools were Anglophile and Episcopalian or Presbyterian. In the 1920s the white Protestant corporate class generally wrapped itself in defensive narcissism and excluded all but a minority of Jews and Blacks from the leading colleges and universities in the nation. The religiously-affiliated colleges became more concerned with denominationalism than they had been before the Civil War, and concern with Christianity actually increased, reaching its peak around 1920.[11]

At the College of the City of New York there was a corresponding combination of social discrimination, secularization, and diffuse Protestantism, at least in the beginning. In the 1870s, as the sons of wealthy German (and some Sephardic) Jews began to enter CCNY, the fraternities excluded them. There were a number of anti-Semitic incidents. Like children dressing up in daddy's clothes, middle-class Protestant CCNY boys proved that even if they did not have the power of the national corporate class, they could certainly aspire to its prejudices. "The professors," said Irving Howe, "maintained a tone of Protestant moralism."[12]

Official policy, however, was more open. In a rare exception to CCNY's regimented program, Jewish students were given special exemption from compulsory attendance at classes on the High Holy days. In 1882, in return for Catholic support in CCNY's fight against one of the perennial legislative efforts to abolish the College, CCNY dropped the requirement for admission that applicants must have spent at least a year in the public schools, and a number of parochial school graduates applied for admission. (As the late nineteenth century was the period of the establishment of a large number of Catholic colleges, however, the number of Catholic students at CCNY never became very large.[13]) By 1904, when a majority of CCNY students were Jewish, chapel attendance was made voluntary.

But for many years City College, with a predominantly Jewish student body, was staffed and administered almost entirely by white Protestants. As late as 1920 Barnard Baruch was the only Jewish trustee, and extremely few Jewish or Catholic names appear on the lists of administration and faculty.[14] President Finley reportedly "managed to overcome . . . some of the anti-Semitism that was endemic in the genteel, Anglo-Saxon milieu in which he moved . . . [and] to create with unmistakable sincerity a more tolerant atmosphere at C.C.N.Y." The elaborateness with which Rudy, Duggan, and Gettleman praise Finley's tolerance, however, gives silent testimony to the pervasiveness of anti-Semitism in this "genteel Anglo-Saxon milieu."[15]

City College's secularization, like that of other public institutions, went hand in hand with a diffuse Protestantism. The head of the

Louisiana State University complained in 1873, "[We are] required by public opinion to have religion, in a general way, somehow, yet forbidden to have it in any particular way." Or as Milton Himmelfarb put it, "While the secular society in the lands that used to be Christendom is neutral in matters of religion, it is more neutral against Judaism than against Christianity."[16]

In sum, like most U.S. colleges and universities at the turn of the century, CCNY was secular in form and Protestant in culture. Unlike the latter-day elite colleges, however, the school was not religiously restrictive in its admissions policies; the administration consistently opposed anti-Semitism, and tuition was free. As a result, the student body was increasingly Jewish and poor. Once there, these students affected the informal culture of the college, forming religious and ethnic clubs and organizations of their own. The school's institutional structure remained a form of secularized Anglo-Protestantism for some time, however, and it is this arena of Anglo-Protestantism that Lower East Side Jewish boys entered.

Scientific Racism

A great paradox of higher education is that the secularization of the schools and the triumph of rationalistic science over dogmatic theology made possible the triumph and scholarly legitimation of systematic and virulent racism. The liberalization of academia let flow academic theories of the racial and cultural inferiority of Blacks, Native Americans, Jews, Italians, and Poles. These theories permeated college curricula.

"Scientific racism" developed in Europe as a "scholarly" justification for the worldwide expansion, plunder, and domination by a Northern European capitalist class over multivaried peoples of the world. According to racial theories, Europeans' innate mental superiority gave them the ability, right, and burdensome responsibility of rule over mere savages.

The adoption of scientific racism in the United States was retarded by the factors that slowed the adoption of European science generally: resistance by educational conservatives and clerics to the expansion of sciences within the college curriculum, and the relative underdevelopment of U.S. capitalism. Racism did not become the substance of college curricula and university scholarship until the academic revolution at the turn of the century, which created the social sciences, organized them into professional disciplines and academic departments, and put them into college curricula.[17] Simultaneously many of the elite colleges—funded, controlled, and attended by the wealthy—became the leading institutions in the new national higher educational system. Despite the many substantial ideological differences among scholars, these institutions generally transmitted upper-class racial, religious, and class prejudices throughout the collegiate system via myriad paths of cultural influence.

The modern U.S. capitalist class merged the southern planter aristocracy, interested in promoting Jim Crow laws to help control Southern populism, with the Northern industrialists, interested in carrying the white man's burden and U.S. industry across Indian lands and beyond the territorial United States. Locked also in conflict with an immigrant working class, the bourgeoisie began to develop a ruling ideology based on social Darwinism and "scientific" racism.[18]

At first, racial theories were applied to Black, Chinese, and native peoples but not to European groups. The white Protestant political leadership needed white unity in controlling both the black population (especially after the Civil War) and the "Indians" (who were still fighting the advance of European colonization). Most white Protestant businessmen also needed to continue importing labor from Europe. These needs led them to emphasize color differences only, and to delay making the kinds of distinctions among European groups that were already part of scientific racism in Europe.[19]

But the influx of immigrants a third again as numerous as the previous population, with their labor militancy and anti-capitalist political activity, made the application of scientific racism to the immigrants politically necessary at precisely the time when the modernization of the curriculum of higher education, the reforms fostering scientific research, and the organization of national scientific associations made it institutionally possible.

"Scientists" traced the capitalist class's right to rule and its riches to its origins in a Germanic "blonde, chaste, warrior" tribe with primeval institutions of democracy. They asserted that the immigrants' innate deficiencies made them unfit to rule themselves and participate in a democratic order. Using the prestigious paraphernalia of science—measurement—the "scientists made a system of the caricatures," codifying common stereotypes. Immigrant inferiority was to be proved through craniology—the measurement of skulls—using the most ingenious and, at times, bizarre techniques.[20]

The "scientific" classification of races was ingeniously flexible, as Thomas Gossett shows:

By a little judicious tampering, the historians and political scientists could adapt racial theory to the needs of the moment. If they wished to demonstrate our racial kinship with England, they could say that both nations were basically Anglo-Saxon. If they wished to maintain that Americans were not all plebian, they could refer to the Norman blood which ran in American veins. If they admired Germany or if they wished to cast aspersions on southern and eastern European immigrants, they could say that we were Teutons—a term which could, on occasion, include the people of England, Germany, Holland and the Scandinavian countries. If they wished to include virtually all of Europe—for example, if they wished to demonstrate the solidarity of the white man against the colored races or Christians against Jews—then they could refer to Americans as Caucasians or Aryans.[21]

This remarkable flexibility of innately fixed characteristics made it possible for racial groups to be promoted into the white group or demoted to inferior classifications without undermining in any way the concept of racial hierarchy, and without, of course, challenging the location of Anglo-Saxons or Teutons at the apex of the racial pyramid. The very flexibility of the concept of race made it extremely useful as an instrument of social control. The Irish, for example, moved from being "foreign Papists" to being among the older immigrants "who were more akin to us" than Italians and Jews. But they could also be "the evil Celt." In the South, when Italians fraternized with Blacks, they were classified by whites as colored, were excluded from white schools, and in at least one case, lynched.[22] Thus a group's innate biological character might well depend on its good behavior: racially superior workers were those who did not yield to foreign socialist ideals. Scientific racism served as a consensus ideology when applied to WASP workers: socialism was just not supposed to be in their blood. All these wide shifts of racial category took place within the conceptual framework of scientific racism, a set of theories that insisted that a group's racial characteristics were fixed, fatal, not reformable.

Although Anglo-Saxonism and Teutonism implicitly excluded all Jews from racial superiority, the Russian Jews received explicit attention as a low breed. E. A. Ross, the leading sociologist, saw the new immigrants as "hirsute, lowbrowed, big-faced persons of obviously low mentality." He pointed to "the shortness and the smallness of [their] crania."[23] Historian Frederick Jackson Turner asserted that "the coming of Italians, Poles, Russian Jews, and Slovaks was 'a loss to the social organism of the United States.' " In particular, the Jews were capable of living under conditions that would exterminate men whom centuries of national selection had not adapted to endure the squalor and the unsanitary and indecent conditions of a dangerously crowded population. [The Jews were] a people of exceptionally stunted stature and deficient lung capacity.[24]

The liberals blamed the Italians and Jews for being organically adapted to their oppression. The conservatives blamed them for being "incapable of democracy," by which they generally meant not sufficiently respectful of law and order. After the Bolshevik Revolution in particular, the Jews were discovered to partake of "the turbulent and anarchic character of the Slavic Race." Carl C. Brigham, Assistant Professor of Psychology at Princeton University, used the Army intelligence tests to "disprove the popular belief that the Jew is highly intelligent." For other social scientists, however, natural selection had developed the Jews' minds unnaturally, at the expense of body and "spirit."[25]

The bearers of higher culture feared that the superior race was in danger of "race suicide" because it was not breeding apace. Ross proposed immigration restriction; Margaret Sanger proposed population control. Charles Eliot was for ethnic assimilation and "Yankee procreation."[26]

Virtually all turn-of-the-century social scientists, liberal and conservative, asserted racial theories. For a quarter of a century, the Teutonic origins theory was the dominant school of thought among American historians. It also captured literature and political science, particularly through John W. Burgess. At Columbia University Burgess set up a most influential department in political science, training several men who were to found and staff social science departments at City College.[27]

Although the work repudiating scientific racism was developed a decade earlier, this environmentalist scholarship had little impact until after the restrictive immigration laws of the 1920s had been passed. Anthropology, which had originated as the science of race, became the science of relativism, through the development by E. B. Tylor and Franz Boas of cultural anthropology. In 1910 Boas undertook an investigation for the U.S. Immigration Commission. Supervising the measurement of seventeen thousand immigrants and their children, Boas used the cephalic index, devised to prove the superior cranial capacity of Anglo-Saxons and Teutons, and showed that the supposedly unchangeable and hereditary index was not necessarily inherited. In fact it changed according to length of stay in the United States.

The theoretical implication of Boas's work was that racial characteristics are not fixed—not even with respect to physical measurements,
let alone mental capacities. The methodological implication was the
undermining of craniology as a means of classifying races. The
political implication was at least initially nil, since Boas's portion of
the Commission report was buried in the study, which was otherwise
overwhelmingly biased in favor of the restriction of immigration. The
cultural implication was that the ethnic hierarchy was culturally rather
than genetically based. Members of the Jewish bourgeoisie, lobbying
against immigration restriction, argued that the Educational Alliance's
Americanization program proved that immigrant deficiencies could be
removed through education.

The adoption of environmentalism with regard to European immigrants did not mean the abandonment of biological racism with regard
to Black people, Orientals, or Indians. Basically the environmentalist
scientists reunited what the racist scientists had divided: the unity of
European descendants. The assimilation of the so-called culturally
inferior Europeans meant their acceptance as ethnic groups as opposed
to racial groups. Now Jews, Italians, and other white Europeans could
be assimilated into the culture of white Protestant racism. They had
been permitted to cross the border of the racist divide.

The 1920s, the period in which environmentalism first started to
make a serious impact on scientific thought, was the period of the
triumph of immigration restriction, the Red Scare, and the most
frenetic pressure for Americanization. The Palmer raids rounded up
aliens and jailed, terrified, and deported them. Sacco and Vanzetti were
murdered by the state for being Italian anarchists, despite a worldwide
protest. Harvard and other elite institutions, headwaters of the Western mainstream, restricted Jews and segregated Blacks. Shortly before
this time Horace Kallen and a number of others had begun to articulate
theories proposing cultural pluralism as against coercive assimilation,
but they had little program for structural or economic change. The
underlying presumption that made environmentalism possible, and
cultural pluralism problematic, was a structure of political and ethnic
inequality. This period, when the scientific consensus on racism was
finally cracked by environmentalist science, is the one which Baltzell
quite plausibly labels "The Anglo-Saxon Decade."[28]

Boas's work was enormously important in establishing a culture of
environmentalism and social reform. It paved the way for the democratic assimilation of members of European ethnic groups. But antagonistic as his work was to biological racism, it did not necessarily
imply equality among ethnic groups. An emphasis on adaptability

does not necessarily attack the hierarchy of superiority and inferiority any more than social mobility destroys the existence of classes. Environmentalism per se merely states that placement in terms of superiority and inferiority is not hopelessly immutable: the inferior head shapes of Russian Jews and Sicilians may change to resemble the superior heads of the Anglo-Saxons.

Boas himself was a cultural relativist, and eschewed judgments of cultural superiority and inferiority.[29] The cultural and political impact of his work, however, was limited by the context of American ethnic and class structure. Consequently his work paved the way for an environmentalism based on the *cultural* rather than *biological* superiority of white Protestants. This was the "mainstream" of Western culture that beckoned immigrant students.

The Spirit of Capitalism

The socialism that permeated the Lower East Side was not part of the definition of social thought in academia. Whereas in Europe socialist scholarship was well developed, and even non-socialist scholars recognized classes and class conflict as relevant to the analysis of capitalist society, American social theory was much more restricted. Scholars sought, in general, to play down class conflict. They tended to ply psychological and/or cultural, rather than economic, definitions of class. Either they saw U.S. society in conceptual terms other than *capitalist*, or they lauded U.S. capitalism as the best of all possible systems.[30] Openly and implicitly, the message of "higher culture" was a defense of the U.S. political and economic system against the social movements that were daily calling that system into question.

Many social theorists were sympathetic toward the working class, and many were ardent reformers. But the spectrum of social science as defined by the influential and recognized theorists of the academic world ranged from conservative to liberal; it went to farther. Lester F. Ward, whose social theory was closest to that of Marx, never read him. His brother, C. Osborne Ward, who had read and met Marx, had no academic influence. Albion Small, founder of the *American Journal of Sociology*, was reputed to be "a critical and sympathetic student of Marx," but he was basically dedicated to cooperation (social harmony), was clearly anti-socialist, and supported the University of Chicago's firing of radicals. Franz Boas basically had no theory of class. All in all, the major social scientists, the theorists who taught at the leading institutions, and whose ideas defined their fields in each profession for the less prestigious institutions, "gave voice to class theories which were, in the final analysis, highly colored by the 'classlessness' of the American scene."[31]

Universities in the United States generally fostered forms of social science which focused on the individual rather than on society or social classes. Behaviorism insisted on the study of behavior rather than institutions, classes, or social forces. Initially established at the Social Science Research Council with a grant from the Laura Spelman Rockefeller fund, behaviorism became the dominant approach in political science, sociology, and psychology. "Social pathologists"— C. Wright Mills's term for persons concerned with dealing with deviance, crime, and other social maladies—sought social reform through immigrant adaptation, the fitting of the individual into society. Such approaches left little room for societal change.

Those theorists who were openly socialist or Marxist, such as Thorstein Veblen, Isaac Hourwich, and Scott Nearing, did not retain their academic posts. John D. Rockefeller's University of Chicago (dubbed the "Standard Oil Laboratories" by the International Socialist Review[32]) fired Hourwich, Veblen, and Edward T. Bemis, a critic of the railroad and gas trusts. Said Lester Ward: "I heard that Veblen was likely to have to leave the University of Chicago. They will all have to go ultimately who are above the wretched chauvinism that is required and expected."[33]

Veblen later taught at Stanford University, worked for the U.S. government as a minor bureaucrat, and taught at the New School for Social Research. When the New School was reorganized in 1922, Veblen had nowhere to go; he was unable to find an academic job.[34]

Hourwich's firing prompted a local paper to say, "Dr. Isaac Hourwich is debarred from teaching because he is an avowed socialist, an infidel, a sympathizer with the People's Party. No self-respecting institution should retain for an hour among its lecturers one who holds such dangerous opinions. . . ."[35] Most university administrations agreed. They worried most about endowments and business benefactors.

The concept of academic freedom, receiving its first North American development and articulation in just this period, ran into "a rather naked double standard." A professor might campaign for Republican candidates as part of civic virtue; to campaign for Debs or even Bryan was to be unacceptably controversial. Especially "in times of marked social unrest, professors were expected to keep silent about issues about which they might otherwise speak" because businessmen might be discouraged from donating funds. That is, professors were free to teach and speak freely except when their speech might have some effect. "The history of academic freedom thus became a rather accurate reflection of the degree of social alarm felt at any given hour by the more substantial elements in the American population."[36]

In the 1890s and early 1900s, professors were fired not only for favoring socialism, but also for supporting strikes and boycotts, opposing monopolies, supporting free trade and the coinage of silver, opposing Asian immigration (when employers favored it), supporting assimilation of Black people in the South, and opposing the firing of other professors for their beliefs.[37] Many professors were intimidated into silence or support for the administration's side of academic freedom disputes. ("Professors always have hungry children," Veysey explained.) Others supported the suppression of radicals out of conviction. They had themselves been selected for their conformity and compatibility with business ideology.[38]

Having organized a national higher education system through directed philanthropy, the corporate elite who stewarded their wealth as trustees or through college presidents made certain that their institutions would sanction neither conviction nor science antagonistic to their power, privileges, or property. On the contrary, they expected their universities to further their interests, investigate and solve their problems, and articulate their ideology.

The social analyst who had the greatest impact by far on the entire academic world was Herbert Spencer. Spencer provided the academic justification that the business class needed for the concentration of wealth and power, the persistence of poverty, and the suppression of movements for social change. Thomas Gossett explains,

> In the United States, the influence of Spencer on the developing discipline of sociology was tremendous. Charles H. Cooley thought that most of the people who took up the study of sociology in this country between 1870 and 1890 were drawn to the subject chiefly through Spencer's writings. Spencer's popularity was not merely academic. As an advocate of laissez faire, he was lionized by the business classes when he visited this country. His prestige among conservatives undoubtedly led many boards of trustees of American universities to look with favor upon the idea of founding departments of sociology.[39]

Although not all social theorists were followers of Spencer, his work set the framework for the academic debate of the era. Even the liberals identified social change with evolution and evolution with progress.

Liberals believed in helping progress along through social reform, whereas conservative followers of Spencer denounced reformers as tampering with the natural "survival of the fittest" by hampering the strong or helping the weak. Spencer's thought ideologically bulwarked conservative opposition to any curbs on corporations, or any poor relief.

One of Spencer's most ardent disciples was Franklin Giddings, the dominant figure in the Department of Sociology at Columbia and a major influence on City College. References to Spencer comprise a full column (half a page) of the index to Giddings's *Principles of Sociology* (1896). Giddings and William Graham Sumner were "the most ardent defenders of the *status quo.*" Like Spencer, Giddings opposed aid to the poor, believing that "all modern experience of poor relief is an overwhelming demonstration that any community can have all the pauperism and criminality that it cares to pay for."[40]

Inequality, according to Giddings, is inevitable. Poverty is innate and an indication of degeneracy. Unfortunately, great inequality of wealth threatens "that perfect fraternity upon which the highest social evolution and resulting social welfare depend."

Giddings saw socialism as a result of the "degeneration of the social constitution"—the radicalism of the poor and the greed and lack of civic interest of the nouveau riche (who withdraw from social association through self-centeredness).

> Many of the poor, though happily not a majority, give ear to anarchism, or seek comfort in the socialistic dream of a world where labour time-checks would buy everything save that the love of which is said to be the root of evil. They withdraw themselves as far as possible from contact with the rich, and cherish the hope of organizing the proletariat into an irresistible force, and of taking possession of all the organs of government.
>
> Thus is civilization menaced by dangers perhaps as grave as those that overshadowed it at the beginning. It was threatened then by barbarism beyond its walls. To-day it is threatened by the savagery within the gates.[41]

To socialists, the "savagery within the gates" was caused by the rich themselves. Giddings's "civilization" rested on murderous labor, tuberculosis, unemployment, hunger, and wage slavery. Capitalism was savagery. Only socialism could end "barbarism" and bring civilization. (In this sense, socialist Jewish students may have been required to make more of a cultural "break" to enter "the Western mainstream" than Talmudists!)

Franklin Giddings, then, was, like his mentor Herbert Spencer, a social Darwinist, an organicist, and a defender of the status quo. Through his student, Howard Brown Woolston, founder of the sociology department at CCNY, Giddings's social thought set the framework for City College sociology.[42] Other conservative Columbia University faculty members such as John W. Burgess and J. B. Clark had their CCNY disciples in William Guthrie, who founded City College's political science department, and Walter B. Clark, CCNY economist. On the liberal side, Columbia's Franz Boas became M. R. Cohen's friend, although Cohen received his graduate training at Harvard.[43] As we shall see in the next chapter, City College reflected and refracted the spirit of the age.

Higher Culture

The trouble with the seemingly all-embracing culture which so dazzled young Joseph Freeman and his fellow students from the Jewish ghetto was not only what it left out but also what it included. The leading colleges were secularized Protestant institutions, dedicated to the reform and protection of the political and economic system which so bountifully benefited their wealthy contributors, trustees, and clientele. Faced with the various challenges posed by an immigrant working class and by political movements which demanded social changes antagonistic to capitalist interests, these institutions promoted ideologies of scientific racism and social Darwinism.

At no point did this higher culture form a unitary body of thought, a consensus of scholars. There were serious disagreements among the various schools of scientific racism, between eugenicists and anti-eugenicists, between immigration restrictionists and non-restrictionists, between social Darwinists and anti-social Darwinists and, within all these divisions, between liberals and conservatives. Those debates were real, and they implied vastly different social policies.

But for all its variety higher culture did not cover the entire range of the contemporary social philosophies, and thus the warring factions had certain limited underlying assumptions. The commonality between scientific racism and environmentalism rested on the ethnic hierarchy. The scholarly debate in social theory, for all its diversity, excluded socialism and Marxism. By various means the corporate trustees of colleges and universities across the country sought to ensure that the radical ideas which confronted them on the railroads, in factories, mines, and city streets would not be sympathetically considered in the schools which they had endowed "to save our families and our money from mobs."[44]

The capitalist class, embarked on worldwide junkets and at war with immigrant labor, knew which side it expected universities to support. The Protestant culture of higher education was often racist, anti-Semitic, anti-socialist and generally anti-labor. This was the mainstream that permeated the formal and informal culture of the leading institutions of higher learning and was promulgated in the newly-formed professional associations, the new professional journals, and the new university presses. It filled the expressed convictions of scholars, their writings and their courses and was repeated in college classes and textbooks all across the country.

The Eastern Jews entering higher education belonged to one of the groups classified by some scientific racists as innately inferior, and by some environmentalists as culturally inferior. That discussion cannot have been irrelevant to these students. Regardless of whether they were attracted to socialism or repelled by it, they resided in a community that seriously discussed it. The Lower East Side was Yiddish, Orthodox, and socialist. "Higher culture" expressed the Protestant ethos and the spirit of capitalism.

Frontispiece from *Songs of Labor* by Morris Rosenfeld.

8

The City College Curriculum in an Age of Cultural Conflict

The City College curriculum between 1903 and 1925 was very much the child of its age. It was more environmentalist than racist, and more social Darwinist than reformist. It was explicitly and assertively pro-capitalist and anti-socialist, and it implicitly and explicitly expressed white Protestant cultural superiority. Through it passed CCNY's Jewish students, many of them from the immigrant, working class, and heavily socialist Lower East Side.

The study of the curriculum as long ago as seventy years is a study of culture at a distance. It is hard to evoke a living presence, to know for sure what actually transpired in the complex interaction of the classrooms. It is possible to sketch a composite picture of CCNY as a cultural institution by examining several different types of data, each of which, considered alone, has certain weaknesses. This analysis rests, therefore, on the *cumulative weight* of the evidence garnered from several sources.

The materials available in the City College Archives are uneven. In economics and history there are detailed lecture notes. In anthropology there are only course descriptions, but some texts are listed, and I have examined them. In sociology there are course descriptions alone, but we may gain additional clues by studying the training and the intellectual output of the faculty. No student notebooks were found.

The lecture notes are the best sources of data. They are extremely detailed, giving a specific outline and specific bibliography for each class session. Where lecture notes are absent, however, we must rely on other data, among them, course descriptions, faculty doctoral dissertations, and texts.

The weakness of texts as a source of data is that one does not know how they were presented. Were they criticized, lauded, or both? Were they included solely because of their influence and importance in the field or did they reflect, as well, the perspective of the instructor? How were they received? Did the students read them, and if so, how much were they affected by what they read? Finally, the texts listed in the catalogue may not have been the only ones used in the course, although earlier CCNY catalogues were more detailed than many are today. Despite these flaws, the texts do give some indication of the content of a course, especially in conjunction with other materials.

Course catalogues are at once the most plentiful and, at first glance, the most problematic sources of data. Every instructor knows that the catalogue description bears only an approximate relation to the course that he or she actually teaches. Instructors tend to revise their course content over the years without revising the descriptions in the catalogue. Moreover, it is impossible to encompass several months of instruction in a single paragraph. Consequently, as an isolated bit of data, a single course description would be an unsatisfactory indicator of course content. Thus the use of course descriptions requires the greatest leaps of interpretation.

But although there may be great disagreement on the meaning or significance of any *one* of them, taken together they present a fairly coherent overall picture, especially in conjunction with other types of evidence, and especially when Columbia University's contemporary curriculum is used for comparison.

Thus we are looking at the City College curriculum as a whole, and examining it both in itself and in contrast with that of another college in New York City. The validity of the data is enhanced by our examination of some of these materials at the point of institutional formation. The social science departments at CCNY were being formed anew.

The social sciences came late to City College. History predated the Progressive reforms, as did economics. (Bernard Baruch was tremendously impressed by the course in political economics he attended at CCNY in the 1880s.)[2] But political science and anthropology were not taught until 1907, and only in 1909 was authorization given for courses in Sociology and Municipal Affairs in the new Department of Political Science.[3] In this perspective, catalogue descriptions are not simply routinized entries that have become outmoded by the passage of time. Rather they present courses, and whole departments, at the point of their formation, and in the pattern in which they grew.

Curriculum at City College

As scientific racism set the framework of much discourse at the turn of the century, it influenced CCNY's curriculum. In general, however, the strident racism characteristic of Ross, Adams, and Burgess is scarcely evident at CCNY.

Anthropology, taught from 1907 on, and devoted entirely to the subject of race, came closest to the predominant thinking. Brinton's *Races and Peoples* was one of the two texts. A work of seemingly detached and dispassionate classification, Brinton's book is chiefly devoted to describing each "race," "branch," "stock," "group," "tribe," "nation," and "ethnos." Brinton asserts: "Peoples low in one point [of civilization] are high in another; they develop along different lines, with scarcely a common measure. . . ." On the other hand the weight of the book reflects his contention that we are "accustomed familiarly to speak of 'higher' and 'lower' races, and we are justified in this even from merely physical considerations." The physical inequalities are said to "bear intimate relations to mental capacity." Brinton continued, "Measured by these criteria [of physical dimensions, including the continuation of the 'heart' line across the hand] the European or white race stands at the head of the list, the African or negro at its foot." The Celtic peoples are "a dangerous element in the body politic of a free country"; "Italic peoples," on the other hand, "acknowledge authority."[4]

Unfortunately for the education of those students who took anthropology, Brinton's classification scheme was favorable to the Jews. Jews even had, Brinton asserted, a greater tendency to be blond than many people realized. "The Semitic stock is a markedly white type of the race, and in all ages fair complexion, light eyes and hair, have been admired as especially beautiful."[5]

Brinton's affinity for "the Semitic Race" was based on his conception of their contribution to his vision of progress:

No man and no race of other lineage dare withstand an attack or disobey an order from a leading European power. Africa and Asia are dismembered and parceled out at London, Berlin and St. Petersburg, and no one dreams of asking the consent of the inhabitants of those countries.

This astonishing progress is not due alone to the North Mediterranean branch of the Eurafrican race. The representatives of the South Mediterranean branch are for a large part in it. In the forefront of it, whether in the great capitals of Europe or in the pioneer towns of the frontiers, we find the acute and versatile Semite, full of energy and knowledge, guiding in councils, his master hand on the levers of the vastest financial schemes, his subtle policy governing the diplomacy of statesmen and the decisions of directors.[6]

I wonder whether City College's poorer Jewish students were flattered by this paean to the role of the Jewish capitalist class in imperialism. Did they perhaps squirm a little at this stereotyped image of the Jew as Master Shylock to the Master Race?

The other text used in anthropology at City College was far more restrained. W. L. H. Duckworth's *Morphology and Anthropology* was a book chiefly on the comparative anatomy of mammals other than man. The word *race* does not appear in the index. Duckworth begins this work with an introductory chapter on the history of anthropology. Concerned chiefly with establishing the history of the field as a science of measurement and observation, Duckworth barely discusses race, and when he does, he declares that the belief in the infertility of the offspring of interracial mating has been "negatively disproved." His discussion of the issues is entirely too meager, however, to serve as a counterfoil to Brinton.

This is the sole direct evidence of racist theorizing at the City College. No instructor is listed for anthropology, so we can gain no further insight into how these texts were treated in class. No other texts are listed. Anthropology was not a required course, and I am told that not many students chose to take it.[7] The works of other social scientists at the College treated non-Anglo-Saxon ethnic and racial groups as inferior, but they did not explicitly posit that inferiority to be racially derived, and some of them saw the members of the various "races" as decidedly culturally redeemable.

IMMIGRANTS AS A SOCIAL PROBLEM

The other social sciences tended to portray the subordinate ethnic groups as a social and cultural, rather than racial, problem. In sociology, this outlook may have been an outgrowth of the pragmatic orientation of the department.

City College's first course in sociology was Practical Sociology. It dealt with "defectives and paupers; criminals and crime."[8] When the College did institute a course in elementary sociology in 1909, it did not list in its description the theorists then revered in the field, but its conceptual framework seems very similar to that outlined in Giddings's early texts.[9] For years sociology at City College consisted of four courses: Elementary Sociology, Municipal Affairs, Applied Sociology—Philanthropy, and Applied Sociology—Criminology.

If the character of sociology and political science at Columbia was set by Franklin Giddings and John W. Burgess, at CCNY it was formed by Howard Brown Woolston and William B. Guthrie, both Columbia products. Woolston, who acknowledges Giddings's influence in his 1909 Columbia Ph.D. dissertation, taught all four initial sociology courses offered at City College from 1909 through 1919.[10] In 1913–1914 he added a course in statistics. It was not until 1914 that he was joined by Norris Briscoe, for a short time only.[11] For the first decade of its existence, then, sociology took its character from one man—Howard Brown Woolston.

Woolston's dissertation, *A Study of the Population of Manhattan-ville*, reveals him to have been very much Giddings's protegé. An empirical and demographic study of "The Hollow Way," a neighborhood situated in the geographical valley between City College and Columbia and now part of Harlem,[12] Woolston's *Study* appears at first glance to be purely descriptive and demographic. He collects many statistics, some of them ingeniously, and presents few conclusions.

But the largest chapter of his dissertation, taking more than a third of the book, is devoted to the description of ethnic character. Entitled "The Social Temper," it is divided into two major subsections, "The Naturalized Sub-races" (Irish, Gemans, English, Scotch and Scandinavians, and French and Swiss) and "Americans in Process" (Native White Americans, Negroes, Italians, Hebrews, Austro-Hungarians, and others). His descriptions are frequently highly sympathetic, but they clearly reveal the intellectual framework within which his perceptions are formed.[13]

For example, Woolston introduces the classification of the population according to "national and ethnic stock" as follows:

> Teutonic and Celtic stock preponderates, with a strain of Latin and Slavic blood. The Mediterranean peoples are represented by Italians, French and a handful of Greeks. Practically all of the Russians and Poles, as well as some Germans and Americans, are Jews, so that there is a small mixed Semitic element. But the Aryan type greatly outnumbers all the others. The Negroes are practically the only exception to racial purity so far as color is concerned, the Chinese and Japanese being a negligible quantity.[14]

Woolston footnotes the word *Celtic* with the statement, "By Celtic stock is here meant the blending of the old Mediterranean and Alpine strains, best represented by Gaelic and Gallic varieties." Table XII, "Nativity, Race and Ethnic Stock, Population, 1905," gives three different classifications: national origin, color (native white, foreign white, colored), and race (Teutons, Celts, and so on). "The Scandinavians," he informs us, "are our most remote Teutonic relatives." Discussing "entangling alliances," he says, "Chromatic race intermixture is rare, except for possible clandestine relations.[15]

Woolston describes each ethnic group with extensive physical detail. ("There is a certain clean blocking-out of the Englishman's frame, that indicates activity and strength.") He adds a revealing footnote to his statement that, contrary to the traditionally tall Englishman, among the English he has observed in Manhattanville, "height is not so noticeable":

> The writer must explain, that in estimating the stature of these people, he may have a tendency to understate impressions; since he is somewhat above average height himself, and leans toward judging by the level of his own eyes.

Somehow the limitations of this quaint rule-of-eyeballs measurement system had not bothered him earlier, when describing the Germans as "under the height of the average American" or the Irishman as "slight and wiry." These observations had not challenged his concept of the nature of "the average American," a rather controversial concept at a time when nearly half of U.S. residents were either Black or of "foreign stock."[16] More important are the larger implications of Woolston's comment for his whole endeavor: if his own height biased his judgments and observations, could his own ethnicity, race, class membership, and political commitments have also influenced them?

The most striking illustration of his operating within the racist theoretical framework of the day is *not* the content of his descriptions, which repeat all the familiar stereotypes in a scientific format (the Irish are impulsive and reckless: "When warmed by a drink, Pat waxes demonstrative, and will not scorn a fight. . . ."). Rather, his immersion in that theoretical framework is best revealed by his unselfconscious use of its terminology. He feels no need to define "chromatic race mixture," "Aryan," "Alpine strain," "racial purity" or "Dogmatic-Emotional" mind type. After six pages of description of the character of the Irish, he says, "To sum up our estimate of the type of mind displayed, we may designate it as 'Ideo-Emotional' active and adaptable."[17]

Woolston cites Giddings for the term "Ideo-Emotional," indicating the intellectual debts of the man who dominated sociological thought at City College for so many years. A revealing footnote also indicates his debt to Giddings: "*Cf.* Giddings, *Inductive Sociology*, pp. 77–9. The definition of character in these sections is based upon the logical analysis presented in Professor Giddings' work." In addition to innumerable references to Giddings, Woolston supports his statement that the German is "concentric and intensive," as follows: "*Cf.* Hans Meyer, *Das deutsche Volkstum*, p. 12 *et seq.* This analysis has furnished the writer several mental hooks on which to hang his observations."[18]

For the Jews, Woolston's "mental hooks" come from Leroy-Beaulieu's *Israel Among the Nations*, which catalogues all the deficiencies of which the Jews have been accused and is dedicated to proving that those characteristics are the effects of environment and discrimination. Contrary to the racists' beliefs, said this French defender of the Jews, "hardly more than one or two generations are necessary to transform the most greasy, the most bigoted Oriental Jew into an Occidental, a Parisian." Furthermore, "rare though we may deem such cases, I, myself, have known French, English, and Italian, aye, and German, Polish and Russian Jews who, for loftiness of feeling, are as deserving as any Christian of the name of gentleman."[19]

Woolston is not Giddings's puppet: he has ideas of his own. He is even critical of the English, saying that they tend to be condescending and can go to cruel lengths, exemplified by current colonial policy in England. But nothing better illustrates his immersion within an intellectual framework than the nature of his deviations from it. He makes apologies to "Professor Giddings" whenever he alters Giddings's classification of ethnic personality type; he modifies the type without abandoning it. The Saxon's mind, he says, is "*dogmatic-motor*," not "Ideo-Motor."[20] No sociologist other than Giddings—neither major nor minor colleagues, neither liberals nor other conservatives, not Ward, Ross, Cooley, or Small—appears in Woolston's text or footnotes. There is little doubt that in general he was a Giddings disciple.

In some ways, though, he seems somewhat more of a reformer than his laissez-faire mentor. For example, he wished to "train the coming generation for effective citizenship by consistently developing their ability to observe and analyze the facts of social life around them. "Thus the citizen and worker might become intelligent as to those local conditions that largely control the choice of occupation and political allegiance."[21]

Beginning in 1911–1912 he focused his course on Municipal Affairs on "the City of New York as the special theme for study." He had served as secretary of the Neighborhood Workers Association of New York City, and in 1906 he had asserted that "the alien element" and "selfish power" were causing communal disunity.[22] Echoes of Franklin Giddings: the wealthy "withdraw from association," and the immigrants rabble-rouse!

Woolston expressed his attitude toward social reform and the ethnic and class structure in the two concluding sentences of his dissertation. Referring to work in areas such as Manhattanville, he said,

> As an experiment in scientific social prophylaxis, the field is a promising one, if cultivated in the spirit of respectful sympathy. The question to be decided within the next ten years is, "Shall Manhattanville be filled with people who are good neighbors; or shall it become a sort of social drain, filled with settlings from the city's economic life?"[23]

For Giddings, courtesy was the social cement that would create social harmony; for Woolston sympathetic neighborhood work would create good neighbors.

It appears that Woolston regarded the immigrants as presenting a problem of social control. Whether "social prophylaxis" was designed to prevent them from becoming dregs in the social drain, or whether the disease to be prevented was more dire, "respectful sympathy" was to be cultivated in the interest of producing "good neighbors," in the interest of social control.[24]

We do not know whether students who took applied sociology at CCNY were taught a racist or an environmentalist conception of "defectives and paupers" or crime and criminals. Although the very concept of "defectives" has biological implications and tended to be used in connection with the "inferior" immigrant stocks, Woolston, the instructor of these courses, made no direct statement on these subjects in his dissertation. Our only clue lies in his discussion of "Economic Conditions" in *Manhattanville:*

> The most fundamental social activity of any group is the economic occupation of its members. On the one hand these occupations indicate *inherent and acquired* characteristics of the people, which lead them to adopt certain lines of work. That is, the vocations express essential qualities of mind and body that induce their possessors to follow specific callings. On the other hand this em-

ployment reveals the social needs that afford business opportunities and professional openings. . . . The occupation in turn fixes its mark upon the individual by developing a certain set of habits and tendencies.[25]

That is, occupational choice is both biologically inherited and environmentally shaped, exactly Giddings's position. The quote, and the chapter from which it is taken, support two conclusions: first, that the sociology instructor at CCNY seemed to combine an acceptance of the hierarchical racial schema of the day with a certain meliorism of a diffuse sort; and second, that he definitely did *not* locate the source of problems of crime and poverty in the social and economic order.

Walter E. Clark taught economics at CCNY from 1906 to 1918. In 1907, Clark was appointed head of the newly established Department of Political Science, upon the recommendation of Columbia's conservative economist, John Bates Clark. Because he taught most of the economics courses, his extremely detailed lecture notes, preserved in the CCNY archives, give an excellent indication of the content of this social science as it was taught at the turn of the century. After all, Walter Clark dominated economics at CCNY, in the same way that Woolston dominated sociology.

Clark's lecture notes were listed under CCNY Teachers Extension Courses, which means that they would have influenced not only his regular CCNY students, but also New York public school teachers. Lectures VI and VII were devoted to The History of Immigration to the United States: Advantages and Disadvantages.[26] The advantages were described as: first, the advantage to the immigrants: coming to America afforded the immigrants a chance for a better life; second, the political advantage to the United States: their numbers increased U.S. military strength; and third, the economic advantage: productivity is increased (he figured their value added, per head, much as Carnegie had in arguing against immigration restriction—$1,000 per immigrant times the number of immigrants). The fourth and final advantage, which he calls "social," is stated much more tentatively: "It is argued that the mixture of races develops the best nation."

The disadvantages listed by Clark were quite formidable:

1. *Political.* Immigrant masses furnish material for corrupting bosses and render successful democracy more difficult.

2. *Economic.* Immigrants with lower standards of living tend to displace native born Americans, to lower wages, to impair the development of labor unions, and to embitter labor struggles.[27]

Since one of Clark's criticisms of socialism (Lecture XXIX) was that "the class emphasis is . . . embittering,"[28] one may speculate that when he asserted that immigrants "embitter labor struggles" he may have meant that one of their disadvantages was their tendency to espouse socialism. In addition, although Clark included Isaac Hourwich's exhaustive study *Immigration and Labor* in his references, he repeated the same wage-lowering, American-displacing generalizations which Hourwich's voluminous statistics, collected for the U.S. Immigration Commission, refuted.[29]

There was a third disadvantage to immigration:

> 3. *Social.* Immigrants and their children yield a disproportion of illiterates, diseased, insane, paupers and criminals. They tend to congest in large cities and to complicate our already difficult urban problems.[30]

Clark was making these contemptuous statements to immigrants and the children of immigrants—his students.

Clark seems to have favored immigration restriction. At least he argued for the constitutional right to legislate against immigration. He presented no counter-arguments, a notable omission in view of his obvious effort to seem impartial and to present pros and cons on other issues. He also predicted more restriction, especially of "applicants for admission who are physically, mentally or morally defective."[31]

There is abundant evidence that Clark's outline was typical of City College courses throughout the period. The other Outline of Economics (1920) preserved in the City College Archives is quite similar to Clark's lecture notes. Both implicitly and explicitly these courses expressed the view that immigrants were a social problem. From the beginning applied economics, chiefly taught by Clark, involved the study of "the practical economic problem of Immigration."[32] Year after year, the catalogues explained that Applied Economics A. would be devoted to the problem of immigration and trade unions, while Applied Economics B. studied the problems of trusts and tariffs. In 1911 the problems were A. Immigration and Socialism, and B. Trusts and Trade Unions.[33] In 1913–1914 Contemporary History of the U.S. included, among other topics, "immigration and resulting problems, civil service and election experiments and reforms, and colonial expansion and the assured position of the U.S. as a world power."[34] In 1925–1926 Race Problems in the United States was described as an "analysis of outstanding facts in the migration to the United States of various racial and national stocks. The negro question, Oriental and European immigration are critically examined."[35]

Economics 2, Evolution of Industry, was not "critically examined"; it was "a study of human progress. . . ."[36] Trusts and Tariffs were not "critically examined." Only immigration and "the negro question" were to be "critically examined"!

Little in the course descriptions for history, social science, or even language or literature suggests that immigrants were peoples bearing cultures that were meaningful for their own lives, let alone interesting to others as "culture." Literature was English, Greek, and Latin. History was European, English, and American—the American taking its virtues from the transplantation of English democratic institutions. When the Jews were not a social problem, they were almost invisible. Livingston B. Morse's History Lecture Guide mentions the Jews as the victims of the Spanish Inquisition (on religious grounds) and as the group which contributed monotheism to Christianity.[37] Commerce under feudalism is given extensive treatment without mention that it was carried on almost exclusively by Jews and Syrians. The Crusades are presented as "a series of military pilgrimages to the Holy Land in an effort to check the western invasions of Asiatic peoples." (The Christian military makes "pilgrimages"; the "Asian" military makes "invasions.") The considerable impact of the Crusades on the Jews is not mentioned.[38] When the Alumni *Quarterly* published the list of those killed in World War I, the overwhelmingly Jewish names appeared under the Latin words, *De Mortuis.*[39]

When the cultures of immigrant groups finally did appear in the City College curriculum in the 1920s, it was the expression of a considerable cultural struggle. Cultural pluralists had begun to attack forced assimilation, and social reformers such as Lillian Wald had fought for the importance of an understanding of immigrant cultures in dealing with social pathology.[40] It was no doubt a reflection of these struggles that the description for the course Racial and Cultural Background of Immigrant Groups, given in 1925–1926, read: "This course is designed especially for social workers and teachers doing work with the foreign-born, and also for students of the general immigration problem."[41]

The most sympathetic and least pejorative course, Immigrant Background: The Social and Cultural Background of the Peoples of Greater New York, given in 1921 in the Department of Government and Sociology of the School of Education, was organized in the form of lectures by "representative scholars, writers, editors, professional men and women chosen from each native group." (There were no workers.) "Our problem," said the catalogue,

> is to lead the social worker and teacher back to Europe, Asia and Africa; and to develop in them the power for a keener and more sympathetic examination of conditions in our cities. The problem is a human one; the material is human and living, and the worker can learn from those whom he teaches and for whom he labors.

Even so the cultures of the twenty-eight different ethnic groups were not to be studied as culture, but as "cultural background." The purpose was not aesthetics, as it might have been with the study of the ancient Greeks, or appreciation, as with English culture. Rather it was problem solving:

> Purposes. Social workers, teachers, librarians, and those whose work is largely with unassimilated foreigners, can do effective work only when they have acquainted themselves with the traditions, habits, customs and psychology of these people. . . . No Americanization is possible without a knowledge of the homelands of these peoples, their peculiar difficulties of readjustment and acclimatization.[42]

This course was quite remarkable in its respectful attitude. Two years later students in Social Forces in Education studied "special problems such as: the immigrant home and the school, particularly the significance for education of the cultural heritages of the foreign-born; the diagnostic and preventive role of the school in the field of juvenile deliquency and defectiveness." The purpose was, again, "dealing intelligently with problems of social adjustment and discipline." Cultural pluralism had made its mark.

At the very least, the study of immigrant cultures, even as the source of "problems," signaled their existence and importance. It was better than being invisible. It was better than pretending that white Protestant ethnocentrism was universal culture. The study of immigrant culture may have been confined within the pitying framework of social pathology, but perhaps in spite of that it led some students to explore with greater respect the cultural worlds of immigrant peoples. Yet with some exceptions, the underlying message of such courses was that immigrant culture was to be used as a weapon in its own destruction.

THE SPIRIT OF CAPITALISM AT CITY COLLEGE

The curriculum at City College, by its omissions and its declarations, not only carried forth the theme of WASP superiority and immigrant defectiveness, it also expressed and inculcated business values and business perspectives.

Of course it was to be expected that the school founded by Townsend Harris would attempt to be of service to businessmen. It was largely begun for that purpose, and for that reason it retained the support of businessmen on its Board of Trustees. In 1919 the College developed a business school, eventually named for Bernard Baruch, financier and statesman of Sephardic Jewish ancestry, a City College alumnus and a member of the CCNY Board of Trustees from 1921 to 1924.[43] So it is not surprising that in 1915–1917, when there was no course available to City College's predominantly Russian Jewish student body on the history or development of Russia, none on the history of the Jews, none in either the Hebrew, Russian, or Yiddish languages, there was a course on "The Development of the South American States . . . in which regard will be had to the needs of those who expect to enter into business or professional relations with the South American States."[44] Analogously, there were courses seeking to solve problems of business management, business finance, foreign trade, and so on, but before 1924 there were none seeking to solve problems of union organizing or workplace conditions.[45] (The point is not as obvious as it may seem, however; as we shall see shortly, Columbia University gave courses far more relevant to these concerns than did CCNY.)

Business perceptions and business values permeated the social science curriculum far beyond those courses of direct interest to businessmen and future businessmen. A working-class student commuting to CCNY from the socialist Lower East Side, a student who had, perhaps, joined a Marx study club in his neighborhood, was confronted in *all* of the social sciences at CCNY with a world view regarding society, the definition of social problems, the nature of ideology, and the nature of science, totally opposite to that of his earlier experience. Walter Clark's course in economics, discussed earlier, described socialism (in the nineteenth lecture) purely as a Utopia—a series of "shoulds" and "oughts," a purely ethical philosophy—and not as a science of society. Karl Marx's *Capital* is among the list of references only for the lecture on socialism, not even for the lecture on capital itself, despite the fact that Marx's three-volume work is an examination of capital (and not socialism). Nor are Marx's works, in which the labor theory of value is vital, included among discussions of theories of value, although one of Clark's criticisms of socialism is that "the surplus value theory is faulty."[46]

In a period of raging public controversy about the distribution of wealth and the control of monopolies, the City College student was taught that, in contradistinction to four other theories of wage, the Productivity Theory holds that,

> under free competition, each factor of production tends to get what it has produced, marginally tested. This widely accepted Productivity Theory, applicable to each of the factors of production, reaches a factual and not an *ethical* conclusion.[47]

No socialist would regard the Productivity Theory as factual. Socialists (and in the present day many non-socialists) criticize this theory's inapplicability to the real world and its ideological (ethical) assumptions.

Clark concluded a presentation of the criticisms and advantages of corporations and their securities with the statement, "The corporation is a business machine necessary to the modern day. Intelligent reform seeks to eliminate its evils without lessening its advantages."[48]

A student who might have worked for the election of socialists Eugene V. Debs or Morris Hillquit was told that among the criticisms of socialism was that it "makes the persistent assumption that its way is the only way to cure the ills of modern life." He also was told that (presumably as a matter of science, not ethics) "whatever may be the controversies as to the socially most expedient system of control over capital, and whatever may be the abuses of capital power under any given system, . . . the largely increasing capital hastens the complete transition to the industrial age of world peace and plenty." That is, matters of enormous controversy in the world of politics were treated by Clark as settled principles of science. Those socialists who saw Marxism as an aspect of Western science, who wished to construct a new social structure by means of that science, were dismissed by Clark as "Utopians"—purveyors of "oughts" and "shoulds." Science, for Clark, equated capitalism with progress.[49]

A socialist student's disagreement with Clark would have gone much farther. A Marxist student would have disagreed with the definition of capital as "a factor in production," with the definition of value as "the estimate of utility," with the definition of production as "the creation of form, place, time and possession utilities," and with the separation of distribution from consumption and production. That is, he would have disagreed with the very organization of Clark's course. Clark was expressing the view dominant then (and now) in the field of economics, and particularly the views of Professors Henry Seager, J. B. Clark, and E. R. A. Seligman, the predominant economists of the day at Columbia. The texts of these three men are among the main texts used in Clark's course.[50]

Seligman's course at Columbia on the history of economics, an exhaustive survey of economic thinkers from Plato through Adam Smith to "recent developments" including Bohm-Bawerk, and Carey, does not include Karl Marx. Marx was a writer to criticize, but not analyze.[51]

Thus Clark presented (as though it was "the only way to cure the ills of modern life") the corporate side of two fiercely contending world views. In 1921, Seligman, Clark's mentor and a member of one of the two or three most important investment banking families in the German Jewish upper class, debated Scott Nearing, the Marxist economist recently fired from the University of Pennsylvania, on the proposition: "Resolved, that capitalism has more to offer the workers of the U.S. than has socialism." According to a City College alumnus, "Nearing had such a debate at CCNY in 1925 or 1926 with then Professor of Economics and later President Frederick B. Robinson in the Great Hall before 3,000 students and faculty. Nearing had the audience with him and 'mopped up the floor' with Robinson, as I recall it."

Apparently these students felt that the "Productivity Theory" did not explain their parents' low wages; that "free competition" had disappeared in the merger movements; and that "the largely increasing capital" was not "offering to the workers" a life of "peace and plenty." Whatever mobility through higher education may have meant for these students, the economic ideology they were being taught was certainly discordant with their own understanding of their world.

City College and Columbia

City College's curriculum may be understood by contrast—by comparison with that of Columbia College and University. The University supplied the bulk of CCNY's faculty; the College was New York's major institution of higher education for the sons of the wealthy.

Columbia's courses were certainly as accepting of the capitalist system as City College's courses, and they were, after all, the main source of Woolston's social wisdom. Nevertheless, when we compare Woolston's CCNY course with that offered by Professor Edward T. Devine at Columbia, we see that Devine's course may have contained more of a critical edge:

Applied Sociology—Philanthropy. Professor Woolston.

This course presents the facts and causes of poverty, describes methods of public and private relief, discusses the care of defectives, indicates lines of constructive philanthropy. Special attention is given to the organization and work of local charitable institutions.[52]

SOCIAL ECONOMY 282—*Efficiency and Relief.* Professor Devine.

This course is a study of the methods by which society undertakes to relieve distress and to promote social efficiency. It includes the social aspects of philanthropy and of education. Special attention is given to constructive social movements, such as those for housing and sanitary reform, and the prevention of disease and of accidents.[53]

Note that Woolston's course stresses established institutions, whereas Devine's stresses constructive social movements. And although it is clear that Devine sought to define which social movements were "constructive" and which were not, social movements are at least mentioned as a positive agent of social change. Nowhere in the City College curricular materials I have examined is there a positive reference to social movements. On the other hand, Woolston's course dealt with "causes of poverty;" Devine's did not.

Devine also offered a course in Misery and Its Causes, described as

a survey of social mal-adjustments (e.g. congestion of population, preventable disease, child-labor, overwork, casual employment, *exploitation of employees and consumers* . . . inefficiency in administration of justice); the *resulting* privation and degeneration.[54]

Nowhere in materials associated with course content at City College does the word *exploitation* occur. Nor does privation appear as a result of exploitation and institutional flaws. Devine was presumably not using the word *exploitation* in the strict Marxian sense, as the employer's theft of the worker's surplus labor. Still, the very use of the word defies complacency; it encourages critical questions.

In 1910–1911 Columbia's Professor Samuel McCune Lindsay taught Social Economy 283—Social Legislation: (I) *Workshop and Factory:*

A comparative study of methods and results of recent legislation in American states and some European countries, dealing with social problems of the wage-earner relating to the place where and conditions under which he works. Topics considered are: Factory legislation, factory inspection, child labor, dangerous occupations, industrial accidents, employers' liability, workmen's compensation, industrial insurance, old-age pensions, regulation of wages and hours of labor, arbitration of labor disputes.[55]

No such course appears at City College. If factory conditions were treated in CCNY curriculum, they were not highlighted in the catalogue descriptions. Factory conditions do not appear in Clark's lecture notes for economics or in the other extant Outline of Economics lectures. Nor did sociology at CCNY deal with factory conditions; as we have seen, sociology's role in the academic division of labor was to deal with pauperism, criminality, urban problems, and ethnic personality.

The difference was one of emphasis. Sociology in both institutions studied social problems, but Devine and Lindsay were defining them in terms of defective *conditions* in need of reform; Woolston tended to view social problems in terms of defective *persons* in need of reform.[56]

Devine may have gone a bit too far in finding problems with U.S. society. On May 1, 1911, the Columbia Board of Trustees received a registered letter from Jacob Schiff, who had endowed the Schiff Chair of Social Economy in 1905. Complaining of "the attitude, on an important question, of the present occupant of the Schiff Chair," Schiff literally pulled the chair out from under E. T. Devine, requesting that the $100,000 endowment be transferred to the general fund. No indication is given of the "important question" in the controversy. The letter bears the single, fatal word: "Done."[57]

Socialism was among the many social movements less evident at City College than at Columbia. J. Salwyn Schapiro, for example, had a reputation as a wise person and an inspiring lecturer. A socialist student who attended CCNY in the early twenties reported being enthralled by his courses.[58] Yet his course on The Intellectual History of Europe During the Nineteenth Century dealt "chiefly with the intellectual heritage bequeathed by the French Revolution . . . the theories of the Individualists, Utopians, and Christian Democrats of the early nineteenth century and the political and social aims and ambitions of labor movements." Socialism was included neither as part of the "intellectual heritage" nor among the "social and political aims." The listing for Main Currents of Contemporary European History is similarly incomplete.[59]

William Guthrie, who taught political science at CCNY, wrote his doctoral dissertation on *Socialism Before the French Revolution*, and we may presume that he taught about the subject in his courses. The book is highly disciplined, carefully analyzed and sympathetic, but it has a rather strange definition of socialism:

> Socialism means, in the large, the carrying the public or social control ever farther into the sphere so far occupied by the individual; it means the setting aside the so-called natural, social and economic laws through the intervention of the social will operating consciously and in an absolute, sovereign manner as against the individual will.[60]

Guthrie's opposition between "social will" and "individual will" reflects the obsession of anti-socialists; for socialists, "the individual will" is enchained, in capitalism, by class structure. At most only a handful of people can exert their individual wills, and they may do so only under the constraints of economic laws and at the expense of the majority of people. A more sympathetic analyst than Guthrie, therefore, would have defined socialism as common ownership and control of the means of production and an end to class rule. "I was a student of Guthrie's in a required course in 'Government' about 1925 or 1926," a CCNY alumnus told me. "He was a popular but hardly a respected lecturer; his reputation was that of a conservative."[61]

At Columbia socialism was given somewhat more explicit attention. In 1910–1911 Vladimir Simkhovitch taught Radicalism and Social Reform as Reflected in the Literature of the Nineteenth Century. Beginning in 1905–1906 John Bates Clark taught Economics 109: Communistic and Socialistic Theories, and Economics 110: Theories of Social Reform.[62]

One may safely assume that the Columbia faculty was not more hostile to capitalism than the CCNY faculty, and that the motivation behind these courses was not to inspire students with an ardor for socialism. J. B. Clark was a world-renowned marginalist theoretician, and his course description suggests that he used marginalist economics as the standard by which "a critical test of these [socialist] theories themselves and of certain counter-arguments" would be made. It is quite clear from the descriptions of Clark's courses that they were dedicated to demonstrating the unsoundness of socialism and the impracticality of the reform movements. Simkhovitch's course seems, from its short description, more sympathetic, being "an interpretation of the various types of modern radicalism, such as socialism, nihilism and anarchism, and of the social and economic conditions on which they are based."

At City College, where critical, questioning, and skeptical students commuted to school from a working-class Russian Jewish milieu, course content underplayed working-class movements and Jewish history. At Columbia—citadel of scientific racism and of the economics of Seligman, Seager and J. B. Clark, where students were primarily from elite homes and where immigrant students on scholarship were in awe of Western civilization and Columbia's all-embracing "culture"—the faculty examined socialism and the labor movement, working conditions, and The Economic and Social Evolution of Russia.[63]

The contrast may seem ironic, but it is not. It is an understandable pattern of social structure, of the stratification of educational institutions according to their class functions, and of the functions of knowledge as power and knowledge as social control. The Columbia College faculty, which presumed its role to be training leaders and defining what was and was not "culture," could include all manner of courses which the City College faculty had neither the budget nor the cultural legitimacy to entertain. Moreover, the different political and social character of the student body would have affected the kinds of courses which the faculties offered. To faculty and administrators, City College was introducing immigrant boys to Western culture; Columbia was a leading institution, training an elite.

John W. Burgess, who taught at Columbia for thirty-six years, expressed the "great hope in founding the school of political science at Columbia . . . that it would become the training school for the future rulers of the country."[64] Perhaps that concern is best expressed in the simultaneous existence at Columbia of Giddings's year-long course in The Relation of Social Theory to Public Policy and Lindsay's four-course sequence on Social Legislation. The first in that series was the course on Workshop and Factory. The fact that it was part of the Social Legislation series better explains its function; it was *not* designed to enable working-class students to better understand their own and their parents' lives.[65]

The other courses in the Social Legislation series focus on (II) Family, Home, and School; (III) Urban and Rural Community Life; and (IV) Methods and Tendencies in Law Making. The latter promised to be

a comparative study of legislative procedure in American states and the Congress . . . with special reference to the preparation and drafting of bills for the enactment of social legislation. Preliminary investigation of social conditions and the presentation of their results; *the organization of public opinion;* work of private societies with legislative programs; committee hearings; co-operation of private societies with public officials and the courts in the administration and interpretation of the law . . . the organization of administrative and judicial machinery for the enforcement of social legislation; the education of citizens; are the chief topics considered.[66]

That is, it was a complete how-to-do-it course for those who rule, whether through commissions, legislative committees, or "private societies," such as, presumably, the Committee of One Hundred, which reorganized public education in New York City.

By "rule" I do not mean control. I mean what some theorists designate as "participate in leadership." It presumes power and often wealth, but not omnipotence. Part of the role of participating in leadership is responding to social forces and movements that are *not* directly controllable. For this task all of the skills listed by Lindsay, including the organization of public opinion, are essential. It is because those who "participate in leadership" must respond to the real threats posed by popular movements that institutions like Columbia teach courses on socialism and the labor movement.

A Columbia student was expected to learn how to create or respond to social forces and movements, make policy, and influence the public. Among the public were the workers and paupers, defectives and immigrants, some of whom sent their children to CCNY to learn how to carry out policy and apply social legislation.[67]

Two Cultural Worlds

To Guthrie, Woolston, and Giddings, the ghetto may have been a social drain of defectives and paupers, but to the people who lived there it was a far more human world. Immigrants could not see themselves as academics saw them, as a distant clinical phenomenon—*those* people having *these* dimensions, mentalities, and behaviors, bringing *these* calculable dollars' worth of benefits, costs, and dangers. Immigrants and their children felt the ghetto's agonies and depredations close-up, in human faces. They felt also strengths and loves, brutality and rage, their own struggle against victimization. The Jewish poor interpreted their own world and made their own culture. In poetry, short stories, plays, and press, they created self-images, analyses, and programs that scarcely penetrated the world of "higher culture."

"Yiddish creative writing in America was not transplanted from old

Europe. It grew out of American soil."[68] But it did not grow out of City College. The four major labor poets—Morris Winchevsky, Morris Rosenfeld, David Edelstadt, and Yossef Bovshover—were Russian Jewish immigrants, penned to the shop floor by necessity and political commitment. They and other Yiddish writers wrote of class struggle, of unemployment, of work conditions, of exploitation, even of the cruelty of workers toward each other, and the harrassment of women workers by men. In *How the Rich Live*—forty-eight caustic portraits of usurers, speculators, lawyers, doctors, and "gentlemen"—Winchevsky provided descriptions far different from the Teutonic hero cult with which elite scholars flattered the wealthy. The poets wrote *Battle Chants* and laments: such as *A Month Without Work*. When they were romanticists, they were not romanticists of bucolic idylls, but of shopfloor struggles and workers' victories.

"The poems echoed in song across the machines and work tables, creating a bond of common feelings and common aspirations." They aroused and thrilled "hundreds of thousands of men and women . . . . The impact of the songs on their wide audience was deep and immediate."[69]

Here, in the most powerful of Morris Rosenfeld's *Songs of Labor*, is the world that the parents of City College students knew, and that the students' inculcation with Western culture generally left out:

In The Shop

Oh, here in the shop the machines roar so wildly, that oft, unaware
That I am, or have been, I sink and am lost in the troubled tumult
And void is my soul . . . I am but a machine.
I work and I work and I work, never ceasing;
Create and create things from morning till e'en;
For what?—and for whom—Oh, I know not!
Oh, ask not!
Who ever has heard of a conscious machine?

No, here is no feeling, no thought and no reason;
This life-crushing labor has ever supprest
Noblest and finest, the truest and richest,
The deepest, the highest and humanly best.
The seconds, the minutes, they pass out forever,
They vanish, swift fleeting like straw in a gale.
I drive the will madly as though to o'ertake them,—
Give chase without wisdom, or weight, or avail.

The Clock in the workshop—it rests not a moment;
It points on, and ticks on: eternity-time;
And once someone told me the clock had a meaning,—
Its pointing and ticking had reason and rhyme.
And this too he told me,—or had I been dreaming—
The clock wakened life in one, forces unseen.
And something besides: . . . . I forget what: O, ask not!
I know not, I know not, I am a machine.

At times, when I listen, I hear the clock plainly;—
The reason of old—the old meaning—is gone!
The maddening pendulum urges me forward
To labor and still labor on.
The tick of the clock is the boss in his anger!
The face of the clock has the eyes of the foe;
The clock—O, I shudder—Dost hear how it draws me?
It calls me "Machine" and it cries to me "Sew"!
.   .   .   .
The sweatshop at midday—I will draw you a picture;
A battlefield bloody; the conflict at rest;
Around and about me the corpses are lying;
The blood cries aloud from the earth's gory breast.
A moment . . . and hard! The loud signal is sounded,
And dead rise again and renewed is the fight . . .
They struggle, these corpses; for strangers, for strangers!
They struggle, they fall, and they sink into night.

I gaze on the battle in bitterest anger,
And pain, hellish pain wakes the rebel in me!
The clock—now I hear it aright!—It is crying:
"An end to this bondage! An end there must be!
It quickens my reason, each feeling within me;
It shows me how precious the moments that fly.
Oh, worthless my life if I longer am silent,
And lost to the world if in silence I die.

The man in me sleeping begins to awaken;
The thing that was slave into slumber has passed:
Now; up with the man in me! Up and be doing!
No misery more! Here is freedom at last!
When sudden: a whistle!—the Boss—an alarum!—
I sink in the slime of the stagnant routine;—

There's tumult, they struggle, oh, lost is my ego;—
I know not, I care not, I am a machine![70]

Pain, rebellion, oppression, but also pride and a call to courage and
justice: where some professors saw defectives and paupers, poets
knew creators of wealth and a new world.

To the Worker

> Be proud of your labor—it gives you the right
> to savor the fruits of the earth.
> Be brave, be human, not a slave,
> learn your proper worth!
> . . . .
> But how reward you, when the world,
> its goods, is yours to own?—
> its bread and wine, its grain and gold,
> its store of precious stones.
>
> Take what's yours by right to take!
> Be bold, base fear disdain!
> Be proud, unawed! And neither make
> nor wear, enslaving chains.[71]

Yiddish literature was not for refined sensibilities. It did not explore
ennui or cultivate attitude. "In Europe [as in America] . . . the learned
and cultured snobbishly ignored it."[72] Only Bovshover and Rosenfeld
received any recognition at all outside of the Jewish labor movement.
Bovshover had one poem published in *Liberty* magazine; Rosenfeld
was "discovered" in 1897 by Leo Wiener of Harvard, who was
working on *The History of Yiddish Literature in the 19th Century*.
Wiener introduced him to an academic audience and to a liberal
audience in *The Nation*.[73]

By 1924 courses on contemporary literature and poetry were given
at City College, but poems such as Rosenfeld's were not included.
Although there were courses explicitly devoted to English literature,
there were no analogous courses in Yiddish literature or the literature
of the workshop. By 1924, the Menorah Society was awarding a prize
for the "best essay on some phase of Jewish life," but CCNY's
curriculum, which had two separate courses on Cicero, two on Vergil,
one on Horace and four on the literature of England, had none on
Yiddish literature.[74]

The proletarian poets provided more than an alternative culture for a Yiddish socialist world; they lived an alternative model of intellectual work. They were what Gramsci later called "organic intellectuals" of the working class, putting their minds at the service of workers rather than wealth or power.[75]

David Edelstadt wrote:

> I was not born for sweet songs,
> For roses, love and beauty;
> I am no poet—I am a worker,
> A child of poverty, and night.
> The struggle for bread is my Muse,
> Factory-hell—my true boss; . . .
> Streams of tears, poison and blood—
> That is sweet nectar for us slaves.[76]

Unable to make a living on the pennies that leftist newspapers could pay for his poems, Morris Rosenfeld felt keenly the commonality between his alienated labor as pants presser and poet:

> For Hire
>
> Work with might and main,
>   Or with hand and heart,
> Work with soul and brain,
>   Or with holy art,
> Thread, or genius' fire—
>   Make a vest, or verse—
> If 'tis done for hire,
>   It is done the worse.[77]

Rather than fueling obsessions of individual escape, this common condition of wage servitude strengthened his solidarity with fellow workers.

> A Fellow Slave
>
> Pale-faced is he, as in the door
> He stands and trembles visibly,—
> With diffidence approaches me,
> And says: "Dear editor,

"Since write you must, in prose or rhyme,
Expose my master's knavery,—
Condemn, I pray, the slavery
That dominates our time.

"I labor for a wicked man
Who holds o'er all my being sway,—
Who keeps me harnessed night and day,
Since work I first began.

"No leisure moments do I store,
Yet harsh words only will he speak;
My days are his, from week to week,
But still he cries for more.

"Oh print, I beg you, all I've said,
And ask the world if this be right:
To give the worker wage so slight
That he must want for bread.

"See, I have sinews powerful,
And I've endurance, subtle skill,—
Yet may not use them at my will,
But live a master's tool.

"But oh, without avail do I
Lay bare the woes of workingmen!
Who earns his living by the pen,
Feels not our misery."

The pallid slave yet paler grew,
And ended here his bitter cry . . .
And thus to him I made reply:
"My friend, you judge untrue.

"My strength and skill, like yours, are gain
For others . . . Sold! . . . You understand?
Your master—well—he owns your hand,
And mine—he owns my brain."[78]

Revolutionary commitment also reduced the alienation of intellectual work, giving it meaning and purpose. Rosenfeld, usually the poet of despair, swore in "Oath":

You see the creators? In factory and mine?
That's Man, making goods for the use of mankind.

They carve and they build, they spin and they weave,
They hew and they forge, they fill all our needs.
Yet ask them, these pale ones, who shiver and sweat,
What is it they own, what reward do they get. . . .

Ask them, also, who's to blame . . .
They lack understanding? Then *you* must explain.
· ·
Use your pen as a fiddle, as well as a sword.
You must punish and play, and sharpen your word.[79]

David Edelstadt asked that his song, "In Battle," sung around the
world from czarist jails to New York sweatshops, be sung at his burial.
And Morris Winchevsky proclaimed that he would accompany the
people with his songs when they march in revolutionary battle.[80] For
writers such as these, the purpose of intellect was service to working
people; the purpose of education was liberation.

CCNY Students in Two Cultural Worlds

The curriculum at City College promoted a conception of service
quite different from that of the Yiddish poets. It filled the Eastern Jews
with a portion of Western culture that was as neglectful of the Western
labor and Western socialist tradition as it was of the Yiddish. Simultaneously the college prepared students for social positions that would
remove them from the social base that made Yiddish proletarian
culture meaningful.

City College graduated teachers and school principals, lawyers,
accountants, engineers, and persons who went into various positions
in business and civil service. The College curriculum gave students
training in commercial languages, economics, and social science for
those entering business; manual training and pedagogy for teachers;
social science for those entering the various caretaking professions;
and history, literature, and philosophy for all students, particularly
those who were to return to academia—perhaps even to City College—
as college faculty. Without conscious aim, the college sought to create
various types of "organic intellectuals" of the bourgeoisie, (in Gramsci's conceptualization)[81]—persons who would put their minds to
solving the problems of U.S. society without undermining the way
that wealth is produced and possessed. The very class society which

Rosenfeld blamed for workers' misery, higher education assumed as either natural or best.

Glazer and Moynihan state that Jews who moved up through business were more likely to retain their ethnic identity than Jews who moved up through college.[82] Having examined the cultural biases of college curricula, we need not wonder why. If Glazer and Moynihan are correct, we may guess that those City College graduates who went into fields that put them into a Jewish milieu (such as accounting, business law, and business itself) would have returned to a more ethnically Jewish context. Perhaps they never left it: anticipatory socialization for them might have meant participation in the Menorah Society and other such informal student activities. If that is so, however, then their ethnic culture would have been a business culture, one quite at odds with the Jewish socialist world and quite at home with Walter E. Clark's economic world view.

Unlike the CCNY graduates who become businessmen, accountants, and lawyers, however, many students who became teachers and social workers became ideological workers. The stuff of their work was what people thought. Many moved into the milieu of administrative bureaucracy, whose purpose was social control and social harmony and whose direction was set by men like Nicholas Murray Butler—a man notorious for his anti-Semitism, a man who repeated the Teutonic origins theory, and who shared his *class* biases with major businessmen like Andrew Carnegie and Jacob Schiff.[83] In the hierarchies of education and social work, a worker's job became Americanization. In the 1920s it became Americanization with a vengeance. Before and after the environmentalist breakthrough, it included racism toward non-white groups. As a condition of employment, if not as internalized belief, a worker's task was often to convince new generations that immigration was a social problem; that the ethnic hierarchy was natural, either biologically or environmentally; that (when mention was absolutely necessary) Marxism was a Utopian vision disproven by marginalist science; that the American economic order was progressive, and that the class emphasis of socialism is needlessly embittering. We do not know what these workers thought—or even what they did. Many may have worked against the tide, stressing other elements of contradictory North American culture—democracy, pluralism, equality. But when the force and prestige of "higher culture," and all systems of reward and punishment, were pressing them to repeat the dominant ideologies, could they long avoid believing them?

Even for Joseph Freeman, who was to retain his radical commitments, higher education at Columbia College produced a duality between home conditions and the seeming universality and liberality of liberal culture. For Freeman, planning to be a writer, the duality was first expressed as a tension between class conflict and a presumed-to-be unified, universal realm of art.

> The more acutely aware we became of these divisions, [between "rich and poor, Negro and white, Jew and gentile, native and alien"], the nearer we approached the day when we would have to participate actively in the social struggle, the greater became our devotion [to] an ideal art. . . .
>
> We understood that in politics there were contradiction, incongruity and conflict. In art, we imagined, there were only differences of opinion capable of harmonious resolution in the imagination. As a result of this dualism, we had two sets of friends. *In the city were the socialist workers with whom we discussed strike tactics, the policies of the Socialist party, the course of the Bolshevik Revolution. On the campus were the students and professors with whom we discussed Plato, Shakespeare, Edwin Arlington Robinson.* The workers listened to us with amused tolerance or sober respect when we showed off our meager knowledge of the classics. The students and professors smiled loftily or argued vehemently when we asserted that the best ideas of mankind inevitably led to communism.
>
> The two worlds were as separate as the earth and heaven of the poet's imagination. There were mundane matters, like earning a living, strikes, wars, revolutions. There was, beyond these, the celestial realm of the imagination where one talked about eternal truths with generous and gifted friends.[84]

For Joseph Freeman the duality was partially resolved, and the myth of universality shattered, when the "generous friends" started throwing some of the socialist friends in jail. Columbia expelled Professors Cattell and Dana for pacifism. The First World War polarized the Realm of Pure Reason, and the Espionage Act cracked the easy Spirit of Toleration. Periodically echoes of class conflict invaded the campus; periodically colleges purged themselves of radical thought and restored the purity of bourgeois spirit to the temples of social harmony and eternal truth.

The realities and ideas of the workers' world challenged the realities and ideas of the campus, and the students who commuted between them brought some of the experiences of the one to bear on the ideas of the other. Yet except for those students who supported their studies through manual work, everything conspired to separate the life of the mind from manual labor, the world of mental phenomena from their own social grounding. The life of the mind denied the validity of the perceptions formed in the world of class struggle. Working-class parents, feeling themselves ignorant of the world of the campus, abjured influence and even understanding in intimidated resignation. And the very definition of college attendance as success reinforces the separation and denies the reality of workers thought.

Yet the minds of the students whom the City College administration and faculty sought to socialize were by no means *tabulae rasae* when they entered CCNY, and we have some evidence that, although they were strongly influenced, they did not accept with total passivity what they were taught. At City College Jewish working-class students formed a critical mass. That is the strength of working-class minority institutions. They can offer some protection from the ideological confusion and schizophrenia that assaults the few token students at elite colleges.[85] No matter how oppressively the official curriculum cloaks them in invisibility or batters them with insults, there is some safety in numbers. This is the value of consensual validation: if many are uncomfortable, they cannot *all* be crazy.

City College students formed organizations that were culturally different both ethnically and politically from the curriculum of City College.[86] Within classes, they questioned the wisdom that was being proffered to them. Stephen Duggan, who was both a student and a faculty member at CCNY, said the Jewish students

> were practically all poor and many of them had been badly persecuted in Russia, Poland, Rumania and in Central Europe generally, and some of them naturally looked upon government with suspicion. But few foreigners absorbed democratic views more readily and became better Americans than the Jews of that time.
>
> No teacher could have had a finer student body to work with. They were studious, keen and forthright. They did not hesitate to analyze any subject down to its fundamentals regardless of tradition or age. . . . I allowed the freest discussion in my classroom and placed no restrictions upon a student putting forward views that were radical or unpopular. I did this from preference but I also discovered that untenable views were frequently demolished by the students themselves. I usually closed the discussion by presenting my own attitude on the subject, which ordinarily carried weight, possibly because of the greater experience behind it. I do not hesitate

to say that I learned a great deal as the result of the keen questioning of these young men. It was fatal to evade; one had always to be on the *qui vive.*

Some of [their] views were quite different from those held by students in a college situated in a less cosmopolitan environment. . . . They formed the most socially-minded group of young people that I know. . . .[87]

Morris Raphael Cohen's observations corroborate those of Stephen Duggan:

In my undergraduate years, and even more in later decades, an increasing proportion of the students was Jewish, many of them foreign-born, and very many of the others children of foreign-born parents. Many of us, therefore, were familiar with what are today provincially called "un-American" ideas. Certainly, a large part of the student body of the College has always been peculiarly open-minded and critical towards the accepted commonplaces of the complacent. These students came prepared to weigh and consider new, as well as old, ideas, and their intellectual eagerness was encouraged rather than restrained by home conditions.[88]

For Cohen, the tolerance made necessary by this lively student skepticism and the interplay of ideas described by Duggan did not produce a reaffirmation and expansion of his own views; it produced a grateful appreciation of liberalism.

It was hard for a teacher who was not a master of his subject to survive this sort of intellectual climate, but many did. . . . Because the College made no effort to impose a single pattern of social behavior upon its graduates, its militarism was not tainted by totalitarianism.[89] Many of its graduates have become rabbis, others have become Christian ministers, communist leaders, financiers, and distinguished statesmen and jurists. The College thus, despite the mediocrity of its teaching staff in those days, embodied what has always seemed to me the essence of liberal education as opposed to dogmatic indoctrination. I do not know of any charge that has been brought against our Jewish boys of the City College that could not have been brought against me personally, at the comparable age, and yet the College was willing to ignore or forgive my defects in the social graces, as well as the unorthodoxy of many of my views. That the College tolerated me became, to me, a symbol of liberalism in education.[90]

If the democratic ethos, mobility, and the structure of work encouraged some students to internalize the City College curriculum, then self-support through manual labor, commuting from the Lower East Side, and (most of all) the vicissitudes of capitalism might encourage them to challenge it, as Stephen Duggan observed with intense displeasure.

> In later years, especially after the disillusionment following the close of World War I, the College acquired the unjust reputation of being "red." Unquestionably some of the students were allured by the promises of the "Bolshevik heaven" established in 1917 in Russia, as was true at the time of the universities in most of the countries of Western civilization. Some of them became members of the Communist Party and followed the "party line" dictated at Moscow. I feel confident that the number of such students was decidedly less than ten percent of the student body. But they were there for the definite purpose which they followed in every country: as agents of Communism to bring about confusion, to arouse hatreds between economic classes, and to destroy confidence in the institutions of the country.[91]

City College's curriculum may have been in part geared for socialization, but its students were not pawns. They influenced the school that sought to influence them, and in so doing they participated in their own socialization. They changed City College, and City College changed them.

Labor demonstration, Union Square. *YIVO Archives*

9

Changing Perspectives

The sociological literature on ethnicity generally asserts that the Jews have experienced remarkable upward mobility by virtue of their passion for education—a transference of traditional predelictions for education to American secular education. The meaning, implications, and explanatory adequacy of that conception have not been sufficiently analyzed. The work contained in this study begins that analysis.

My major criticisms of this literature are that it is too abstract, overgeneralized, and inattentive to the relevance and complexities of the processes of social change. Social analysis cannot profitably leap five generations at once. I have thus focused on the period between 1880 and 1924, the period of the great Jewish proletarian migration. Although any carving of a period out of the flux of historical reality is in a sense arbitrary, I have selected this period for several reasons relevant to the sociological questions at hand. Chief among them are: first, 1880 is the beginning of the existence of a large Jewish proletariat in the United States; 1924 is the year of the Immigration Restriction Act, a law which had great effect on ethnic relations within the United States, and hence great impact on the character of the Jewish group; and second, the period between 1880 and 1924 was a time of major institutional change in the United States, in terms of education, class structure, ethnicity, and politics.

In this book I have concentrated on higher education and the professions, particularly the profession of education. I have thus focused on a type case for the ethnic literature: poor Jewish males of the first Jewish proletarian migrations, who moved into professional occupations via higher education, chiefly at the College of the City of New York. I have analyzed the changing institutional matrix in which their social mobility took place. I have examined that institutional matrix in its social systemic context, focusing particularly on educational institutions, which played a far more complex role in Jewish mobility than has heretofore been discussed. The Jewish experience in business, law, dentistry, medicine, and crime await similar specific treatment in terms of the transformation of the whole system. And the experiences of Jewish women with work and education must be integrated into the hitherto male-centered sociology and history of the Jews.

In this study I have also shown that the conception of culture—and of education—in this literature has been too abstract, too far removed from the actual content of Jewish education. Culture and education within the various segments of the Jewish community were developed in different forms, which in turn differed from the content of education and culture as they were being developed in U.S. colleges and universities at the turn of the century.

I have argued that the analysis of the economic experience of an ethnic group in terms of the character of the group and the occupational structure at the time of the group's arrival in this country is insufficient because such a model is both too simple and too static. Consequently, I have analyzed the experience of the Jews in terms of a total socioeconomic system as a historically changing phenomenon, including in the analysis the *changing* Jewish culture and the impact of the Jewish immigrants on that system.

Before the last quarter of the nineteenth century, widespread social mobility by means of educational attainment was impossible. Most of the bureaucratic structures which were to employ Eastern European Jews did not exist. The teaching profession was much smaller, both absolutely and in proportion to population. There were few high schools, and thus few jobs for principals and specialized teachers. Social work, and its predecessor, social philanthropy, were yet to be developed. Business was much simpler: there were fewer accountants, bookkeepers, and clerks. Law, engineering, and science were less developed.

Before the turn-of-the-century reforms, education was scarcely a channel of mobility. College was largely irrelevant to most occupations. Public elementary school was irrelevant to college preparation. Public secondary schools were barely developed. Their curricula did not mesh with college entrance requirements. In short, educational institutions did not form much of an inter-linked *system*. Except for the College of the City of New York and one or two Midwestern universities, there were simply no public educational ladders linking school levels to each other and to the world of work. Most students dropped out of school early.

In the course of this study I have discussed the processes within the American socioeconomic system that changed education and occupations into an articulated system of roughly interlocking hierarchies.

That discussion is merely a beginning; the process was highly complex. The concept of industrialization, often used to explain this transformation, is inadequate. As it is usually applied, it is an excessively mechanical abstraction. The social changes of the period between 1880 and 1924 involved far more than mechanization, urbanization, and the mere quantitative expansion in the size of industrial enterprise that increased the size of the working class. The transformation involved *qualitative* changes in the nature of capitalism: the development of monopolies and oligopolies; the sharing of ownership and the hiring of managers; the development of planned scientific and technical research. But it was still more than that. Crucial to the transformation of the educational, occupational, and class system—and in fact crucial to most of the processes just mentioned—was the conflict between capital and labor, and the attendant problems of social control.

The role of social control has been virtually completely neglected in the sociological literature on the social mobility of the Jews. It has been my central thesis that the systemic need for social control and political socialization played a major role in the upward mobility of the Eastern European Jews at the end of the nineteenth and the beginning of the twentieth century.

The need or desire for social control does not "explain" Eastern European Jewish social mobility, any more than the passion for education "explains" Eastern European Jewish mobility. An adequate analysis of the occupational distribution of the Eastern Jews will require an understanding of social process much more complex than either the currently overstressed cultural factors or the currently understressed political factors. The contribution of the present work does not lie in discovering a new determining variable, but in beginning the construction of a conceptual framework that will systematically relate social control *and* cultural factors to systemic change. Moreover, as I shall indicate below, that analysis will require a conception of culture that is broader than values, and a conception of social control that is broader than politics. The present work has focused most closely on that aspect of social control most obviously related to the conflicts between capital and labor.

The conflict between capital and labor played a major role in the transformation of American capitalism even before the great waves of Southern and Eastern European immigrants arrived. The conflict between capital and labor contributed to the conflicts over the establishment of high schools; to the effort to pass child labor laws and establish elementary school education; to the mechanization of industry and hence to the century-long effort to introduce scientifically relevant instruction in the colleges. The conflict between capital and labor contributed to the manual training movement, and the manual training movement fanned the conflict. And, ironically, the conflict between capital and labor acted as an incentive to employers to recruit labor in Southern and Eastern Europe.

Yet that conflict was only exacerbated and complicated by the arrival of these immigrants. Packed into working-class slums, they increased the problems of social control. Their ethnic and class concentration facilitated working-class organization in radical and self-help activities. Their poverty and concentration fostered problems that came to be defined by philanthropists, settlement workers, and concerned citizens as "social disorganization (disease, paupers, and criminals)." Both their organization, and their disorganization threatened social control. The immigrants presented anew to the business class the problem of socialization of a work force—the destruction of an organized and coherent peasant and artisan work culture and the substitution of the culture of factory discipline. They contributed new vigor to the ferocity of labor disputes. Most important, they contributed not only to social conflicts *within* the system, but to the crisis of the system itself. The developments of capitalism, which created a national economy, drew the immigrants from Europe and created a nationwide, socially and politically organized capitalist class and a nationwide ethnically diverse working class. These developments also called forth political movements whose adherents called that same capitalist system into question. In retrospect those movements now may appear to have posed a much less serious threat to the capitalist order than some publicists then feared. But at the time they were taken very seriously.

I have focused particular attention on the socialist and labor movements. Eastern European Jews played an important role in socialism and the labor movement, and the socialist and labor movements played an important, although indirect, role in the institutional changes that made Jewish social mobility possible. At the very least, it was the socialist threat that enabled the Progressives to promulgate policies (such as the reform of higher education) which had long been thwarted by conservatives among businessmen, educators, and politicians.

The socialism and labor militancy of the Jewish workers contributed to the changes in education in New York City on lower and higher levels. Their effects were indirect—many other factors were important—but labor militancy and the socialist movement provided part of the justification for the reform of higher education toward greater business relevance, as we have seen in Chapter 3. Most important, labor militancy and the socialist movement provided an impetus for the creation of systematic linkages, making possible educational career ladders, ladders of mobility through education.

Labor militancy and the socialist movement helped to inspire the Progressives' expansion of the schools for the purpose of achieving social control over the work force. Labor militancy and the socialist movement among immigrants provoked the Americanization movement. The effort to use the schools to combat labor militancy and the socialist movement contributed to the enormous expansion of the teaching profession and to the creation of hierarchies and control systems within that profession. The use of the schools for the purpose of Americanization and social control infused education at the turn of the century with much of its specific cultural content.

It is a logical extension of the empirical work of this study, and of the work of Gutman and Braverman elsewhere, that the recalcitrance of laborers themselves contributed to the expansion of that part of clerical work devoted to the control and accountability of labor. The recalcitrance of labor to the speed-up of the pace of work contributed to the development of Taylorism, which ramified hierarchies within business enterprise and within education. Insofar as the recalcitrance of labor helped inspire mechanization, it contributed to the expansion of the scientific and technical professions. And the problems of the social control of immigrant labor contributed to the growth of social work as a profession. Thus the problems of social control caused by the behavior of immigrant labor itself played an important role in the changing occupational structure that the children of these immigrants entered.

The need for social control was articulated by the Progressives—that movement of intellectuals, social reformers, corporate liberals, and reformist labor leaders. It was the Progressives who responded to the radicalism of the age, who formulated the theories and promulgated the policies of reform and social harmony. There were many differences among them; they were influenced by those whom they sought to influence, and their particular policies changed over the years. But through such organizations as the National Civic Federation, the National Education Association, the U.S. Bureau of Education, and various formal and informal governmental and private bodies, the Progressives made major institutional changes in the United States at the turn of the century.

In their effort to use ideological weapons in their conflict with labor, the Progressive leadership of the business class defined socialism as foreign. They defined Americanization as becoming loyal, obedient, and similar to their conception of an American—a white Protestant of Northern European descent. They thereby imposed conceptions of economic and social harmony on the "old" immigrants as well as conditons of acceptability on the "new." Many Jewish business leaders, men like Schiff and Seligman, similarly defined Americanization as loyalty, obedience, and patriotism.

Labor militancy and the socialist movement among Eastern European Jews were among the factors that directly and indirectly led the assimilationist German Jews to take the role of Americanizers in the Jewish community. There they created educational and social institutions, such as the Educational Alliance, geared toward co-optation within the Jewish community and toward the creation of institutional models for adoption by the public schools and other local and national institutions. There they sought to substitute Americanizing educational activities for the cultural activities of the Orthodox and socialist Jews. Their particular position as Jewish big businessmen pushed them to take a leadership role both within the Jewish community and nationally. That the Eastern European Jews were not easily resocialized may be seen by the German Jews' movement toward pluralism, symbolized by both the creation and the demise of the *Kehillah*. The German Jews were brought to recognize respectable unionism, Yiddish, and Jewish education even as they sought to remake these cultural elements along what they conceived to be more "American" lines. That is, co-optation within the Jewish community, as nationally, was a profoundly interactive process.

Once the Progressives succeeded in turning higher education into a national, loosely pyramidal system, they began to have great influence over its cultural content. In the course of developing teaching as a profession of social control, they gave to that profession its professional ideology. One of the consequences of their triumph in establishing the priority of secular learning over the classical tradition was the ramification of "scientific" racism and social Darwinism as ideological justifications for the hegemony of a predominantly Northern European business class. Although environmentalism gained influence toward the 1920s, as did some forms of cultural pluralism, the most coercive aspects of the Americanization movement also grew during the same period. Thus social science in higher education generally stressed the cultural, and in some versions, the racial, superiority of the Northern European group. In all its varieties, social scientists generally viewed the immigrants, including the Eastern European Jews, as primarily a threat, occasionally as a resource, but rarely as different but equal peoples. Political science, economics, and sociology were uniformly anti-socialist.

The content of schooling is not the same as the content of socialization. Socialization is a *process*, not an imprint. City College students, it will be remembered, kept their instructors on their toes. Nevertheless, insofar as mobility through higher education required or produced some internalization of the dominant culture, mobility was an aspect of social control. We have seen, in Chapter 3, that the conception of ladders of success—of opportunity for mobility—was in part a conception of social control, albeit one that was particularly suited to the technological needs of developing capitalism.

Jewish mobility through higher education was particularly facilitated by the existence of free public higher education at the College of the City of New York. Like the rest of the educational system in New York City, CCNY was in advance of the nation in some educational developments and behind it in others. Established in 1847 as part of the effort by forward-looking businessmen to make higher education relevant to business and the changing socioeconomic order, and in response to the Working Men's Party's demand for universal free education (and the redistribution of wealth), City College sank back into the classical mold until long after most other educational institutions had been "modernized." Nevertheless, even in the early years the College produced graduates in the more "modern" subjects: business and education. In effect, City College was an early precursor of the educational ladders. The College was only substantially transformed in Progressive directions in the early twentieth century, however, when its student body was largely Russian Jewish.

The immigrant groups, including the Russian Jews, had a great impact on both Progressivism and on the New York schools, including City College. Despite the College's mission of introducing underdeveloped poor Jews to Western culture, the students created their own milieu. Most important, members of the faculty and administration came to justify the school's existence in terms of developing educated immigrants who would have special facility in Americanizing other immigrants in schools and neighborhoods.

Consequently, not only was the widespread need for social control of recalcitrant and political immigrant workers a factor in the social mobility of the children of immigrants, the children's social mobility was also, in many complex ways, a factor in social control of both the immigrants and their children. Mobility placed the children of immigrants in a different social position from which to form their social perceptions. Moreover, mobility in most of the "caretaker roles" encouraged the internalization of a set of perceptions about "social problems" which, needless to say, did not include capitalism.

Like their fellow workers, proletarian Jews found factory work and tenement work oppressive. Like their fellow workers, they sought to end that oppression: politically, by ending the wage-labor relationship; or economically, through the "wage-bargain"; or individually, through personal escape. The possibilities for any of these alternatives are specific within historical circumstances. "Culture" plays a role within a specific economic and historical context. Group membership shapes both the knowledge of alternatives and the actual alternatives available, including patterns of acquaintanceship, apprenticeship, trust, and advice.

To explore this matter further, we can look at the structure of the specific industries in which the different ethnic groups were concentrated. For the Jews we can examine the structure of the garment industry, for example, and the influence of its seasonal nature, general instability, periodic unemployment, and low capitalization in leading, enabling, and forcing workers to seek alternatives for themselves and their children.

Culture is neither as arid nor as ethereal as it appears in the sociological literature. It is not as arid as an "inventory of values," because culture is more active than a warehouse full of attitudes. It is not as ethereal as it appears in the literature because it is not confined to the realm of pure spirit. Culture is the expression of the life process of real human beings living their daily lives. Culture shapes perception and influences social structure, but social structure also shapes culture.

The German Jews and the Russian Jews had very different ways of perceiving each other, and different ways of perceiving charity, politics, and the value of labor. The fundamental reason does not lie in the one group having come from Germany and the other group having come from Russia. It lies in their different structural positions within the United States and in the way that their previous experiences as Jews in Germany and Russia had shaped them into structurally different groups. Those in the Russian Jewish business class were different from those in the German Jewish business class partly because they had participated in a different history, partly because they were in a different segment of American business, and partly because at the end of the nineteenth century in Russia they were in a different kind of socioeconomic structure. Even so, a segment of the Russian Jewish business group was developing assimilationist tendencies in Russia just as the German Jews had in Germany, although they were seeking assimilation into a very different kind of state.

As for those in the Russian Jewish proletariat, their perceptions, their culture, and their language differed from the Russian Jewish business class and from the German Jewish business class because their lives and their interests differed. Even to gain a conception of how the Russian Jews lived, the German Jews had to carry on deliberate investigations into how "the other half" lived, and indeed they only investigated sympathetically after non-Jewish muckrakers had shown the way, and after the Russian Jews' efforts on their own behalf had become an embarrassment to respectable Jewry. Bankers and basting-pullers simply led different lives, and those different lives led them to perceive and understand the world in different ways.

On the other hand, to seek a one-to-one correspondence between position and social perception is to have as static a conception of culture as that of the cultural determinists. Some workers who became businessmen remained socialists, as did some teachers, despite the cultural influence of higher education and the requisites of the role of the socializer. Some workers who remained workers were consumed by the ambition to be exactly like Jacob Schiff, even if it was not clear how to go about being like Jacob Schiff while living on the Lower East Side and working as a house painter.

If the gap in social perception between Russian Jews and German Jews changed somewhat, it is not because of any metaphysical "unity principle" or instinct for "Jewish survival" (a concept with at least as many meanings as "Jewish identity"). Insofar as the gap was breached, it was because of many complex factors, including the larger historical context described in the preceding chapters. Among those factors were the conditions favorable to Russian Jewish mobility into business, and the German Jewish efforts to mold a new Jewish cultural unity centered around North American liberalism. Even this effort was not purely cognitive. It would have had little effect had it not been bolstered by the creation of institutions and by the structural changes such as the creation of the ladders of mobility. On the one hand, the existence of the ladders of mobility may have had more to do with the removal of "Oriental tendencies" than the purely cultural/cognitive efforts of the Breadwinners' College, the Educational Alliance, and the *Kehillah*. On the other hand, insofar as mobility was contingent on being socialized away from such tendencies as orthodoxy and socialism, Jewish upward mobility may have been as much a product of the *loss* of Jewish values as of their expression, and as much a product of the requirements of loyalty, patriotism, and obedience as of the Jewish passion for education.

But those who celebrate Jewish mobility often fail to ask the price. Poor Jewish students came to higher education from a world fired by the socialist movement. It was a world of the labor poets, where intellectuals, united in factory and labor movement with rank-and-file workers, forged a Yiddish culture which decried their oppression and demanded major change. These students entered a world of higher education, dominant culture, and caretaker bureaucracies which proposed to change the immigrants rather than their social circumstances. The secular spring at which Jewish students were invited to quench their thirst for learning was a heady brew of racism and contempt for socialism. Upward mobility offered them an opportunity to hone their brains "for hire." Yet some of them thought differently, keeping their professors on their toes and, once they began work, determining that wherever they worked, they would "neither make, nor wear, enslaving chains."

Given the tendency of cultural proclivities which are not structurally encouraged to die out, what is remarkable is not the continuance of the Jewish propensity towards education; as we have seen, that passion was institutionally encouraged. Rather, what is remarkable is the persistence, despite equally intensive efforts at discouragement, of Jewish radicalism.

Afterword

The Open Admissions students brought to their work a motivation that was like a hunger.

—Theodore Gross, 1978[1]

By 1961 City College had been joined by Brooklyn, Hunter and Queens Colleges, three community colleges, and a Graduate Center, forming, in all, The City University of New York. In the 1960s a combination of social forces reminiscent of those that gave rise to the Free Academy in the 1840s and enlarged it in the 1900s expanded CUNY into the third largest university in the country with eighteen colleges, serving two-hundred and seventy thousand students. Once again in a context of general radicalization (the Vietnam War, ghetto rebellion, and widespread disaffection) social reformers and representatives of the capitalist class called for the training of more social workers, teachers, and other social service agents. Once more they promoted individual mobility through education against socialism and collectivism. Businessmen called for adapting universities to better train a potential work force for the ever-changing structure of work. Once again social reformers faced working-class demands for social change, greater equality and educational expansion. But now the new occupations offered by industry were more likely to be paraprofessional jobs. The education-occupation nexus created at the turn of the century had become so tight that higher schooling became a condition of employment. Now working-class communities *had* to demand access to education with an urgency unprecedented in previous times.

Chancellor Albert Bowker of the Board of Higher Education had already drawn up plans for the expansion of CUNY by 1975 to a system offering 100 percent tuition-free post-high school education in a tracked system of senior colleges, community colleges, special programs and Educational Skills centers. In 1969 a student strike and sit-in at City College forced his hand, and Bowker's program for Open Admissions was begun in modified form five years earlier than planned.

Demonstrators demanded that the racial composition of all entering classes reflect the Black and Puerto Rican population of New York City high schools. They demanded that rather than defining human needs in corporate terms, the colleges must serve the needs of working-class minority communities—including their need for fundamental social change. Facing the inadequacies and failures of lower schooling, they demanded that all persons training to become teachers in the New York public schools study Black and Puerto Rican culture. Confronting a curriculum which remained as ignorant of Black, Hispanic, and Asian culture as it had been of working-class Jewish culture, as ignorant and contemptuous of the world of workers in the 1960s as it had been in the 1920s, demonstrators demanded that the narrowness of City College's curriculum be corrected by the inclusion of Black and Puerto Rican Studies programs.

The City University had its heritage as the first free public educational ladder, but that ladder had served a very small proportion of the working class. Now the university began a new experiment in democratic schooling: mass higher education. City University was expanded, a number of new colleges were founded, and a semi-tracked system of Open Admissions began. Thousands of Jewish, Italian, Puerto Rican, Black, and Asian students entered the 1970 freshman class. Black, Puerto Rican, Jewish, and Asian Studies programs were begun, finally moving the City University curriculum beyond "that narrow learning and art which . . . glowed over the isolated circles of a few Western capitals. . . ."[2]

But the response did not exactly match the demonstrators' demands. Official rhetoric confined Open Admissions to opportunity for individual mobility, underplaying the goals of service to the community and fundamental social change. Spanish language was never required for prospective teachers; it was treated as merely a remedial tool for Hispanic students. Remedial work, which everyone had understood was necessary to counteract the failures of the lower schools, was underfunded. Professors who worshipped the "books that from the Anglo-Saxon point of view represent the best that has been thought and said" balked at teaching Shakespeare to "plebeian minds" and treated the study of other cultures as a threat to their own "intellectual capital." They portrayed the new courses as an intellectual copout, a lowering of standards, and at best an unfortunately necessary form of therapy for the underprivileged.[3] Some faculty nostalgically "remembered" a glorious City College past, when poor Jewish immigrant students with brilliant intellectual preparation and docile, grateful demeanor inspired an appreciative faculty. They forgot or did not even know the *real* past, when professors like themselves had expressed repugnance and distaste for the cultural and personal mannerisms of the Jewish poor, fresh from homes where English was not spoken. Romanticizing a reconstructed, mythologized past, they helped to destroy past, present, and future.

A City College alumnus remembers it differently:

> When I entered CCNY in 1924 the entrance requirement was simply 60% high-school average (or 65% Regents average). When I started teaching [there] in 1928, the entrance requirement was *still* 60% high school average. In 1930, with the influx of applications for admission from high school graduates affected by the Depression, I watched the entrance requirement screwed upward year by year from 60 to 65, 68, 70, 72, 75, 78, 80, 82, 85 and 88 by the time I left the college in 1941. The reason for this escalation had absolutely nothing to do with academic standards but everything to do with economics: the College had [only] so many seats that could be filled by entering freshmen. Those for whom there was no room had to be excluded. The escalating entrance average was an economically-based exclusionary technique designed to cope with the surge of students towards higher education (a surge that gave birth to Brooklyn, Queens . . . etc.). Therefore, Open Admissions in 1970 was a *reversion* to the tradition of Open Admissions for high school graduates that had obtained from 1847 to 1930. All the Jewish students considered in your study were the beneficiaries of Open Admissions. Neither I nor many other Jewish students could have entered CCNY had the entrance requirements been 88 (as in 1941–1969):[4]

But free higher education with Open Admissions threatened the entire system of higher education based on the sorting of an elite and private payment for schooling. The vast expansion of higher education threatened to glut the labor market with people schooled in rebellion, expecting that they would get a better job because they now had gotten a better education. Educational and business leaders became alarmed.

In 1976 CUNY's bold experiment, born in an atmosphere of expansiveness and growth, came to an end. In an atmosphere of fiscal crisis, an inability of the economy to offer the kinds of jobs to college students that had been promised as the rewards to greater schooling, a general increase in unemployment, attacks by private colleges on their competition in public education, and the resurgeance of reactionary ideology and scientific racism, the policy of Open Admissions was ended just six short years after it had begun. Tuition was imposed, terminating 129 years of free public higher education.[5]

This book, rooted in the past, began with a dedication to the past. I end it with a dedication for the future:

> *to all those who have struggled and who struggle now,*
> *at City University and elsewhere, for "a democratic*
> *and free system of higher education for the working masses"*[6]*—*
> *a liberating education.*

Notes

Chapter 1: Uneasy Questions on the Mobility Miracle
1. Glazer, "The American Jew and the Attainment of Middle Class Rank: Some Trends and Explanations," in Marshall Sklare, *The Jews*, p. 146.
2. Ben Halpern, "America Is Different," in Sklare, *The Jews*, pp. 23–39.
3. The question of Jewish mobility must focus on the fate of the Eastern European Jews because only they were a substantially proletarian group. The Sephardic and German Jews who preceded them in North America were largely a business group, some of whom had connections with European wealth. Statistical documentations of Jewish success sometimes neglect this important distinction.
4. Glazer, "The American Jew," in Sklare, *The Jews*, pp. 142, 143.
5. Milton M. Gordon, *Assimilation in American Life*, pp. 186, 187. For other scholars who state that the Jews have been "remarkably upwardly mobile" because of their "passion for education" and middle-class values, see virtually all the essays in Sklare, *The Jews*; Talcott Parsons, "The Sociology of Modern Anti-Semitism," in *Jews in a Gentile World*, ed. Isacque Graeber and Steward Britt; Moses Rischin, *The Promised City*; Charles Bernheimer, ed., *The Russian Jew in the United States*; "What the Hebrew Has Done in Business, the Professions, Art, Science, Literature, and Philanthropy," *New York Herald*, Sunday Magazine, 16 November 1905, pp. 2–3; and Diane Ravitch, *The Great School Wars*.
6. Walter E. Clark, *Outline of Lectures on Economics*, p. 12.
7. Norman Podhoretz, *Making It*, p. 3.
8. "The Torah has spoken concerning four sons—one wise, and one wicked, and one simple, and one who wits not to ask" (Passover *Haggadah*).
9. Nathan Glazer, "The American Jew and the Attainment of Middle Class Rank: Some Trends and Explanations," in Sklare, *The Jews*, p. 144; Abraham Karp, *Golden Door to America: The Jewish Immigrant Experience*, p. 183.

Chapter 2: Remolding Jewish Culture
1. S. Joseph Fauman, "Occupational Selection among Detroit Jews," cited in Sklare, *The Jews*, pp. 119–120.
2. Oscar Handlin, *Adventure in Freedom*, p. 144.
3. Nathan Glazer, *American Judaism*, chaps. 1–4.
4. Cited in Moses Rischin, *The Promised City*, p. 97.

5. Howard Morley Sachar, *The Course of Modern Jewish History*, pp. 77, 74–80; Nora Levin, *While Messiah Tarried*, pp. 6–7.

6. In the 1840s, after three-quarters of a century, the division between Hasidism and Talmudism began to close, with the reform of some of the more cramping and sterile aspects of Talmudic study, and the muting of some of the anti-intellectualism of the Hasidic movement.

7. Melech Epstein, *Jewish Labor in USA*, vol. 1, p. 4. Epstein cites A. Litvin, in *Forward*, 7 December 1912. The original source was the *Pinkus*, the official chronicle of the ghetto.

8. Joshua Kunitz, *Russian Literature and the Jew* (New York: Columbia University Press).

9. Bernard Weinryb, "Jewish Immigration and Accommodation to America," in Sklare, *The Jews*, p. 628, n. 43.

10. "But what is the origin of these values that are associated with success in middle-class pursuits? Max Weber argues that they originated in a certain kind of religious outlook on the world, the outlook of Calvinism. There is no question that Judaism emphasizes the traits that businessmen and intellectuals require, and has done so since at least 1,500 years before Calvinism. . . . The strong emphasis on learning and study can be traced that far back too. The Jewish habits of foresight, care, moderation probably arose early during the two thousand years that the Jews have lived primarily as strangers among other peoples." Nathan Glazer, "The American Jew," in Sklare, *The Jews*, p. 143.

11. See Abram Leon, *The Jewish Question;* Ezra Mendelsohn, *Class Struggle in the Pale;* Sachar, *Modern Jewish History;* Rischin, *The Promised City;* Epstein, *Jewish Labor;* Adolf Kober, "Emancipation's Impact on the Education and Vocational Training of German Jewry," pp. 3–32, 151–169; Milton Himmelfarb, "Secular Society? A Jewish Perspective"; pp. 220–236; Levin, *While Messiah Tarried;* and Ber Borochov, *Nationalism and the Class Struggle.*

12. For more detailed accounts of nineteenth-century industrialization, see Rischin, *The Promised City*, p. 28, and A. Yuditzky, *Jewish Bourgeoisie and Jewish Proletariat in the First Half of the Nineteenth Century.* Emma S. Gorelick translated this Yiddish work for me. I am grateful to her for her painstaking and dedicated work.

13. See Rischin, *The Promised City*, chaps. 2 and 3; Epstein, *Jewish Labor*, chap. 1; and Glazer, *American Judaism*, chap. 5. Apparently the workers resented the fact that the industrialists' exercise of "care and moderation" was to be achieved by the workers' "postponement of pleasure."

14. David Singer, "David Levinsky's Fall," p. 697; Salo Baron, *The Russian Jew Under Tsars and Soviets*, pp. 148–168.

15. Epstein, *Jewish Labor*, p. 9.

16. Mendelsohn, *Class Struggle*, p. viii. Emphasis added.

17. Ibid., p. ix; Simon Dubnow, *History of the Jews in Poland and Russia*, vol. 3, pp. 55–58; and Levin, *While Messiah Tarried*, Part 3, especially chap. 16; and Baron, *The Russian Jew*, pp. 168–172.

18. For a sensitive account of the many motivations for emigration and the ways these motivations changed with changing conditions in Europe, see Irving Howe, *World of Our Fathers*, pp. 57–63.
19. Herbert G. Gutman, "Work, Culture, and Society in Industrializing America," pp. 3–76; Epstein, *Jewish Labor*, vol. 1, pp. 98–99; Weinryb, "Jewish Immigration," in Sklare, *The Jews*, pp. 4–22; Singer, "David Levinsky's Fall," pp. 697–698; and Charles S. Liebman, "Orthodoxy in American Jewish Life." pp. 27–30.
20. Glazer, *American Judaism*, p. 67.
21. Epstein, *Jewish Labor*, vol. 1, pp. 61–62.
22. Ibid., pp. 278–279. See also Jeremy Brecher, *Strike!*, chaps. 1–3.
23. On the many cultural divisions within the Jewish community as late as 1918, see Alexander M. Dushkin, *Jewish Education in New York City*, chap. 1.
24. For illustrations of the role of habit and of patterns of personal acquaintanceship and personal connections, see the analysis of the relative tendencies of Jews and Poles to enter business in Jacob Lestchinsky, "The Position of Jews in the Economic Life in America," in *Jews in a Gentile World*, ed. Isacque Graeber and Stewart Britt, p. 402. See also the discussion of the same factors in apprenticeship in various trades in Rischin, *The Promised City*, p. 8. For the role of culture in trust see Gerald D. Suttles, *The Social Order of the Slum*, esp. pp. 45–47. Patterns of advice would make an excellent study of culture-as-process. Examine, from that point of view, the letters in Isaac Metzker, ed., *A Bintel Brief*.
25. I am omitting entirely consideration of the various strains of Zionism, which were important during this period. In the following discussion I am treating both orthodoxy and Jewish socialism in general. One must keep in mind, however, that there were numerous differences and divisions among Orthodox Jews and among Jewish socialists.
26. Gilbert Klaperman, *The Story of Yeshiva University*, pp. 3–4.
27. Herbert Gutman, *Work, Culture, and Society in Industrializing America*, pp. 23–26.
28. Klaperman, *Yeshiva University*, p. 21.
29. Ibid., pp. 18, 19; also pp. 8, 13.
30. *Di Tageblatt*, 4 May 1888 and 2 October 1910, cited in Klaperman, *Yeshiva University*, pp. 28, 32.
31. On the collapse of early nineteenth-century synagogue schools, see Glazer, *American Judaism*, p. 34. For a description of the Polish gymnasium from the point of view of Jewish parents, see Tamara Deutscher, "Introduction: The Education of a Jewish Child," in Isaac Deutscher, *The Non-Jewish Jew and Other Essays*, pp. 12–15. See also Howard Sachar, *Modern Jewish History*, pp. 90–95, for the Russian school system.
32. Handlin, *Adventure in Freedom*, pp. 116–117.
33. Dushkin, *Jewish Education*, pp. 497–504.
34. *Landsmanschaften* were (and are) organizations of persons who had

emigrated from the same town in Europe. (Irish and Italian immigrants founded similar societies.) The organizations usually originated as burial and sickness-relief societies. On Orthodox self-help efforts see especially Rischin, *The Promised City*, chap. 6; Epstein, *Jewish Labor*, p. 51; and Morris Isaiah Berger, "The Settlement, the Immigrant and the Public School," p. 53.

35. Marshall, quoted in Arthur A. Goren, *New York Jews and the Quest for Community*, pp. 66, 67. Marshall learned Yiddish in order to be able to communicate more directly with the "downtown Jews," and founded a Yiddish newspaper in order to create a more "responsible" Yiddish press.

36. Epstein, *Jewish Labor*, vol. 1, chap. 7.

37. Isaac Hourwich, *Immigration and Labor*, p. 373.

38. Goren, *New York Jews*, p. 191; Epstein, *Jewish Labor*, vol. 1, chap. 17.

39. See for example Handlin, *Adventure in Freedom*, pp. 135–137, and Werner Cohn, "The Politics of American Jews" in Sklare, *The Jews*, pp. 114–126.

40. Handlin, *Adventure in Freedom*, p. 130.

41. Daniel Bell, "Marxian Socialism in the United States."

42. Handlin, *Adventure in Freedom*, pp. 126–127.

43. Sachar, *Modern Jewish History*, pp. 324–325. See also Glazer, *American Judaism*, p. 67.

44. Howe, *World of Our Fathers*, pp. 302–303, 322–324. On socialism and the Jewish labor movement see also Morris U. Schappes, *The Jews in the United States: A Pictorial History, 1654 to the Present*, chaps. 9–11; John Laslett, *Labor and the Left*, chap. 4.

45. Howe, *World of Our Fathers*, pp. 302, 310.

46. Epstein, *Jewish Labor*, vol. 1, pp. 274–275.

47. Epstein, *Jewish Labor*, vol. 1, p. 274.

48. *Jewish Messenger*, vol. 50, no. 19, pp. 5, 6. Cited in Levin, *While Messiah Tarried*, p. 68.

49. See Sachar, *Modern Jewish History*, chap. 15; and Rischin, *The Promised City*, chap. 6. Baron de Hirsch floated a loan to the Russian government in the midst of the 1880s pogroms, refused to use the loan as leverage for a change of czarist policy, and suppressed efforts by Oscar Straus to send food to Russian famine areas. Straus, who was especially anti-Zionist, and who prided himself on *not* favoring the Jews while ambassador to Turkey, supported Jewish settlement in the Ottoman Empire as a solution to the "immigrant problem." See Naomi W. Cohen, *A Dual Heritage*, pp. 65, 28.

50. Cited by Weinryb, "Jewish Immigration," in Sklare, *The Jews*, p. 18.

51. Rischin, *The Promised City*, pp. 51–58; Barry Supple, "A Business Elite," Goren, *New York Jews*, chap. 1.

52. Supple, "A Business Elite," p. 157. See also Ellis Rivkin, *The Shaping of Jewish History*, chaps. 6–8; Glazer, *American Judaism*, chaps. 3–5;

Stephen Birmingham, *Our Crowd*, parts 3 and 4; and E. Digby Baltzell, *The Protestant Establishment*, passim.

53. Cyrus Adler, *Jacob H. Schiff*, vol. 1, pp. 163, 169, 171–182, 194–207, and chap. 7. See also Goren, *New York Jews*, pp. 16–17. It is impossible to exaggerate the importance of Schiff, especially in the Jewish world. I have not come across a single book dealing with this period which does not at least mention his name. Even Michael Gold's autobiographical novel, *Jews Without Money*, mentions his name and influence.

54. Glazer, *American Judaism*, p. 46.

55. Progressivism was a very complex movement incorporating groups and persons of different and often conflicting ideas, motivations, and interests. As a result, different students of the Progressive movement, coming to it with their own diverse interests, concerns, and political persuasions, have seized upon different aspects of Progressivism, and therefore define "the essence of Progressivism" differently. Robert H. Wiebe, *The Search for Order: 1877–1920*, for example, sees Progressivism as a movement of a "new middle class," primarily of professionals, interested in forming a new social order based on efficiency and bureaucracy. Weinstein, in *The Corporate Ideal in the Liberal State*, sees Progressivism as a movement dominated by liberal corporate leaders concerned with efficiency and co-optation. Some authors stress Progressivism's humanitarian aspects, others stress its coercive side. Ultimately these differences are matters of emphasis rather than total truth or falsity. Synthesizing these diverse views is possible, although different authors would disagree on the truth or falsity of various attempts at synthesis.

Diane Ravitch, in *The Revisionists Revised*, correctly cautions against oversimplifying the thoughts of individual Progressive thinkers, endowing them with omniscient foresight, or ignoring their diversity. One must not ignore the trees for the forest. But surely one must *see* the forest, and a work of social science must present central tendencies.

56. It should be obvious that the two concepts of "charity" are fundamentally different, ethically, psychologically, and politically. (See especially Rischin, *The Promised City*, p. 104; also Gold, *Jews Without Money*, pp. 211–213.) This transformation of the meaning of *zedakah* into virtually its opposite renders meaningless the efforts of recent sociologists to explain current political behavior of the Jews in terms of "enduring Jewish values," such as *zedakah*. See, for example, Lawrence Fuchs, "Sources of Jewish Internationalism and Liberalism" in Sklare, *The Jews*. Fuchs's article is a particularly striking example, since he spends considerable space in discussing *zedakah* without once mentioning that its core was gutted and replaced by totally opposite materials.

57. Cohen, *A Dual Heritage*, p. 10.

58. *Jewish Messenger*, 14 September 1891. Cited in Berger, "The Settlement, the Immigrant and the Public School," p. 52.

59. First Annual Report of the Educational Alliance, 1893, p. 29, cited in

Berger, "The Settlement, the Immigrant and the Public School," p. 12. See also Second Annual Report of the Educational Alliance, 1894, pp. 6–8.

60. The Board of Trustees of Temple Emanu-El included Schiff, a Seligman, a Lehman, Louis Marshall, Daniel Guggenheim, and Louis Stern. The overlap among the Boards of Trustees of the Educational Alliance, Temple Emanu-El, the Jewish Theological Seminary, and the New York *Kehillah* (discussed later in this chapter) is considerable. See Goren, *New York Jews*, esp. p. 15.

61. "The Hebrew Educational Fair and Its Bearing on the Immigrant question," *The American Hebrew*, December 6, 1889, p. 119. This was an extract of the lecture. Emphasis is in the original. The long quotation that follows is from the same source.

62. Ibid., pp. 119–120.

63. Rischin's subtitle to chap. 6 of *The Promised City*, "Philanthropy Versus Self-Help," is suggestive, but he doesn't carry through its implications.

64. Cited in Richard F. W. Whittemore, "Nicholas Murray Butler and Public Education," p. 118.

65. Andrew Carnegie, "Wealth," p. 663.

66. Second Annual Report of the Educational Alliance, 1894, p. 7. The first annual report had a similar statement.

67. The political dimension of Americanization is insufficiently emphasized by scholars. The point may be clarified by asking what the immigrants were doing to inspire such prodigious efforts. Berger's major answer seems to be that they were "different": "The immigrant, posing the problem of being different, compelled the school to shape a program that would remove the difference" (Berger, "The Settlement," pp. ii–iii). Lawrence Cremin, in *The Transformation of the School*, sees the Progressives as responding to suffering. Handlin, in *Adventure in Freedom*, ascribes the philanthropic efforts of the German Jews to compassion based on religio-ethnic fellow-feeling. In his view the "two communities" were merely "different," and their conflicts were the result of "misunderstanding." No aspect of the behavior of the German Jewish business class is seen by Handlin as related to social control, and the word *Progressivism* does not appear in his book. As Silverman's statements, the Alliance's aims, and material in the rest of this chapter will show, social control, and political socialization, were essential to the German Jews' efforts. See Epstein, *Jewish Labor*, chap. 9.

68. Thomas Davidson, *The Education of Wage-Earners*, pp. 96–97.

69. Morris Raphael Cohen, *A Dreamer's Journey*, pp. 70–71, 77–78, 82.

70. Ibid., chaps. 7–9.

71. Ibid., p. 66–67.

72. Ibid., p. 103.

73. Ibid., pp. 103–104; Berger, "The Settlement, the Immigrant and the Public School," p. 60.

74. M. R. Cohen, *A Dreamer's Journey*, p. 104.
75. Ibid.
76. Ibid., p. 71.
77. Ibid., p. 119. It is curious that the Breadwinners' College is known as the achievement of Thomas Davidson. Lawrence Cremin, in his account *The Transformation of the School*, does not mention Cohen, who was principal of the College for almost seventeen years, and Berger mentions him only as Davidson's disciple.
78. M. R. Cohen, *A Dreamer's Journey*, p. 99; Rischin, *The Promised City*, p. 216.
79. M. R. Cohen, *A Dreamer's Journey*, p. 110.
80. Bernard Bailyn, *Education in the Formation of American Society*, p. 7. Even M. R. Cohen indicates some awareness of Davidson's superficiality; see *A Dreamer's Journey*, p. 108.
81. M. R. Cohen, *A Dreamer's Journey*, pp. 215, 168; Bailyn, *Education*, pp. 7–8.
82. It is highly unlikely that the rich were attracted to the Breadwinners' College, so the phrase is probably mere hyperbole. It is important as an indicator of Cohen and his friends' changing outlook.
83. M. R. Cohen, *A Dreamer's Journey*, pp. 167, 166.
84. Ibid., p. 112.
85. Berger, "The Settlement, the Immigrant and the Public School," pp. 69, 76, 63.
86. S. Willis Rudy, *The College of the City of New York*, pp. 313–315; Frederick Rudolph, *The American College and University*, p. 344.
87. Rischin, "The Promised City, p 102. In their alienation from the settlement, adult Russian Jews were like the Italians described by Gans, *The Urban Villagers*; and Whyte, *Street Corner Society*. Both authors clearly locate that alienation in "caretaker attitudes," which are, in turn, an expression of the culture conflict inherent in the socializing purpose of the settlements. According to Rischin, the fact that the Educational Alliance's caretakers were Jews did not alleviate that alienation but aggravated it.
88. Charles Seligman Bernheimer, ed., *The Russian Jew in America*, pp. 410, 411. Looking backward from the fifties, Glazer ("The Attainment of Middle-Class Rank," in Sklare, *The Jews*) constructed a never-never past: "the pattern of foresight and sobriety so essential for middle-class success was so well established in Jewish life that it was maintained even when there was no prospect of going into business. The Jewish students were docile, accepting—as lower-class children rarely do today—today's restraints for tomorrow's rewards; the Jewish workers stayed out of jail" (p. 144).
89. See Goren, *New York Jews*, chap. 1.
90. See Second Annual Report of the Educational Alliance, p. 7.
91. Dushkin, *Jewish Education*; Isaac B. Berkson, *Theories of Americaniza-*

tion: A Critical Study with Special Reference to the Jewish Group.

92. Judah Magnes, cited in Goren, *New York Jews,* p. 204.

93. Goren, *New York Jews,* pp. 196–197.

94. Ibid., p. 196.

95. Educational reformers of mid-nineteenth-century Massachusetts faced a similar dilemma. See Michael Katz, *The Irony of Early School Reform,* part 1. Says Katz of the middle-class reformers: "Ironically, their ideology and style could not have been better designed to alienate the very people whom they strove to accommodate in a more closely knit social order" (p. 112).

96. Klaperman, *Yeshiva University,* chap. 6.

97. This crucial distinction—that unlike the liberal and official Americanization programs, leftist Americanizing efforts were not permeated with hostility to socialism—is usually missed by writers on this subject, probably because they are not very attentive to the political nature of assimilation.

    In *The Revisionists Revised,* Diane Ravitch's liberal polemic against radical scholarship, she correctly points to the Achilles' heel of those revisionists who see schooling and Americanization as purely impositions from above. She argues that Americanization "was not simply a one-way transaction between victim and oppressor. Immigrant groups were themselves sponsors of many assimilation and Americanization programs" (p. 69). Furthermore, they often *modified* the culture imposed upon them. She attributes these facts to American pluralism. Since the immigrants did not pry into the families of the upper class, however, or intervene in *their* schooling, "pluralism"—with its egalitarian implications—seems hardly an apt description. Rather we should see the influence of the immigrants on U.S. society and their modification of dominant culture as an expression of the dialectics of class relations: the dominance (oppression) of one class over the other calls forth varied and often creative responses of resistance and adaptation in the oppressed. See Ravitch, *The Revisionists Revised,* pp. 44–47, 150–151; and Sherry Gorelick, "Undermining Hierarchy," pp. 25–28.

98. Goren, *New York Jews,* chaps. 10 and 11.

99. James Weinstein, *The Decline of Socialism in America,* p. 327.

100. Both Weinstein, *The Decline of Socialism* (1967), and Dubofsky, "Success and Failure of Socialism in New York City," (1968), demonstrate the strength of radicalism in the twenties. Both state that radicalism as a popular politics outlived the decline of the Socialist Party; but they have opposite explanations of that decline. Weinstein blames the dogmatism of the Communists, whereas Dubofsky blames the decreasing militancy of the socialists.

101. Stephen P. Duggan, *A Professor at Large,* pp. 11–13; M. R. Cohen, *A Dreamer's Journey,* p. 157; and Rudolph, *The American College,* p. 467.

102. N. W. Cohen, *A Dual Heritage*, p. 70.
103. Goren, *New York Jews*, p. 21.
104. James Weinstein, *The Corporate Ideal in the Liberal State*, pp. 11–14. Of course the distinction between the behavior of industrial and financial capitalists is not absolute. Marcus Marx, President of the National Association of Clothiers, was a founder of the Educational Alliance, and he "intervened on behalf of the National Civic Federation" in the 1909 waistmakers' strike. See Goren, *New York Jews*, p. 197.
105. Handlin, *Adventure in Freedom*, pp. 135–136; Nathan Glazer and Daniel Patrick Moynihan, *Beyond the Melting Pot*, p. 140.

Chapter 3: The Creation of Educational Opportunity

1. Stephen Birmingham, *Our Crowd*, pp. 183, 218–221; Naomi W. Cohen, *A Dual Heritage*, pp. 7–14, chaps. 1, 2.
2. Natalie Naylor, "The Antebellum College Movement," p. 269.
3. Frederick Rudolph, *The American College and University*, chaps. 1–5; Richard Hofstadter and Wilson Smith, eds., *American Higher Education*, vol. 1, pp. 265–296; Stanley M. Guralnick, *Science and the Ante-Bellum American Colleges*, chap. 1.
4. Rudolph, *The American College and University*, p. 207; Michael B. Katz, *The Irony of Early School Reform*, esp. introduction and pt. 1.
5. Guralnick, *Science and the Ante-Bellum American Colleges*; Douglas Sloan, "Harmony, Chaos and Consensus," passim; David B. Potts, "College Enthusiasm;" pp. 31, 37–41; David F. Allmendinger, Jr., "New England Students and the Revolution in Higher Education," pp. 381–385.
6. *Reports on the Course of Instruction in Yale College by a Committee of the Corporation and the Academical Faculty*, pp. 324, 328, 329, 323. (This work is hereafter referred to as the "Yale *Report*.")
7. Rudolph, *The American College and University*, p. 137. Recently a number of historians have argued that the established interpretation grossly mislabels the Yale *Report* as a conservative document. It was, they assert, "comprehensive, openminded, and liberal" (Guralnick, *Science and the Ante-Bellum American Colleges*, p. 30); it was "a thoughtful, realistic, and effective approach" (Potts, "College Enthusiasm," p. 39). These writers appear to be much taken with the *Report's* general statements in favor of change. I disagree. The *Report* espouses change in the abstract, but defends *every single feature* of the status quo as indispensable to a college education. It does defend liberal education against vocationalism, but it has a very restrictive (and conservative) view of the necessary content of liberal education. In my reading, it lives up to its elitist and conservative ill-repute.
8. W. Bruce Leslie, "Localism, Denominationalism, and Institutional Strat-

egies in Urbanizing America"; Guralnick, *Science and the Ante-Bellum American Colleges,* p. 119.

9. Rudolph, *The American College and University,* p. 130; Guralnick, *Science and the Ante-Bellum American Colleges,* p. 131; Joseph S. Wood, "A Comparison Between the Courses of Study at the College of the City of New York and Yale University."

10. Katz, *The Irony of Early School Reform,* pp' 133–134, pts. 1 and 2.

11. Naylor, "The Ante-Bellum College Movement," p. 263; Guralnick, *Science and the Ante-Bellum American Colleges,* p. 14.

12. Rudolph, *The American College and University,* pp. 129–130.

13. Philip Foner's analysis, in his *History of the Labor Movement in the United States,* of the limitations of the labor movment in the pre-Civil War period may have some applicability to college reform as well: "The national labor organizations of the [eighteen] thirties [spurred by the expansion of the economy via the building of railroads and canals] did not last very long. The movement was premature, for although the market was expanding it had not as yet become a truly national market. Until it did, no national labor organization could become really stabilized, for unionism could not develop further than the limits imposed by the economy of the country" (pp. 113–114). Similarly a national system of higher education, oriented to and controlled by a national corporate class, would not become possible before the development of the economy which made that class and its needs possible.

14. For a fuller treatment of the early nineteenth-century reforms, the forces producing them, and the forces restraining them, see Sherry Gorelick, "We Are Climbing Carnegie's Ladders."

15. E. Digby Baltzell, *The Protestant Establishment,* pp. 339–352; Christopher Jencks and David Riesman, *The Academic Revolution,* chaps. 1 and 3; C. Wright Mills, *The Power Elite,* chap. 3; G. William Domhoff, *Who Rules America?,* pp. 16–22; Antonio Gramsci, *The Modern Prince and Other Writings,* pp. 118, 127.

16. See Herbert Gutman, *Work, Culture and Society in Industrializing America,* pp. 3–76, esp. pp. 18, 68.

17. Jeremy Brecher, *Strike!,* chaps. 1–4, esp. pp. 5–12; 76–78.

18. James Weinstein, *The Decline of Socialism in America,* p. 103.

19. Most of the lands were "free" by virtue of military conquest. "Land grants" were part of the involuntary contribution by "American Indians" to non-native wealth, furthering the process of native impoverishment. By the end of the nineteenth century, three-quarters of the native population was destroyed, in what may be termed the United States attempt at a "final solution" of the Indian problem. Protestant denominations aided the process of absorbing new territories through missionary work and college founding in the West. See James Findlay, "The Congregationalists and American Education," pp. 449–453. Consequently, if accumulation through land grants aided the colleges, the

college land grants also aided in securing acquired territory, helping to nail down land won through colonial expansion, attracting settlers, and thereby helping the railroads to prosper. See Fred Albert Shannon, *The Farmer's Last Frontier*, (New York, Farrar and Rinehart, 1945) pp. 52–65; Rudolph, *The American College and University*, pp. 247–263, and Lawrence Veysey, *The Emergence of the American University*, p. 70.

20. Rudolph, *The American College and University*, p. 244; Veysey, *Emergence of the American University*, p. 3.

21. Andrew Carnegie, "Wealth," pp. 653, 656, 657.

22. Ibid., pp. 656–657, 660, 661, 663.

23. Charles Eliot, then president of Harvard, was among the twenty-two college presidents (and three bankers) on the board. See Henry J. Perkinson, *The Imperfect Panacea*, p. 137.

24. David Horowitz, "Billion Dollar Brains: How Wealth Puts Knowledge in Its Pocket," p. 303; Perkinson, *The Imperfect Panacea*, chap. 4.

25. See Richard F. W. Whittemore, "Nicholas Murray Butler and Public Education," chap. 7; Smith, *Who Rules the Universities?* chap. 5; and Harold Wechsler, *The Qualified Student*, Chaps. 4, 5, and 6.

26. David B. Potts, "American Colleges in the Nineteenth Century," p. 374. Potts questions the effectiveness of Carnegie funds in breaking denominational control, but Bruce Leslie, "Localism, Denominationalism, and Institutional Strategies in Urbanizing America," pp. 248-249, shows that the combined effect of the Carnegie Fund and Rockefeller's General Education Board was considerable.

27. Horowitz, "Billion Dollar Brains," p. 302.

28. Milton Mankoff points out in his essay on "The Knowledge Industry" (in Mankoff, *The Poverty of Progress*, pp. 289–297) that U. S. government funding for research, when it became available in the 1960s, went predominantly to the same "lead institutions." This history points out the limitations of a purely behavioristic approach to prestige, which asks people which institutions or occupations have prestige and then tries to explain their answers in terms of their values. This approach fails by looking at respondents' valuations while failing to examine the historical processes and material conditions which make it more likely that certain institutions (or occupations) will be seen as more prestigious. The fact that prestige is both a reflection and a mechanism of power is discussed in Max Weber's famous but often misinterpreted essay, "Class, Status and Party," in *From Max Weber: Essays In Sociology*, ed. H. H. Gerth and C. Wright Mills.

29. Technically speaking, with respect to the creation of public "ladders," the Carnegie Foundation innovations had actually been preceded in the Midwest by the University of Michigan's certification program, which admitted graduates of those public schools that had been certified as offering instruction suitable as college preparation. The purpose of this certification program was to free the universities to operate on the

German university model of research and higher scholarship by shifting college prepatory work from the university to the lower public schools. See Rudolph, *The American College and University,* pp. 282–286.

30. Linda Schneider concludes on the basis of her detailed and painstaking study of workers' consciousness that "in general it appears that in the 1870s iron and coal workers were not highly preoccupied with mobility other than mobility within their own craft based on the evaluation of their peers. They were not oriented toward management-controlled career ladders." See her unpublished Ph.D. dissertation, "Workmen and Citizens," chap. VI.

31. Phillip R. V. Curoe, *Educational Attitudes and Policies of Organized Labor in the United States,* p. 98.

32. Perkinson, *The Imperfect Panacea,* pp. 103–106; Brecher, *Strike!,* chaps. 1 and 3; James Weinstein, *The Corporate Ideal in the Liberal State,* pp. 191–195.

33. Horowitz, "Billion Dollar Brains," p. 298.

34. Stephen Steinberg, *The Academic Melting Pot,* p. 168.

Chapter 4: The Rise and Reform of City College

1. Women were admitted to the extension division in 1910, and to various schools established after the turn of the century, for example the School of Education, the School of Technology, and the School of Business. (The latter excluded women between 1934 and 1936.) After 1870, young women could attend the Normal College, later named Hunter College. But women were not admitted to the College of Arts and Sciences, the core undergraduate school of CCNY, until 1950. See Israel E. Levine, "Coeds on the Campus," *The Alumnus* 48, no. 1 (October 1952) pp. 8–10. (*The Alumnus* succeeded *The City College Quarterly.*)

2. S. Willis Rudy, *The College of the City of New York,* p. 13. Karl Marx's influence was not as confined to the "Old World" as Rudy's statement seems to imply. In 1852 Joseph Weydeymer, a close associate of Marx and Engels, began publishing a German revolutionary newspaper in New York City. Although only two issues appeared, the first was entirely devoted to Marx's *Eighteenth Brumaire of Louis Bonaparte,* which was not to be published in Europe until seventeen years later.

3. Philip S. Foner, *History of the Labor Movement in the United States,* vol. 1, pp. 130–140; Sydney Jackson, *America's Struggle for Free Public Schools,* part 5, esp. pp. 165–169.

4. *Report of the Select Committee Appointed to Inquire into the Application of That Part of the Literature Fund Which Is Apportioned by the Regents of the University to the City and County of New York* (New York, 1847), pp. 1–9. Cited in Rudy, *The College of the City of New York,* p. 12.

5. Ellwood Cubberly, *Public Education in the United States,* pp. 376–377, 245–248, 255.

6. This combination was not as unusual as it may seem. Rudolph notes, "Some colleges had of necessity found themselves in the preparatory business at the very beginning. Insisting upon erecting colleges that neither need nor intelligence justified, college governing boards often had the choice of giving up or of taking any student who came along and starting with him at whatever point his ignorance required. The result was that . . . it had become the classical academy as well as the college for the district that it served." See Frederick Rudolph, *The Ameican College and University*, p. 282.

7. See Joseph S. Wood, "A Comparison Between the Courses of Study at the College of the City of New York and Yale University," and Rudy, *The College of the City of New York*, p. 23.

8. Cited in Rudy, *The College of the City of New York*, p. 33.

9. Although it is possible that Benedict was defending the Free Academy's right to be equal to any private academy or college, the content of his defense presupposed the different destinies of those with different class origins.

10. Rudy, *The College of the City of New York*, pp. 164–165, 229.

11. Phillip J. Mosenthal and Charles F. Horne, *The City College*.

12. On the differing college milieus of schools populated by working-class and middle-class students, see Arthur B. Shostak, *Blue-Collar Life*, chaps. 9 and 10.

13. *The College Journal*, 17 October 1887, pp. 34–41, cited in Rudy, *The College of the City of New York*, p. 195.

14. Rudy, *The College of the City of New York*, p. 82.

15. The reader will note that the first graduating class of City College, in 1853, had a higher proportion of students entering the ministry than did Columbia, but within a handful of years both the number and proportion of City College graduates becoming clergy declined much faster than at Columbia. The tables are based on the "academic department" of Columbia. If data on "all departments" of Columbia University were used instead, the contrasts would be even more extreme.

16. Rudy, *The College of the City of New York*, pp. 203–204.

17. Ibid., p. 171; Rudolph, *The American College and University*, p. 302. Of the 97 institutions, 34 "offered courses of study that were between 50 percent and 70 percent elective, and . . . 51 or over half offered courses that were less than 50 percent elective." Yale freed upperclassmen entirely from course requirements in 1901. But at Yale and elsewhere this freedom was restrained by sequence or graded courses, grouping and requirements in concentration and distribution.

   At CCNY in 1901 juniors and seniors were permitted to select special subjects, and entering students were to select from five distinct, but internally prescribed, courses of study.

18. Letter to R. R. Bowker cited in Rudy, *The College of the City of New York*, p. 163.

19. The Yale *Report,* p. 315.
20. Rudy, *The College of the City of New York,* p. 224.
21. The term *demonstration project* is of course anachronistic, but the process which the term describes is not. An analogy may be made between the use of demonstration projects and the process by which large businesses allow small businesses to take the risks of experimentation and research, and then buy up the successful survivors.
22. "Climbing capitalization and titanic mergers drew the country's industrial leaders to Wall Street, and adopted and native New Yorkers came to own or control much of American industry. Of the 185 largest industrial combinations in the nation at the turn of the century, 69 . . . had their main offices in New York." (Moses Rischin, *The Promised City,* pp. 5–6.)
23. James Weinstein, *The Corporate Ideal in the Liberal State,* chap. 4.
24. In addition to public resentment, the Progressive defeat was due to a split in the Progressive vote, when the Citizens Union nominated Seth Low, and the Republicans nominated Benjamin F. Tracy. See Gustavus Myers, *The History of Tammany Hall,* p. 282.
25. Richard F. W. Whittemore, "Nicholas Murray Butler and Public Education," p. 139.
26. David Hammack, "The Centralization of New York City's Public School System, 1896," p. 76.
27. The development of the Normal College (later to be called Hunter College) is discussed in Chapter 5.
28. It was typical for colleges and academies to oppose the development of high schools. See Cubberly, *Public Education,* p. 260.
29. Hammack, "New York City's Public School System," p. 10.
30. Ibid., p. 104. In theory the "melting pot" was to be an egalitarian and voluntary melding of all racial and ethnic groups. In practice it often served as an ideological cover for forced assimilation.
31. Hewitt, cited in Ibid., p. 27.
32. Not all CCNY Progressives supported centralization. For example, Edward Lauterbach, an important figure in the Republican Party and a major force in the Progressive transformation of CCNY, was strongly opposed to centralization. See Hammack, "New York City's Public School System," pp. 92, 103.
33. Ibid., p. 80.
34. Reverend Rainsford, member of the Committee of One Hundred, cited in Ibid., p. 92.
35. Ibid., pp. 21–22, 52. See also Diane Ravitch, *The Great School Wars,* p. 135.
36. Letter from Butler to Garrett A. Hobart, 16 December 1893, in Whittemore, "Nicholas Murray Butler," pp. 120–121.
37. Hammack, "New York City's Public School System," p. 4.

38. Ibid., p. 110.
39. Manual workers made up only 4 percent of the members of the school boards of 104 U. S. cities, according to a study by Scott Nearing. Clerical workers were only 5 percent, while businessmen were 45 percent. See "Who's Who on Our Boards of Education," *School and Society* 5 (January 1917), cited in Samuel Bowles and Herbert Gintis, *Schooling in Capitalist America*.
40. Until 1904 the Regents were appointed for life by the State Legislature. They were for at least some time dominated by the Trustees of Columbia University, and showed a distinct proclivity for private schooling. The reforms promulgated by the Progressives over the years involved reorganizing the Regents, reducing their tenure to eleven years, and expanding their power over the public schools. See Frank C. Abbott, *Government Policy and Higher Education*, p. 53. See also pp. 11–12, 39-40, 63-64, 89 and chaps. 2-4, *passim*, and Whittemore, "Nicholas Murray Butler," pp. 147–161.
41. Rudy, *The College of the City of New York*, p. 231.
42. After some negotiation, the three sub-freshman years at CCNY were treated as equivalent to four years of high school because of the more intensive character of the College's preparatory program.
43. The Dartmouth College case of 1819 is generally known as having established the legal rights of corporations as "persons." The decision had wide implications for higher education as well. According to Rudolph, *The American College and University* (pp. 207–212, esp. p. 211) the decision established the rights of private trustees against public authorities, "and put the American college beyond the control of popular prejudice and passion; it assured the further alienation of the people from the colleges" and it endorsed "the American principle of academic organization whereby control resides not in the hands of the faculty but in an external board."
44. Rudy, *The College of the City of New York*, p. 209.
45. Ibid., p. 235.
46. Ibid., p. 236.
47. *Minutes of the Board of Trustees*, CCNY, 1900, pp. 17–20 (CCNY archives).
48. Rudy, *The College of the City of New York*, pp. 236–238.
49. Among them were *The French in the Heart of America* (New York: Charles Scribner's Sons, 1915); *The Coming of the Scot* (New York: Charles Scribner's Sons, 1940); and *A Pilgrim in Palestine: Being an Account of Journeys on Foot by the First American Pilgrim after General Allenby's Recovery of the Holy Land* (New York: Charles Scribner's Sons, 1919). Finley was also the organizer of the first *Dictionary of American Biography* in 1928. He also wrote "A Tribute to Jacob H. Schiff," a poem appearing with Schiff's portrait in the Chamber of

Commerce of the State of New York. See Cyrus Adler, *Jacob H. Schiff*, vol. 1, pp. 323–324.

50. Marvin E. Gettleman, "John H. Finley at CCNY—1903–1913," pp. 430, 434–435.

51. Rudy, *The College of the City of New York*, pp. 281–283.

52. For the control aspects of formally free academic careers, see David Horowitz, "Billion Dollar Brains," in *The Poverty of Progress: The Political Economy of American Social Problems*, ed. Milton Mankoff, pp. 305–306; and Theodore Caplow and Reece McGee, "The American Academic Marketplace," in A. H. Halsey, Jean Floud, and C. Arnold Anderson, eds., *Education, Economy and Society*, pp. 589–601.

53. In Mosenthal and Horne, *The City College*, p. 548. He was actually quoting James Bryce, who had made the remark on a visit to the campus.

54. Statement of the Society for the Diffusion of Knowledge among the Working Classes, Philadelphia, 1835, as quoted in Foner, *History of the Labor Movement*, vol. 1, pp. 115n.

55. Bureau of Jewish Social Research, "Professional Tendencies Among Jewish Students in Colleges, Universities, and Professional Schools," p. 388 and calculations made from data on pp. 388 and 386.

56. Stephen Steinberg, *The Academic Melting Pot*, pp. 25, 11, 26 (citing Lawrence Veysey, *The Emergence of the American University*, p. 238, and Lewis S. Gannett, "Is America Anti-Semitic?" in *The Nation*, vol. 115, 14 March 1923, p. 331).

Chapter 5: The Creation of Occupational Opportunity

1. See Isaeque Graeber and Stewart Britt, eds., *Jews in a Gentile World*, p. 408; Bailey B. Burritt, "Professional Distribution of College and University Graduates (1912)," pp. 77, 78; Mortimer Karpp, "Vocations of College Men, 1849–1934," pp. 158–160; B'nai B'rith Vocational Service, *Jewish Youth in College*, pp. 9–10; Nathan Goldberg, "Occupational Patterns of American Jews" (April 1945), p. 12.

   Many contemporary observers commented on the number of Eastern Jews going into the teaching profession. See Norman Hapgood, "Schools, Colleges and Jews," New York *Herald*, Magazine Section, (Sunday, 26 November 1905), p. 3; Isaac M. Rubinow, "Economic and Industrial Condition: New York," in *The Russian Jew in America*, ed. Charles Bernheimer, p. 107.

   According to Goldberg teachers were almost a quarter of the Russian Jewish professionals in the 1900 U.S. census; they were the largest category of professionals. The Bureau of Jewish Social Research (1920–1921) data for 1918–1919 show teaching to be primarily a profession for Jewish female college graduates; they reported that Jewish male graduates were less likely than non-Jewish male graduates to enter teaching. All three of these sources are for the United States as a whole. The 1918 and 1935 studies would include both German and Russian Jews. Gutman shows teachers as second only to doctors among male Jews on the Lower East Side in 1905. See Herbert Gutman, *The Black Family in Slavery and Freedom*, p. 528.

2. Phillip R. V. Curoe, *Educational Attitudes and Policies of Organized Labor in the United States*, chaps. 2, 4; David Hogan, "Education and the Making of the Chicago Working Class, 1880–1930," pp. 232–245, esp. pp. 232–234.

3. Mary Stevenson Callcott, *Child Labor Legislation in New York*, p. 252.

4. John T. Buchanan, "How to Assimilate the Foreign Element in Our Population," p. 688.

5. U.S. Bureau of Education *Bulletin*, no. 11 (1920); Forest C. Ensign, *Compulsory School Attendance and Child Labor*, pp. 119, 118.

6. Ensign, *Compulsory School Attendance*, pp. 120, 121, 143–151; Callcott, *Child Labor Legislation*, pp. 21, 252; A. Emerson Palmer, *The New York Public School*, pp. 167, 312.

7. Buchanan, "How to Assimilate the Foreign Element," p. 693.

8. Walter Laidlaw, *Statistical Sources for Demographic Studies of Greater New York*, vol. 1, p. 5.

9. Diane Ravitch, *The Great School Wars*, p. 180.

10. Data compiled from Palmer, *The New York Public School*, pp. 161, 193, 195, 248, and 316; and the *Journal of the Board of Education of the City of New York*, 1925, Board of Education Professional Library.

11. Burritt, "Professional Distribution," pp. 19, 77.

12. Lotus Delta Coffman, *The Social Composition of the Teaching Population*, pp. 54, 65.

13. Ibid., pp. 31–36. These averages are undoubtedly influenced by the inclusion of rural schools. The school system of New York City, although basically exemplifying national trends and relationships, had its own particular variations. In capsule, the City led in certification and unionization, trailed in the development of the high school and probably trailed in feminization. See Walter A. Jessup, *The Teaching Staff*, pp. 42, 54.

14. Coffman, *Social Composition of the Teaching Population*, p. 65; Charles Seligman Bernheimer, ed., *The Russian Jew in America*, p. 191; Joseph Van Denburg, *Causes of the Elimination of Students from the Secondary Schools of New York City*; pp. 46–47, and pt. 7; Leonard Covello, *The Teacher in the Urban Community*, chaps. 5 and 6.

15. Van Denburg himself suggests this link. His data are based on a 1906 questionnaire survey of high school freshmen. I have used data on his pp. 49–68, basing my calculations on those with definite occupational aspirations and on brothers and sisters with known occupational destinies. One caveat as to this procedure is in order: girls who stayed in school tended to be older daughters with dead fathers. They stayed in high school in order to become teachers and support their families. Boys who stayed in school tended to be the youngest brothers; their older

siblings had gone to work so that they might stay in school. Consequently the boys might not have uniformly followed the paths of their older brothers. (Morris Raphael Cohen's older brother Sam went to work while Morris continued elementary school and college; see Morris Raphael Cohen, *A Dreamer's Journey*, pp. 77, 91.)

16. Ellwood Cubberly, *Public Education in the United States*, pp. 390–391.
17. Coffman, *Social Composition of the Teaching Population*, p. 54.
18. Cubberly, *Public Education*, p. 384, fig. 107.
19. Ibid., pp. 384, 400; Richard F. W. Whittemore, "Nicholas Murray Butler and Public Education," p. 65; Anonymous, *An Historical Sketch of the State Normal College at Albany, New York and a History of Its Graduates for Fifty Years*; Lawrence A. Cremin, *The Transformation of the School*, p. 169.
20. Coffman, *Social Composition of the Teaching Population*, p. 77; Walter A. Jessup, *The Social Factors Affecting Special Supervision in the Public Schools of the United States*, p. 112.
21. Cremin, *The Transformation of the School*, p. 175; Whittemore, "Nicholas Murray Butler," p. 63.
22. Whittemore, "Nicholas Murray Butler," pp. 62–63.
23. Ibid., pp. 86, 89, 97–98.
24. Herbert G. Gutman, *Work, Culture, and Society in Industrializing America*, p. 68–69.
25. Cremin, *The Transformation of the School*, p. 33.
26. Curoe, *Educational Attitudes*, p. 84, citing an editorial in *Journal of United Labor*, 14 May 1887; p. 163, citing "Manual and Technical Education," *American Federationist*, 11 (1895), pp. 82ff.; p. 164, citing "Address of President Van Cleave before the National Society for Promotion of Industrial Education," 1908; and pp. 112 and 164 citing a speech by Samuel Gompers in *History, Encyclopedia and Reference Book* of the American Federation of Labor, p. 209. Businessmen backed up their interest in manual training by insuring its adoption in the public schools. As we have already seen, the F. W. Devoe Company rescued manual training from the attack of the classicists at CCNY by establishing commencement prizes for the best wood and metal work. Jessup, *The Social Factors*, chap. 12, esp. pp. 112–114, notes that many of the new programs introduced into the public schools in the early twentieth century owed their existence to the initial financial support of "private interests," chiefly business. Once these innovations were adopted, they became part of the school budget and were publicly financed. Business continued to reap the gains at no further cost.

The Baron de Hirsch Fund pioneered in manual training as part of the effort to "productivize" the Jews, turn their overabundant peddlers into proletarians, and ensure that they did not become "public wards." There was also a Baronness de Hirsch Training School for Girls. The Trade

School trained the boys to become plumbers, carpenters, sign painters, machinists, and electricians. The Training School taught girls millinery, cooking, washing, machine operating, hand sewing, and dressmaking. See J. K. Paulding, "Educational Influences: New York," in Bernheimer, *The Russian Jew in America*, pp. 194–195. Many of these activities were later taken over by the Educational Alliance.

27. Nicholas Murray Butler, "The Beginnings of Teachers College," p. 345.

28. Current theorists see the manual training movement as the beginning of an effort systematically to stratify public education according to class, as well as to use public education to train manpower both politically and technically. See, for example, David Cohen and Marvin Lazerson, "Education and the Labor Force," in R. Edwards, M. Reich, and T. Weisskopf, eds., *The Capitalist System*. See also C. Karier, "Elite Views in American Education," in Walter Laqueur and George L. Mosse, eds., *Education and Social Structure in the Twentieth Century*. A similar analysis was made by Norton Grubb at the New Haven History Conference, March, 1973. Samuel Bowles and Herbert Gintis, *Schooling in Capitalist America*, pp. 191–195, analyze vocationalism in a similar light.

29. John Higham, *Strangers in the Land*, p. 243. See also chap. 9, "Crusade for Americanization," passim, but especially p. 247. In the great 1950s Jewish tercentenary celebration, B. Halpern rejoiced that "America is Different" (in Sklare, *The Jews*, pp. 23–39). Assimilation in America, he said, has been a question of "freedom," of "give and take." "In America [unlike France] there was no urgency about the procedure [of Emancipation]. The Jews, like other immigrants, could make their way into the real American community as swiftly or as slowly as they themselves chose. They could, if they preferred, remain in their ghetto seclusion indefinitely" (pp. 30, 31). For the contrary experience of one who lived through this alleged expansive voluntarism in the 1920s, see Robert A. Carlson, "Americanization As An Early Twentieth-Century Adult Education Movement," p. 456. The quote beginning "every schoolhouse . . ." is from Governor Roswell P. Flower, quoted in Rudy, *The College of the City of New York*, p. 213.

30. Morris Isaiah Berger, "The Settlement, the Immigrant and the Public School," p. 117.

31. See Covello, *The Teacher in the Urban Community*, chaps. 14, 17, p. 118.

32. Cited by C. H. Grabo in Oscar Handlin, ed., *Immigration as a Factor in American History*, p. 155.

33. See, for example, Hannah Margaret Harris, *Lessons in Civics for the Elementary Grades of City Schools*.

34. John J. Mahoney, "Training Teachers for Americanization," p. 9.

35. Isaac Rosengarten, "The Jewish Teacher in the New York Public Schools," p. 328.

36. Ibid., pp. 336, 325. The case caused a public outcry, drawing comment

from John Dewey, Charles A. Beard, and the New York *Evening Post*, among others. As a result, the decision was reversed.

37. Coffman, *Social Composition of the Teaching Population*, p. 82.

38. Walter A. Jessup, *The Social Factors*, p. 110; Margery Davies, "Women's Place is at the Typewriter," pp. 250–252.

Farm labor and domestic service were the two occupations most common for women from 1870 through 1920, when teaching supplanted farm labor as one of the two most common women's occupations. See U.S. Bureau of the Census, *Historical Statistics of the United States from Colonial Times to the Present*, pp. 167–188; and Rosalyn Baxendall, et al, eds., *America's Working Women*, pp. 406–407.

39. David Hammack, "The Centralization of New York City's Public School System, 1896," p. 10.

40. Raymond Callahan, *Education and the Cult of Efficiency*, pp. 86–87, citing Franklin Bobbitt, *The Supervision of City Schools: Some General Principles of Management Applied to the Problems of City-School Systems*, "Twelfth Yearbook of the National Society for the Study of Education," part I, (Bloomington, Ill., 1913), pp. 51–52.

41. Beginning around 1905 the center of professional educational administration was Teachers College. There George Strayer promulgated the business model of educational administration, while fellow graduate Ellwood Cubberly united his zeal for centralization with his zeal for coercive Americanization, and E. L. Thorndike fostered a measurement movement which served both educational Taylorism and social Darwinism.

Beyond their direct influence and their specific programs, the men at Teachers College had a profound, general cultural impact in establishing the idea of the school administrator as a professional. Beyond Cubberly, Thorndike, and Strayer (and of course the perennial influence of Butler), Teachers College's influence included the work of Coffman, whose concern over the social origins of teachers was expressed in his dissertation; Van Denberg, whose dissertation presented a manual training-oriented critique of the New York high school dropout rate, and who was to become a member of the Board of Examiners; as well as Dushkin, Benderly, and the eighteen others at the Jewish Bureau of Education who sought to apply scientific social efficiency to the Talmud Torahs. By the 1920s Columbia had established Columbia House, which offered a comprehensive program of Americanization courses for teachers. (See John J. Mahoney, "Training Teachers for Americanization.") Thus professional pedagogy as both philosophy and practice, and the social control and socialization of the professional socializers were strongly and manifoldly influenced by Teachers College, the leading institution in education.

42. On school management see Raymond Callahan's exhaustive study,

Education and the Cult of Efficiency. On Taylorism in industry and clerical work, see Harry Braverman, *Labor and Monopoly Capital.* For the division within Progressivism on the Gary plan, see Diane Ravitch, *The Great School Wars,* chaps. 17 and 18.

43. I am grateful to Ms. Cathryn O'Dea, Librarian of the New York Board of Education, for this information.

44. See Curoe, *Educational Attitudes and Policies of Organized Labor,* pp. 137–142; Josephine H. McGurk, "History of the Department and School of Education of the College of the City of New York," p. 74.

45. See Callahan, *Education and the Cult of Efficiency,* pp. 120–121.

46. A. Emerson Palmer, *The New York Public School,* pp. 112, 143.

47. S. Willis Rudy, *The College of the City of New York,* p. 1.

48. Cubberly, *Public Education in the United States,* p. 250.

49. Palmer, *The New York Public School,* pp. 327–328.

50. Ibid., pp. 328–329; Curoe, *Educational Attitudes and Policies of Organized Labor,* p. 80.

51. Palmer, *The New York Public School,* pp. 330, 349–350; Rudy, *The College of the City of New York,* pp. 134–135, 229–230.

52. Magnus Gross, "The College of the City of New York: Some of Its Real Functions." *City College Alumni Quarterly,* December 30, 1904, pp. 2–3.

53. Ibid., p. 4. Gross does not express any fears of competition from the Normal College. I presume that male advantage protected the graduates of City College from the Normal College graduates.

54. Ibid., p. 3.

55. Ibid., p. 4.

56. Stephen Duggan, "The Department of Education," p. 29. Morris Raphael Cohen had studied pedagogy with Duggan in 1899–1900, Cohen's senior year at CCNY. M. R. Cohen, *A Dreamer's Journey,* p. 93.

57. Duggan, "The Department of Education," p. 28.

58. Ibid., pp. 28–30.

59. Ibid., p. 29.

60. Ibid., p. 31. Emphasis added.

61. Stephen P. Duggan, *A Student's Textbook in the History of Education* (1936), pp. viii-ix. In his 1916 preface Duggan explains that the text was the result of the syllabus he developed for his classes in History of Education both for CCNY undergraduates and in extension courses for teachers. His 1927 preface notes revisions to bring the history "down to date" with respect to the educational systems of Russia, Germany, and Italy. It would appear then that the rest of the book reflects Duggan's views up to 1916—of course as constructed by him around 1916.

62. Ibid., pp. 302–303.

63. Duggan, "The Department of Education," p. 30.

64. See *School of Education Bulletin* 1911–1913, 1916–1927.

65.   R. R. Bowker, "The College of the Past," in Philip J. Mosenthal and Charles F. Horne, *The City College*, p. 20; S. Willis Rudy, *The College of the City of New York*, p. 229.

66.   McGurk, "History of the Department and School of Education of the College of the City of New York," p. 74.

67.   See *City College Quarterly*, vol. 1–16. Note that the first volume was called *The City College Alumni Quarterly*; the word *Alumni* was removed in subsequent volumes. (CCNY archives.)

68.   See Frederick Rudolph, *American College and University*, p. 176.

69.   Joseph Van Denburg, *Causes of the Elimination of Students from the Secondary Schools of New York City 1906–1910*, pp. 46–47, and pt. 7.

70.   Curoe, *Educational Attitudes and Policies of Organized Labor*, pp. 137–150, esp. p. 142.

71.   Coffman, *The Social Composition of the Teaching Population*, p. 83. Emphasis added.

72.   Rabbi Silverman, "The Hebrew Educational Fair," *American Hebrew*, December 6, 1889, p. 119, quoted above, p. 30.

73.   See Covello, *The Teacher in the Urban Community* (Mario Cosenza of City College helped Covello to get the Board of Education to pass a by-law giving Italian equal recognition as a foreign language within the city schools), pp. 135–136; Ravitch, *The Great School Wars*, p. 224; and Irving Howe, *World of Our Fathers*, p. 280.

Chapter 6: Jobs and Schooling of the Jewish Poor

1.   Abraham Cahan, *The Rise of David Levinsky*, pp. 168–169.

2.   Thomas Kessner, *The Golden Door*, chaps. 3–4; Herbert Gutman, *The Black Family in Slavery and Freedom*, appendix B; Lloyd Gartner, "The Jews of New York's East Side," pp. 264–275 (Gartner presents the Baron de Hirsch Fund study). Also Ben Seligman, "The Jewish Population of New York City: 1952," in Sklare, *The Jews*, pp. 94–106; Simon Kuznets, "Economic Structure and Life of the Jews," pp. 1635–1640 (Kuznets presents the New York State Census results); Jacob Lestchinsky, "The Economic and Social Development of American Jewry," esp. pp. 75–85, 93–95.

3.   Nathan Goldberg, "Occupational Patterns of American Jews," pp. 14, 15.

4.   Seligman, "The Jewish Population," p. 101.

5.   "The Jewish worker in America was typically a man of one generation: he was 'neither the son nor the father' of a proletarian. In the 'old country,' his father, or he himself, had most probably been a petty merchant or artisan; in this country he had become a factory worker; his son and daughter, however, were not following him into the factory or trade, but were going into business, office work, or the professions" (Will Herberg, "The Jewish Labor Movement in the U.S.," p. 53).

6.   An unknown proportion of these offspring are themselves immigrants,

and hence technically "first generation." We have no data systematically tracing the occupations of American-born children of East European Jewish immigrant parents. In Chapter 5 of *The Golden Door*, Kessner traces a very small subsample of individuals from 1880 through 1892 and 1905. He shows considerable upward (and downward) mobility for both Italian and Jewish household heads and their offspring. Those data are the only statistics which approach a rigorous test of the common assertions about intergenerational mobility, and they fall far short of the celebratory claims. Had Kessner been able to trace the offspring later in life, they might have shown more movement out of manual trades. The point is that we have no data adequate to affirm or deny this conjecture.

7. Ibid., pp. 91, 111. Read these words with caution, however. Kessner's distinctions between skilled, semi-skilled, and unskilled labor (I have simply aggregated them in my text) are based on Abba Edward's classification system. Edward's system has been extensively criticized by Harry Braverman, in *Labor and Monopoly Capital*, pp. 428–432, for elaborating false distinctions. According to Gutman, *The Black Family in Slavery and Freedom* (p. 527), fully 73 percent of New York Jewish males were manual workers in 1905. Gutman used the same manuscript census as Kessner, but he surveyed *every* household in selected blocks, while Kessner surveyed every *fifth* household in a stratified sample. Their categories also differ: Gutman's data refer to all males, but males only; Kessner counts household heads, sons, and daughters. Occupational categories differ as well. The resulting statistics are quite discrepant from one another, but neither set contradicts the general analysis which I make in the text.

8. For some of the effects of the seasonal unemployment in the garment industry, see John Laslett, "Jewish Socialism and the Ladies Garment Workers of New York," in his *Labor and the Left*, pp. 102, 104.

9. Seymour Martin Lipset and Reinhard Bendix, *Social Mobility in Industrial Society*, p. 60; Sherry Gorelick, "Jewish Success and the Great American Celebration; pp. 46–47. Seligman, "The Jewish Population of New York," in Sklare, *The Jews*, pp. 94–106; and B. W. Seligman and Aaron Antonovsky, "Some Aspects of Jewish Demography," in Sklare, *The Jews*, pp. 45–93.

10. Lestchinsky, "The Economic and Social Development of American Jewry," pp. 81, 83.

11. Kessner, *The Golden Door*, p. 110.

12. "Among the first generation immigrants it was not medicine, law, or even their vaunted thirst for education that carried them forward. It was business" (Kessner, *The Golden Door*, p. 65). According to Gutman, in *The Black Family* (p. 528), only 3 percent of Jewish males were in "high enterprise." The difference undoubtedly hinges on the classification of "high enterprise."

13. Lestchinsky, "American Jewry," pp. 79–88, esp. p. 88; Gorelick, "Jewish

Success," pp. 41–43; Goldberg, "Occupational Patterns," pp. 21–22; The Editors of Fortune, *Jews in America*, pp. 34–48.

14. On the growth of clerical and sales occupations see Braverman, *Labor and Monopoly Capital*, chaps. 13, 15, 16.

15. Kuznets, "Economic Structure," p. 1639; Goldberg, "Occupational Patterns," pp. 12–13; Kessner, *The Golden Door*, p. 91.

16. Kessner's data in *The Golden Door*, presented in terms of status categories, lumps big businessmen with professionals in a "higher white collar," category. He has very kindly and painstakingly given me the raw data on professionals, on which these calculations and the following information is based. Kessner points out that offspring who became professionals may have tended to be older, and to have left the household. They would then not appear in the census enumeration. They should, however, show up as heads or members of *other* households. When I recalculated the percentages combining generations, the proportion of professionals remained extremely small. The 1900 statistics are taken from Lestchinsky, "American Jewry," p. 82. Gutman, *The Black Family* (p. 528) found that 4 percent of Jewish males were in professional occupations in 1905.

17. Lestchinsky, "American Jewry," p. 82; Thomas Kessner, private communication. On males, see Gutman, *The Black Family*, p. 528.

18. Nathan Goldberg presented statistics gathered by others in "Occupational Patterns of American Jews" in the 1920s (p. 162), but the studies he compiled generally exclude New York City, and the one which includes New York State among five other states has data Goldberg himself considered questionable.

19. Lestchinsky, "American Jewry," p. 83.

20. Kuznets, "Economic Structure," p. 1637.

21. Although the 1930s migrations were smaller, and thus less likely to distort the overall figures, the numbers of professionals had been small in any case, and thus might have been affected by even minor additions from immigration. Further investigation is needed in order to tell.

22. Lestchinsky, "American Jewry," p. 93. The depression caused even more unemployment among Jews than among non-Jews. Almost one-quarter of the whole labor force was still unemployed or only partially employed by 1937. Had unemployed workers been included in the data, the proportion of New York Jews in the working class would undoubtedly have been much larger. Nathan Goldberg notes that "unemployed Jewish workers began to engage in petty trade," experiencing, no doubt, more banana-wagon mobility. By 1937 both domestic service and professional occupations had increased substantially. See Goldberg, "Occupational Patterns of American Jews," pp. 169–175.

23. Irving Howe, *World of Our Fathers*, p. 144.

24. Selma C. Berrol, *Immigration and the New York City Schools*, p. 86; Colin Greer, *The Great School Legend*, p. 118.

25. Selma C. Berrol, "Education and Economic Mobility," p. 260. M. R. Cohen was able to leap over these strict promotion policies enforced by *each* school, by moving from school to school. That was before school centralization coordinated school records. See M. R. Cohen, *A Dreamer's Journey*, pp. 70–71, 77–78, 82.
26. Berrol, *Immigration and New York City Schools*, pp. 200, 208, 201, 65.
27. Julia Richman, "A Social Need of the Public School," pp. 161–169, esp. pp. 164–168.
28. Ibid., pp. 65, 321, 230; Greer, *The Great School Legend*, pp. 116, 179.
29. Berrol, *Immigrants and New York City Schools*, pp. 120–121.
30. Howe, *World of Our Fathers*, pp. 278, 277.
31. On child labor in the garment and "tenement-home industry," see Mary Stevenson Callcott, *Child Labor Legislation in New York*, pp. 195–200; Isaac M. Rubinow, "Economic and Industrial Condition: New York," in Charles Seligman Bernheimer, *The Russian Jew in the United States*, p. 120; Isaac A. Hourwich, *Immigration and Labor*, p. 319; Melech Epstein, *Jewish Labor in U.S.A.*, vol. 1, p. 103; Berrol, "Education and Economic Mobility," pp. 262–263; See also the photographs of child labor taken by Jacob Riis and housed in the Photographic Archives of the Museum of the City of New York. The very fact that Rubinow could present the wage rates for child labor in the garment industry indicates that a considerable proportion of working-class Jews dropped out of school early, or at least interrupted their attendance.

    On the relationship between child labor and school attendance for other ethnic groups, see David Hogan, "Education and the Making of the Chicago Working Class, 1880–1930." "It was only the compulsion of extreme poverty that led [Italian] parents to take their children from school" (Berrol, "Education and Economic Mobility," pp. 70–71).
32. For discussions of the fate of daughters as compared with sons, see Kessner, *The Golden Door*, p. 91; Marshall Sklare, *America's Jews*, p. 100n.
33. See Moses Rischin, *The Promised City*, p. 200; and Diane Ravitch, *The Great School Wars*, pp. 179–180.
34. Berrol, "Education and Economic Mobility," p. 261.
35. Joseph Van Denburg, *Causes of the Elimination of Students from the Secondary Schools of New York City*, pp. 96–98, 127. Van Denburg's overall data is based on a total sample of 9,186 grammar school graduates and 5,871 high school entrants. The study of national background is based on a special questionnaire study of a carefully selected subsample of 958 students. Unfortunately the study does not include Townsend Harris Hall, which was the high school associated with City College. Boys who wished to attend City College would have applied to Townsend Harris. In the absence of a similar ethnic breakdown of the students attending Townsend Harris, we may surmise that the proportion of Russian Jews would have been larger there, since CCNY was itself

largely Russian Jewish by the time of Van Denburg's study. He does indicate that the other public high schools received a good number of Townsend Harris dropouts.

36. Ibid., p. 78. The figure of 1 percent of elementary school students is obtained by taking 2 percent (the proportion of high school entrants reaching the freshman year of college) of 60 percent (the proportion of elementary school graduates reaching the freshman year of high school). If both Berrol's figures and Van Denberg's were employed, the estimate of the proportion of Russian first graders to enter the freshman year of college would be 0.2 percent, but this method is slightly problematic. Berrol's data, drawn from the U.S. Congress's Immigration Commission study, refers to the distribution of all students in 1908, whereas Van Denberg followed students who were high school freshmen in 1906 and seniors in 1910.

37. These figures are somewhat controversial. Berrol claims, on the basis of an analysis of the CCNY *Alumni Register*, that "the proportion of Russian and Polish names increased from less than 1% in 1883 to 11% in 1923 but German Jewish names out-numbered all others [until the thirties]. Admittedly, establishing origins from surnames is far from exact" ("Education and Economic Mobility," p. 262). Irving Howe, on the other hand, claims, "By 1903 . . . more than 75 percent of the students were Jewish; in the graduating class of 1910 at least 90 of the 112 students were Jewish, and of these the great bulk came from east European families" (*World of Our Fathers*, p. 281). Nevertheless he gives no source for his figures.

38. Howe, *World of Our Fathers*, p. 270.

39. Bureau of Jewish Social Research, "Professional Tendencies Among Jewish Students in Colleges, Universities, and Professional Schools," p. 384.

40. Howe, *World of Our Fathers*, pp. 141–144, using data supplied by Gutman.

41. Stephen Steinberg, *The Academic Melting Pot*, p. 92. Unfortunately Steinberg's data do not distinguish between German and Russian Jews. In addition, since it is based on a nationwide sample, it may not represent the patterning of class transmission and mobility in New York City. But it is the best we have.

42. Berrol, "Education and Economic Mobility," pp. 265, 271. "Most New York City Jews did not make the leap from poverty to the middle class by going to college. Rather, widespread utilization of secondary and higher education *followed* improvements in economic status and was as much a result as a cause of upward mobility." (Author's emphasis.) See also Colin Greer, *The Great School Legend*, pp. 83–86, 95; and Goldberg, "Occupational Patterns," p. 19.

43. Morris Friedman, "The Jewish College Student," p. 301.

44. S. Willis Rudy, *The College of the City of New York*, p. 397.

45. For further discussion of these ideologies see Sherry Gorelick, "Jewish Success and the Great American Celebration," pp. 43–47.
46. Kessner, *The Golden Door*, pp. 52, 60, 79, 107, 110; Gutman, *The Black Family*, p. 527.
47. Steinberg, *The Academic Melting Pot*, pp. 92, 93, 100, 101. Steinberg's study of college faculty does not distinguish among Catholic ethnic groups. Other studies indicate that the Irish were more successful in school than the Italians, and we do not know whether Steinberg's data include more Irish than Italian Catholics.
48. Steinberg, *The Academic Melting Pot*, chaps. 2–5, esp. chap. 4; Lestchinsky, "The Position of the Jews in the Economic Life of America," in Graeber and Britt, *Jews in a Gentile World*, pp. 402–409; Bernard Weinryb, "Jewish Immigration and Accomodation to America," in Sklare, *The Jews*, pp. 4–22; and Francesco Cordasco, *The Italians: Social Background of an Italian Group*, pts. 4 and 5.
49. Steinberg, *Academic Melting Pot*, p. 87.
50. Van Denburg, *Causes of the Elimination of Students*, p. 96.
51. Berrol, *Immigration and the New York City Schools*, p. 71.

Chapter 7: Dominant Culture
1. Milton Gordon, *Assimilation in American Life*, p. 186.
2. S. Joseph Fauman, "Occupational Selection among Detroit Jews," in Sklare, *The Jews: Social Patterns of an American Group*, p. 121.
3. Mariam Slater, "My Son the Doctor" p. 365.
4. Werner J. Cahnman, "A Comment on 'My Son, The Doctor,'" pp. 935–936. Cahnman criticized Slater's sources and methodology.
5. In addition to several books, Freeman wrote the Introduction and contributed two poems to *Proletarian Literature in the United States: An Anthology* (New York: International Publishers, 1935).
6. Joseph Freeman, *An American Testament*, pp. 151–152, 156.
7. Frederick Rudolph, *The American College and University*, pp. 4, 24, 12, 26, 53; James Findlay, "The Congregationalists and American Education," p. 452.
8. David B. Potts, "American Colleges in the Nineteenth Century," W. Bruce Leslie; "Localism, Denominationalism, and Institutional Strategies in Urbanizing America;" David Horowitz, "Billion Dollar Brains," in Milton Mankoff, ed. *The Poverty of Problems*.
9. Christopher Jencks and David Riesman, *The Academic Revolution*, pp. 313–314.
10. Ibid., chaps. 1, 7, 8, 9, and 10.
11. Natalie Naylor, "The Antebellum College Movement," p. 268; Potts, "American Colleges in the Nineteenth Century," pp. 363–375, esp. pp. 363, 373; Findlay, "The Congregationalists," pp. 452–453; Lawrence R. Veysey, *The Emergence of the American University*, pp. 40–50, 203–204; E. Digby Baltzell, *The Protestant Establishment*, chap. V, esp. pp.

113–121 and 127–131, *et passim;* Stephen Steinberg, *The Academic Melting Pot,* chap. 1; Harold S. Wechsler, *The Qualified Student,* chap. 7; Marcia Synnott, *The Half-Opened Door,* chaps. 1–3, 5, 6.

12.   Irving Howe, *World of Our Fathers,* p. 281.

13.   Andrew M. Greeley, *From Backwater to Mainstream,* p. 7.

14.   Irving Louis Horowitz first mentioned this fact to me and suggested its implications for the cultural ambience into which Jewish students entered. The "Directory of Officers," list of "Officers of Administration and Instruction," and list of "The Faculty and Instructing Staff," of the City College *Register,* 1919–1920, overwhelmingly bear him out.

15.   Stephen Duggan, *A Professor At Large,* p. 7; S. Willis Rudy, *The College of the City of New York,* chaps. 18–23, esp. pp. 295, 269; Gettleman, pp. 427–429.

16.   See Frederick Rudolph, *American College and University,* p. 280, and Milton Himmelfarb, "Secular Society? A Jewish Perspective," p. 224.

17.   The American Historical Association was formed in 1884, and The American Economics Association in 1885. The American Political Science Association and the American Sociological Society began in 1905. Many of the major professional journals were established in this period.

18.   See C. Vann Woodward, *The Strange Career of Jim Crow,* chap. 3.

19.   Thomas F. Gossett, *Race: The History of an Idea in America,* p. 84; Oscar Handlin, *Race and Nationality in American Life,* pp. 62–63.

20.   Oscar Handlin, *Race and Nationality in American Life,* p. 91. See also Handlin's excellent critique of the fetishism of measurement in chap. 4, "The Linnaean Web." For the mental acrobatics of psychological testers, see the fascinating account in Gossett, *Race,* pp. 408–429.

21.   Gossett, *Race,* pp. 118–119.

22.   See John T. Buchanan, "How to Assimilate the Foreign Element in Our Population," p. 688; John Higham, *Strangers in the Land,* pp. 29, 169; Gosset, p. 96.

23.   Gossett, *Race,* p. 293; E. A. Ross, *The Old World in the New* (New York: The Century Company, 1914) p. 286, cited by Robert A. Carlson, "Americanization as an Early Twentieth Century Adult Education Movement," p. 446.

24.   Gossett, *Race,* p. 293.

25.   Gossett, *Race,* pp. 34, 375; Anatole Leroy-Beaulieu, *Israel Among the Nations,* p. 191.

26.   E. Digby Baltzell, *The Protestant Establishment,* p. 146; Clarence Karier et al, *Roots of Crisis,* p. 54; Gossett, *Race,* p. 171; Milton Gordon, *Assimilation in American Life,* pp. 283–288. On Sanger's argument that birth control was necessary to produce more children of "the fit, and less of the unfit," see Linda Gordon, *Woman's Body, Woman's Right,* pp. 281–282, 332, 333, 350, and Margaret Sanger, *Woman and the New Race,* pp. 31–36.

27. Gossett, *Race*, pp. 110–114; Edward N. Saveth, *American Historians and European Immigrants*, pp. 9, 10, chaps. 1, 2.

28. Baltzell, *The Protestant Establishment*, chap. 9; Milton Gordon, *Assimilation in American Life*, chap. 6; Seymour Itzkoff, *Cultural Pluralism and American Education*, pp. 54–59; Horace Kallen, *Culture and Democracy in the United States* (New York: Boni & Liveright, 1924) pp. 120, 130, and *passim*; Higham, *Strangers in the Land*, chaps. 8, 9. All of these cultural contradictions and changes must be rooted in a specific social structural analysis of the period, which is a particularly important time for understanding the sociology of ethnicity and American Jewry.

29. See Bernhard Stern's fascinating essay, "Franz Boas as Scientist and Citizen," in Stern, *Historical Sociology*.

30. Charles Hunt Page, *Class and American Sociology*, chap. 8.; Robert K. Merton, *Social Theory and Social Structure*, chap. 7.

31. Page, *Class and American Sociology*, pp. 249, 250, 32, 136, 137; Bernhard J. Stern, *Historical Sociology*, pp. 237–238; Peggy Ann, "Thorstein Bunde Veblen: A Preliminary Investigation into the Development of His Methodology." p. 10; C. Wright Mills, "The Professional Ideology of Social Pathologists," in *Power, Politics and People*, pp. 525–552, ed. Irving Horowitz; David Horowitz, "Billion Dollar Brains," in *The Poverty of Progress*, ed. Milton Mankoff.

32. Veysey, *The Emergence of the American University*, p. 378, claims that unlike other founder/benefactors, Rockefeller scrupulously avoided interfering with internal policies, but he also makes clear that the University president, William R. Harper, attempted to tailor his decisions to Rockefeller's anticipated wishes.

33. Ann, "Thorstein Bunde Veblen," p. 11.

34. Ibid., pp. 10–25.

35. *The Elgin News*, cited in ibid., p. 10.

36. Veysey, *Emergence of the American University*, pp. 409, 410, 412.

37. Frederick Rudolph, *The American College and University*, p. 414; Veysey, *Emergence of the American University*, pp. 394–418.

38. See the statement of the Board of Trustees of Johns Hopkins University, stipulating that faculty be hired for their political acceptability. Veysey, *Emergence of the American University*, p. 411.

39. Gossett, *Race*, p. 153. See also Richard Hofstadter, *Social Darwinism in American Thought*, pp. 5–6 *et passim*; Baltzell, *The Protestant Establishment*, pp. 98–102; Page, *Class and American Sociology*, p. 20.

40. Franklin Giddings, *The Principles of Sociology*, p. 129; Page, *Class and American Sociology*, p. 23.

41. Giddings, *Principles of Sociology*, pp. 351, 243.

42. Giddings was on the school board that dismissed three Jewish socialist teachers in 1918. (See Chapter 5.) After a public outcry, he and another member "reconsidered" their votes, thereby breaking the majority and

permitting the reversal of the dismissal. See Isaac Rosengarten, "The Jewish Teacher in the New York Public Schools," p. 326.

43.   Burgess was probably too racist to have had much influence at CCNY. S. P. Duggan, who also studied under Burgess at Columbia, considered him a man of "great mental powers" but undemocratic views. See Stephen P. Duggan, *A Professor at Large*, p. 6.

  See also M. R. Cohen, *A Dreamer's Journey*, pp. 169, 186, 222, 245; and Leonora Cohen Rosenfield, *Portrait of a Philosopher*, pp. 71, 442.

44.   Henry Lee Higginson, in a Harvard fund-raising letter, March 1886, cited by David Horowitz, "Billion Dollar Brains" in Mankoff, *The Poverty of Progress*, p. 298.

Chapter 8: The City College Curriculum in an Age of Cultural Conflict

1.   Personal interview, December 1974. The respondent attended Columbia University between 1916 and 1920.

2.   Bernard M. Baruch, *Baruch: My Own Story*, p. 55.

3.   City College Archives, Special Collections.

4.   Daniel G. Brinton, *Races and Peoples*, pp. 103, 102, 47, 48, 156, 157.

5.   Ibid., p. 139.

6.   Ibid., pp. 298–299.

7.   A Rutgers University Press reviewer who attended CCNY from 1924–1928 pointed this out to me. The reviewer also noted that Anthropology *was* a required science course at Hunter College. His many comments and careful reading were very helpful to me.

8.   City College Archives, City College *Register* 1908–1909, p. 72.

9.   In 1903–1904 Professor Giddings's course in Principles of Sociology at Columbia included "lectures. . . on the sociological systems of important writers, including Montesquieu, Comte, Spencer, Schaffle, DeGreef, Gumplowicz, Ward and Tarde." Columbiana Collection, Columbia University Bulletin, 1903–1904, p. 27.

10.   The first course in sociology at CCNY was Practical Sociology, offered in the 1908–1909 academic year. No instructor is listed for it. Its description is identical with the two courses Woolston taught in 1909–1910 on applied sociology. Municipal Affairs, offered by Woolston in 1909–1910 as a sociology course, was listed, in identical form, in 1908–1909 as a political science course, also without a designated instructor.

11.   See City College Archives, Special Collection.

12.   The neighborhood is smaller than Harlem, being bounded by Convent Hill on the north, 125th Street on the south, the Hudson River on the west, and St. Nicholas Avenue on the east.

13.   Howard Brown Woolston, *A Study of the Population of Manhattanville*, p. 11.

14.   Ibid., p. 50.

15.   Ibid., pp. 50, 72, 51.

16.   Ibid., pp. 62, 55. Over 11 percent of U.S. residents were classified as

"Negro and other" in the 1910 census. Thirty-nine and one-half percent of white residents were counted as "foreign stock," that is, either foreign-born or the children of the foreign-born. Thus over 46.5 percent of the population were either non-white or "foreign stock." These data exclude "American Indians," and count the grandchildren of immigrants as "native whites." If these two groups could be counted, then the "old-time" descendents of Northern European settlers would be a minority indeed—which is exactly what frightened many of them! For the data on which these calculations are based, see U.S. Bureau of the Census, *Historical Statistics of the United States*, pt. 1, p. 9; and Edward P. Hutchinson, *Immigrants and Their Children*, pp. 2, 3.

17. Woolston, *A Study of the Population of Manhattanville*, p. 59.
18. Ibid., pp. 59, 63.
19. Anatole Leroy-Beaulieu, *Israel Among the Nations;* pp. 178, 220.
20. Woolston, *A Study of the Population of Manhattanville*, p. 69. Original emphasis.
21. Ibid., p. 6.
22. Morris Isaiah Berger, "The Settlement, the Immigrant and the Public School," p. 129.
23. Woolston, *Manhattanville*, p. 158.
24. On the political nature of definitions of "deviance" and "social problems" see Howard Becker, *Outsiders*, chap. 1; C. Wright Mills, "The Professional Ideology of Social Pathologists," in *Power, Politics and People: The Collected Essays of C. Wright Mills*, ed. Irving Louis Horowltz, pp. 525 552, esp pp. 527, 531–532, and Irving Louis Horowitz, "Social Deviance and Political Marginality: Toward a Redefinition of the Relation Between Sociology and Politics," in Irving Horowitz, *Professing Sociology*, chap. 8.
25. Woolston, *Manhattanville*, p. 102. Emphasis added.
26. Walter E. Clark, *Outline of Lectures on Economics*, pp. 10–12. See also other materials located in the City College Archives, Special Collections.
27. Ibid., p. 11–12.
28. Ibid., p. 36.
29. See especially Hourwich's Summary.
30. Clark, *Lectures on Economics*, p. 12.
31. Ibid.
32. The words *practical problem of* do not appear until the 1909–1910 *Register*, but "Immigration" was part of "the study" of applied economics from its beginning in 1907.
33. CCNY *Register*, 1911–1912, p. 83. The themes moved around slightly between A. and B. courses. See the *Register* for these years.
34. Ibid., 1913–1914, p. 73.
35. Ibid., 1925–1926, p. 186.
36. Ibid., p. 126.
37. In *Chinese Americans*, pp. 189–190, Stanford Lyman criticized the

concept of "immigrant contributions" as being sociologically invalid because they are entirely *post hoc* evaluations, retrospectively measuring the past in terms of the dominant group's ephemeral values of the present. He might have added that the concept also carries the arrogant assumption that the given and unquestioned culture of the dominant group provides the standard by which immigrant contributions are to be measured.

38. On the treatment of the Crusades as an element of Christian propaganda within Western secular culture, see Milton Himmelfarb, "Secular Society? A Jewish Perspective," p. 225.

39. Alumni *Quarterly* vols. 14–16, 1918–1920.

40. See the account of Jane Addams's Labor Museum and the discussion of the works of Horace Kallen and John Dewey in Milton Gordon, *Assimilation in American Life*, chap. 6.

41. CCNY *Register*, 1925–1926, p. 186.

42. Ibid., 1921–1922, pp. 64–65.

43. Baruch is listed on the faculty in 1919–1920 as instructor of a course on textiles for salesmen (CCNY *Register*, 1919–1920, p. 25).

44. CCNY *Register*, 1915–1917, p. 73.

45. In 1924 a course on Labor and Employment Problems promised to be a "study of the general principles of collective bargaining, labor legislation, wage systems, labor turnover, job analysis, and placement methods. . ." (CCNY *Register*, 1924–1925, p. 123). Labor turnover and placement methods are problems for management, not for labor. "Job analysis" is a method of restructuring work, usually to gain greater management control at the expense of skilled workers, and often involving speed-up. (See Braverman, *Labor and Monopoly Capital*, chaps. 4, 5.) Absent from the course description is consideration of work conditions and problems of organizing labor.

46. Clark, *Lectures on Economics*, pp. 36, 17.

47. Ibid., p. 34. Original emphasis.

48. Ibid., p. 17.

49. Ibid., pp. 36, 17.

50. Ibid., pp. 16, 5, 7, and *passim*.

51. Marx criticized Carey in his *Grundrisse*, pp. 883–893. In 1896 Bohm-Bawerk published a severe critique of Marx. See *Karl Marx and the Close of His System and Bohm-Bawerk's Criticism of Marx*, ed. Paul Sweezy (Clifton, N.J.: Augustus M. Kelley, 1975), pp. 3–118.

52. CCNY *Register*, 1911–1912, p. 85.

53. Columbia University *Bulletin*, 1910–1911, p. 42. See also other materials located in the Columbiana Collection, Columbia University.

54. CU *Bulletin*, 1910–1911, p. 42. Emphasis added.

55. Ibid.

56. The contrast should not be overdrawn: Devine also had a course called Social Aspects of Crime and Abnormality, which dealt with "the more extreme deviations found in criminal and anti-social classes."

Moses Rischin mentions the courses of Lindsay and Devine and their interest in the Lower East Side: "During these years [around 1909] Columbia University was closer to the heart of New York's civic problems than it ever had been before or has been since. . ." (Rischin, *The Promised City*, p. 237). Columbia's relative neglect of its neighbors would return to haunt it in the late 1960s.

57. "Charters, Acts of the Legislature, Official Documents and Records," 1920 (Columbiana Collection).

58. Personal interview, January 1975.

59. CCNY Register, 1915–1917, p. 74; 1912–1913, p. 57.

60. William B. Guthrie, *Socialism Before the French Revolution*, pp. 7–8.

61. Written communication.

62. CU *Bulletin*, 1910–1911, p. 44; 1905–1906, p. 26.

63. Ibid., 1910–1911, p. 44.

64. Thomas F. Gossett, *Race*, p. 114.

65. CU *Bulletin*, 1910–1911, p. 42.

66. Ibid., p. 43. Emphasis added.

67. That is not to deny that many CCNY alumni became public figures. The generalization refers to the typical social role and the class positions of graduates of the two schools. Furthermore, it reflects the perceived social role of the two institutions.

68. Melech Epstein, *Jewish Labor in U.S.A.*, vol. 1, p. 275.

69. Ibid., pp. 276, 295. See also Nora Levin, *While Messiah Tarried*, chaps. 8, 9.

70. Morris Rosenfeld, *Songs of Labor and Other Poems*, pp. 7–9. Translated from the Yiddish by Rose Paster Stokes and Helena Frank. Also translated (in other editions) as "In the Sweatshop" and "In the Factory."

71. Ibid., p. 41.

72. Epstein, *Jewish Labor*, vol. 1, p. 275.

73. Ibid., p. 286.

74. CCNY *Register*, 1924–1925, pp. 122, 168. A former instructor at CCNY comments: "There were no courses in Yiddish literature in any college in the country, not even in the Jewish colleges (Jewish Theological Seminary, Yeshiva University, Hebrew Union College, etc.) This had to do with the widespread contempt for Yiddish as a "jargon." [You must understand the] context [at City College]. There was only one course (an elective) in American literature up to the 1930s, when some of us younger teachers in the English Department won a struggle to add a few more courses (all elective) in American literature. It was [not] until 1918 that the *Cambridge History of American Literature* (3 vols.) had a chapter on Yiddish Literature in America" (Written communication).

75. Antonio Gramsci, *The Modern Prince and Other Writings*, pp. 118–125, esp. p. 118.

76. Translated by Emma Gorelick from the original Russian and from the Yiddish translation in N. B. Minkoff, "David Edelstat: Revolutionary, Romantic and Aesthetic Lyrics," in B. J. Bialostotzky, ed., *David Edelstat*

[Memorial] Book (Los Angeles: Edelstat-Memorial Committees, 1953), p. 561.

77. Rosenfeld, *Songs of Labor*, p. 58.
78. Ibid., pp. 59–60.
79. Ibid., p. 40.
80. Epstein, *Jewish Labor*, vol. 1, pp. 280, 289; Levin, *While Messiah Tarried*, p. 125.
81. Gramsci, "The Formation of the Intellectuals," in *The Modern Prince*, pp. 118–125.
82. Nathan Glazer and Daniel Patrick Moynihan, *Beyond the Melting Pot*, p. 150.
83. Thomas F. Gossett, *Race*, p. 122. Gossett reports that in 1908 Butler still repeated the Teutonic origins theory and still repeated statements of Anglo-Saxon superiority. As Harold Wechsler shows, Butler bent extraordinary efforts at excluding Jews from Columbia and encouraging the development of standardized tests on which Jews would not succeed. His anti-Semitism was unabashed. See Wechsler, *The Qualified Student*, pt. 2, esp. chap. 7. For the Christian—and often anti-Jewish character of elementary schools during this period, see Rosengarten, "The Jewish Teacher in the New York Public Schools," pp. 320–329.
84. Joseph Freeman, *An American Testament*, pp. 151–152. Emphasis added.
85. Compare Norman Hapgood's description, in "Jews and College Life," pp. 53–55, of the experience of Jews at elite colleges with Allen Ballard's description of Black students' experiences at such institutions, in *The Education of Black Folk*, pp. 52–59. The similarities are striking.
86. Organizations such as the Menorah Society and the Socialist Club were formed at many institutions. They were not unique to City College. In fact ethnic organizations are often stronger at schools where Jewish students form a beleagured minority. Nevertheless these clubs were very important at CCNY. Thus, because of deficiencies in the curriculum, Jewish students had to learn of Jewish life in extracurricular activities created for themselves, just as, before the Civil War, students at the unreformed colleges across the United States had to learn in extracurricular literary societies what they could not study in the official curriculum. See Rudolph, *The American College and University*, pp. 137–144.
87. Stephen P. Duggan, *Professor at Large*, pp. 10–11.
88. Morris Raphael Cohen, *A Dreamer's Journey*, pp. 89–90.
89. By "militarism" Cohen is referring to "a tradition of military discipline which had been fixed upon the College by its first two presidents, both West Pointers. . .," which "protected" the "worthy pedagogues and scholastic drill masters" from the intellectual eagerness of students such as himself (p. 90). By the time the CCNY student, Morris Raphael Cohen, had become a CCNY instructor, the pedagogic method was

changing to less rigid forms, as the reported styles of both Duggan and Cohen himself exemplify. Cohen was a near-mythic figure as a CCNY professor. Whenever I have mentioned that I was writing a book on CCNY, anyone familiar with the institution, and virtually *all* former students, have exclaimed immediately: "Oh yes, and about Morris Raphael Cohen!" See Irving Howe's rather charming account of Cohen's influence in *World of Our Fathers*, pp. 283–286.

90. M. R. Cohen, *A Dreamer's Journey*, p. 90.
91. Duggan, *Professor at Large*, p. 11.

Afterword

1. Theodore L. Gross, "How to Kill a College: The Private Papers of a College Dean," *Saturday Review*, February 4, 1978. This statement is an unusual concession in an article otherwise dedicated to claiming that such students were unsuited to college.
2. Joseph Freeman, cited in chap. 7, note 6.
3. Gross, pp. 13, 14, 15, 17, and 18.
4. Written communication. (His emphasis.) The history remembered by this observer is consistent with Harold Wechsler's meticulous account in *The Qualified Student*, Chapter 11. See the latter for the struggle to establish Brooklyn College and to expand public education against the opposition of Columbia University.
5. For a more complete analysis of the ending of Open Admissions and the imposition of tuition, see Sherry Gorelick, "Open Admissions: Design for Failure?" and "City College: Rise and Fall of the Free Academy"; Allen Ballard, *The Education of Black Folk*, chap. 7; Josephine Nieves, *Puerto Ricans in United States Higher Education*, pt. 2.
6. Manifesto establishing the Free Academy, according to S. Willis Rudy, cited in Chapter 4.

Glossary

Arbeiter Ring   Workers' Circle (usually translated as "Workmen's Circle"). A social and benefit organization similar in many functions to the *landsmanschaften* but supported by the labor movement and supportive of the socialist movement in the United States and Russia.

Chasidic, Chasidim   See *Hasidim.*

cheder   See *heder.*

Hasidim   Followers of *Hasidism.*

Hasidism   A fundamentalist movement of religious revival, beginning in the last half of the eighteenth century and stressing faith and personal spontaneity rather than learning of the Torah.

Haskalah   The Jewish enlightenment: a movement for assimilation of Jews into the Western enlightenment, taking place in Germany and Eastern Europe in the eighteenth and nineteenth centuries.

hedarim   Plural of *heder.*

heder   A one-room elementary Hebrew religious school run in the home of a private tutor.

jargon   Disparaging term for the Yiddish language. In Yiddish, *jargón*, with the accent on the second syllable, means the vernacular. It does not have the same meaning as the word *jargon* in English.

kaftan   Long black traditional coat worn by *Hasidim.*

Kahal   See *Kehillah.*

Kehillah   1. The local communal organization in Eastern Europe; the communal administration of Jewish self-government. 2. A social reform and philanthropic organization that attempted to serve as a communal organization and coordinating body for Lower East Side Jews between 1908 and 1922.

landsman   One who comes from the same town in the old country (similar to "homeboy" among Black Americans and "compueblano" among Puerto Ricans, or "paisan" among Italians).

233

Landsmanschaft   Social organization of immigrants who came from the same town in the old country. Generally a social, welfare, and benefit organization of and for people from the same hometown or region.

landsmanschaften   Plural of *landsmanschaft.*

malamdim   Religious tutors.

New York Kehillah   See *Kehillah.*

Orthodox Jewry   Adherents of strict traditional Judaism resting on strict observance of religious rules regarding daily life, ceremonies, Sabbath restrictions, and belief in traditional religious doctrines.

Reform Judaism   Movement beginning in the nineteenth century in Germany and the United States, modifying some of the basic practices, rituals, and beliefs of traditional Judaism and seeking a more "modern" Jewish religious practice.

Rosh Hashonah   The Jewish New Year.

Talmud   Jewish Code of Law.

Talmud Torah   Communally supported elementary religious Hebrew school.

shtetl   Small Jewish town.

Yom Kippur   The Day of Atonement, the most solemn holy day of the Jewish religion, observed by prayer and abstinence from all food, drink, and frivolity.

Zedakah   Religiously mandated tradition of charity in which both donor and recipient remain anonymous.

Bibliography

Abbott, Frank C. *Government Policy and Higher Education: A Study of the Regents of the University of the State of New York 1784–1949.* Ithaca, New York: Cornell University Press, 1958.

Adler, Cyrus. *Jacob H. Schiff: His Life and Letters.* Vol. 1. New York: Doubleday, 1928.

Allmendinger, David F., Jr. "New England Students and the Revolution in Higher Education, 1800–1900." *History of Education Quarterly* 11 (Winter 1971):381–389.

Alofsin, Dorothy. *The Nightingale's Song.* Philadelphia: The Jewish Publication Society of America, 1945.

Ann, Peggy. "Thorstein Bunde Veblen: A Preliminary Investigation into the Development of His Methodology." Unpublished manuscript, Rutgers University, 1979.

Axtell, James. "The Death of the Liberal Arts College." *History of Education Quarterly* 11 (Winter 1971):339–352.

Bailyn, Bernard. *Education in the Formation of American Society.* New York: W. W. Norton, 1972.

Balbus, Isaac. "Ruling-class Elite Theory vs. Marxian Class Analysis." *Monthly Review* 23, no. 1 (May 1971):36–46.

Ballard, Allen B. *The Education of Black Folk.* New York: Harper Colophon, 1974.

Baltzell, E. Digby. *The Protestant Establishment: Aristocracy and Caste in America.* New York: Vintage, 1966.

Baron, Salo. *The Russian Jew Under Tsars and Soviets.* 2nd ed. New York: Macmillan, 1976.

Baruch, Bernard M. *Baruch: My Own Story.* New York: Holt, 1957.

Baxendall, Rosalyn; Gordon, Linda; and Reverby, Susan, eds. *America's Working Women: A Documentary History 1600 to the Present.* New York: Vintage, 1976.

Beck, Robert H. "Progressive Education and American Progressivism: Felix Adler." *Teachers College Record* 60 (1958–1959):77–89.

Becker, Howard S. *Outsiders: Studies in the Sociology of Deviance.* New York: Free Press, 1966.

Bell, Daniel. "Marxian Socialism in the United States." In *Socialism and*

American Life, edited by Donald D. Egbert and Stow Persons, Vol. 1 of 2, pp. 213–405. Princeton: Princeton University Press, 1952.

Bendix, Reinhard, and Lipset, Seymour Martin, eds. *Class, Status and Power: Social Stratification in Comparative Perspective.* 2nd ed. New York: Free Press, 1966.

Berg, Ivar, ed. *The Business of America.* New York: Harcourt, Brace and World, 1968.

————, with the assistance of Sherry Gorelick. *Education and Jobs: The Great Training Robbery.* Boston: Beacon Press, 1971.

Berger, Morris Isaiah. "The Settlement, the Immigrant and the Public School." Ph.D. dissertation, Teachers College, New York, 1956.

Berkson, Isaac B. *Theories of Americanization: A Critical Study with Special Reference to the Jewish Group.* New York: Teachers College, 1920.

Bernheimer, Charles Seligman, ed. *The Russian Jew in the United States.* Philadelphia: The J. C. Winston Co., 1905.

Berrol, Selma C. "Education and Economic Mobility: The Jewish Experience in New York City, 1880–1920." *American Jewish Historical Quarterly* 65 (March 1976):257–271.

————. *Immigration and the New York City Schools, 1880–1920.* Ph.D. dissertation, City University of New York, 1967.

Birmingham, Stephen. *Our Crowd.* New York: Dell Publishing Co., 1967.

Blaug, M., ed. *Economics of Education 1.* Middlesex, England: Penguin, 1968.

B'nai B'rith Vocational Service. *Jewish Youth in College: Summary Report of the 3rd Decennial Census of Jewish College Students in the United States and Canada.* Washington, D.C.: B'nai B'rith Vocational Service Pamphlet, 1957.

Boggs, Grace Lee. "Education: The Great Obsession," *Monthly Review* 22 (September 1970):18.

Borochov, Ber. *Nationalism and the Class Struggle.* 1937. Reprint. Westport, Conn.: Greenwood Press, 1972.

Bowles, Samuel. "Contradictions in Higher Education in the United States." In *The Capitalist System,* edited by Richard Edwards, Michael Reich, and Thomas E. Weisskopf, pp. 491–506. Englewood Cliffs, N.J.: Prentice Hall, 1972.

————. "Unequal Education and the Reproduction of the Hierarchical Division of Labor." In *The Capitalist System,* edited by Richard Edwards, Michael Reich, and Thomas Weisskopf, pp. 218–229. Englewood Cliffs, N.J.: Prentice Hall, 1972.

Bowles, Samuel, and Gintis, Herbert. *Schooling in Capitalist America: Educational Reform and the Contradictions of Economic Life.* New York: Basic Books, 1976.

Braithwaite, Richard Bevan. *Scientific Explanation: A Study of the Function of Theory, Probability and Law in Science.* Cambridge: Cambridge University Press, 1968.

Braverman, Harry. *Labor and Monopoly Capital: The Degradation of Work in the Twentieth Century.* New York: Monthly Review Press, 1974.

Brecher, Jeremy. *Strike!* San Francisco: Straight Arrow Books, 1972.

Brim, Orville G., Jr. *Sociology and the Field of Education.* New York: Russell Sage Foundation, 1958.

Brinton, Daniel G. *Races and Peoples: Lectures on the Science of Ethnography.* Philadelphia: David McKay, 1901.

Bronner, H. R., ed. "Statistics of State School Systems, 1917–1918." Bureau of Education *Bulletin,* 11 (1920).

Broun, Heywood, and Britt, George. *Christians Only: A Study in Prejudice.* New York: The Vanguard Press, 1931.

Brown, Bernard. "Minorities and Public Education: An Economic Aspect of the Education of the Children of Minority Groups." *American Journal of Economics and Sociology* 30 (January, 1971):1–13.

Buchanan, John T. "How to Assimilate the Foreign Element in Our Population." *Forum,* 32 (1902):686–694.

Bullough, Vern. "Education and Professionalization: An Historical Example." *History of Education Quarterly* 10 (Summer 1970):160–169.

Bureau of Jewish Social Research. "Professional Tendencies Among Jewish Students in Colleges, Universities, and Professional Schools." *American Jewish Year Book* 22 (1920–1921):383–393.

Burritt, Bailey B. "Professional Distribution of College and University Graduates (1912)." *U.S. Bureau of Education Bulletin* 19, (1912):9–147.

Butler, Nicholas Murray. *Across the Busy Years: Recollections and Reflections.* Vol. 1. New York: Teachers College, 1939.

—————. "The Beginnings of Teachers College." *Columbia University Quarterly* 1 (September 1899):342–346.

—————. "The Training of the Teacher." *Century Magazine* 16 (1889):916–917.

Cahan, Abraham. *The Rise of David Levinsky.* Harper and Brothers, 1917. Reprint. New York: Peter Smith, 1951.

Cahnman, Werner J. "A Comment on 'My Son, the Doctor.'" *American Sociological Review* 34 (December 1969):935–936.

Callahan, Raymond. *Education and the Cult of Efficiency.* Chicago: University of Chicago Press, 1960.

Callcott, Mary Stevenson. *Child Labor Legislation in New York.* New York: Macmillan, 1931.

Carlson, Robert A. "Americanization as an Early Twentieth-Century Adult Education Movement." *History of Education Quarterly* 10 (Winter 1970):440–464.

Carnegie, Andrew. *Triumphant Democracy, or Fifty Years' March of the Republic.* Norwood, Conn.: Norwood Editions, 1888.

Carnegie, Andrew. "Wealth." *North American Review* 148 (June 1889):653–664.

Cicourel, Aaron V. *Method and Measurement in Sociology.* Glencoe, Ill.: Free Press, 1964.

Clark, Walter E. *Outline of Lectures on Economics.* New York, 1916. (New York: City College Archives, Box 7.)

Cockburn, Alexander, and Blackburn, Robin. *Student Power.* Middlesex, England: Penguin Special S266, 1969.

Coffman, Lotus Delta. *The Social Composition of the Teaching Population.* New York: Teachers College Press, 1911.

Cohen, David K., and Lazerson, Marvin. "Education and the Corporate Order." *Socialist Revolution* 2 (March–April, 1972):47–72.

Cohen, George. *The Jews in the Making of America.* Boston: The Stratford Company, 1924.

Cohen, Morris Raphael. *A Dreamer's Journey.* Glencoe, Ill.: Free Press, 1949.

Cohen, Naomi W. *A Dual Heritage: The Public Career of Oscar S. Straus.* Philadelphia: Jewish Publication Society of America, 1969.

Cohen, Sol. *Progressives and Urban School Reform: The Public Education Association of New York City 1895–1954.* New York: Teachers College Press, 1964.

College Entrance Examination Board. *Examination Questions in History, 1901–1905.* Boston: Ginn and Co., 1905. (In City College Archives.)

Cooper, David. *Psychiatry and Anti-Psychiatry.* London: Tavistock Publications, 1967.

Cordasco, Francesco, and Bucchioni, Eugene. *The Italians: Social Background of an American Group.* Clifton, N.J.: Augustus Kelley, 1974.

Cosenza, Mario Emilio. *The Establishment of the College of the City of New York as the Free Academy in 1847, Townsend Harris, Founder: A Chapter in the History of Education.* New York: The Associate Alumni of the College of the City of New York, 1925.

Covello, Leonard. *The Teacher in the Urban Community: A Half Century in City Schools: The Heart Is the Teacher.* Totowa, N.J.: Littlefield, Adams and Co., 1970.

Cowen, Philip. *Memories of an American Jew.* New York: The International Press, 1932.

Cox, Oliver Cromwell. *Caste, Class and Race.* New York: Modern Reader Paperback, 1970.

Cremin, Lawrence A. *The Transformation of the School: Progressivism in American Education 1876–1957.* New York: Random House, 1961.

Cruse, Harold. *Crisis of the Negro Intellectual.* New York: William Morrow and Co., 1967.

Cubberly, Ellwood. *Public Education in the United States.* Boston: Houghton Mifflin, 1934 (written 1919).

Curoe, Phillip R. V. *Educational Attitudes and Policies of Organized Labor in the United States.* New York: Teachers College Press, 1926.

Davidson, Thomas. *The Education of Wage-Earners.* New York: Ginn and Co., 1904.

Davies, Margery. "Women's Place Is at the Typewriter: The Feminization of the Clerical Labor Force." In *Capitalist Patriarchy and the Case for Socialist Feminism*, edited by Zillah R. Eisenstein. New York: Monthly Review Press, 1979.

de Kadt, Maarten. "Management and Labor" Review of Harry Braverman, *Labor and Monopoly Capital: the Degradation of Work in the Twentieth Century. Review of Radical Political Economics*, 7 (Spring 1975): 84–90.

de Kadt, Maarten; Garrett, Richard; Hill, John; Niehouse, Douglas; and Schechter, Gerald. "Merchant's Capital and Feudalism: 1000–1400." Mimeographed, New School for Social Research, 1972.

Deutscher, Isaac. *The Non-Jewish Jew and Other Essays.* London: Oxford University Press, 1968.

Directory of the Board of Education of the City of New York. Department of Education of the City of New York, 1904, 1911, 1915, 1927.

Domhoff, G. William. *Who Rules America?* Englewood Cliffs, N.J.: Prentice Hall, 1967.

Dubnow, Simon. *History of the Jews in Poland and Russia.* 3 vols. Philadelphia: Jewish Publication Society, 1916.

Dubofsky, Melvyn. "Success and Failure of Socialism in New York City, 1900–1918: A Case Study." *Labor History* 9 (Fall 1968):361–375.

Duckworth, W. L. H. *Morphology and Anthropology: A Handbook for Students.* Cambridge: Cambridge University Press, 1915.

Duggan, Stephen P. "The Department of Education." In City College of New York *Alumni Quarterly* 7, no. 1 (1911):28–34.

———. *A Professor at Large.* New York: Macmillan, 1943.

———. *A Student's Textbook in the History of Education.* New York and London: D. Appleton-Century Co., 1936.

Durkeim, Emile. *The Division of Labor.* Translated by George Simpson. New York: Free Press, 1966.

———. *Suicide: A Study in Sociology.* Translated by John A. Spaulding and George Simpson. New York: Free Press, 1951.

Dushkin, Alexander M. *Jewish Education in New York City.* New York: Bureau of Jewish Education, 1918.

Editors of *Fortune. Jews in America.* New York: Random House, 1936.

Educational Alliance. Annual Reports, 1893, 1894, 1900. New York: Philip Cowen, printer, 1895, 1901.

Edwards, Richard C.; Reich, Michael; and Weisskopf, Thomas E. *The Capitalist System: A Radical Analysis of American Society.* Englewood Cliffs, N.J.: Prentice Hall, 1972.

Emden, Paul H. *Jews of Britain: A Series of Biographies.* London: Sampson Low, Marston and Co., 1943.

"Enrollment of Jewish Students in American Colleges and Universities in 1915–1916." *American Jewish Yearbook* 14 (1917–1918):407.

Ensign, Forest C. *Compulsory School Attendance and Child Labor.* Iowa City: Athens Press, 1921.

Epstein, Melech. *Jewish Labor in U.S.A.: An Industrial, Political, and Cultural History of the Jewish Labor Movement.* 2 vols. New York: KTAV Publishing House, 1970.

Fauman, S. Joseph. "Occupational Selection among Detroit Jews." In Sklare, Marshall. *The Jews:* 119–137.

Feldblum, Mary Alice. The Formation of the First Factory Labor Force in the New England Cotton Textile Industry, 1800–1848. Ph. D. dissertation, The New School for Social Research, 1977.

Festinger, Leon. *A Theory of Cognitive Dissonance.* Evanston, Ill.: Row, Peterson and Company, 1957.

Findlay, James. "The Congregationalists and American Education." *History of Education Quarterly* (Winter 1977):449–455.

Foner, Philip S. *History of the Labor Movement in the United States.* Vol. 1. 1947. Reprint. New York: International Publishers, 1972.

Freeman, Joseph. *An American Testament: A Narrative of Rebels and Romantics.* New York: Farrar and Rinehart, 1936.

Friedman, Morris. "The Jewish College Student: 1951 Model." *Commentary* 12 (September 1951):305–313.

Fuchs, Lawrence H. "Sources of Jewish Internationalism and Liberalism." In Sklare, *The Jews:* 595–613.

Gans, Herbert J. *The Urban Villagers: Group and Class in the Life of Italian-Americans.* Glencoe, Ill.: Free Press, 1962.

Gartner, Lloyd. "The Jews of New York's East Side, 1890–1893." *American Jewish Historical Quarterly* (March 1964):264–275.

Gersman, Elinor Mondale. "Progressive Reform of the St. Louis School Board, 1897." *History of Education Quarterly* 10 (Spring 1970):3–21.

Gerth, H. H. and Mills, C. Wright, eds. and trans. *From Max Weber: Essays in Sociology.* New York: Oxford University Press, 1958.

Gettleman, Marvin E. "John H. Finley at CCNY—1903–1913." *History of Education Quarterly* 10 (Winter 1970):423–439.

Giddings, Franklin. *Elements of Sociology.* New York: Macmillan, 1898.

———. *Inductive Sociology: A Syllabus of Methods, Analyses and Classifications, and Provisionally Formulated Laws.* New York: Macmillan, 1901.

———. *The Principles of Sociology: An Analysis of the Phenomena of Association and of Social Organization.* New York: Macmillan, 1896.

Glazer, Nathan. *American Judaism.* Chicago: University of Chicago Press, 1957.

———. "The American Jew and the Attainment of Middle-Class Rank: Some Trends and Explanations." In Sklare, *The Jews:* 138–146.

Glazer, Nathan, and Moynihan, Daniel Patrick. *Beyond the Melting Pot.* Cambridge, Mass.: M.I.T. Press, 1963.

Gold, Michael. *Jews Without Money.* New York: International Publishers, 1935.

Goldberg, Nathan. "Occupational Patterns of American Jews." *Jewish Review* (April and October–December 1945):3–23, 161–186.

Gordis, Robert. "Marxism and Religion." *The Menorah Journal.* January–March 1937. Reprinted in *The Menorah Treasury,* edited by Leo W. Schwarz. Philadelphia: Jewish Publication Society, 1964.

Gordon, Linda. *Woman's Body, Woman's Right.* New York: Penguin Books, 1977.

Gordon, Milton M. *Assimilation in American Life.* New York: Oxford University Press, 1964.

Gorelick, Sherry, "City College: Rise and Fall of the Free Academy." *Radical America* 14 (September–October 1980).

———. "Jewish Success and the Great American Celebration: The Cold War vs. The World War in Social Science." *Contemporary Jewry* 5 (Spring–Summer 1980): pp. 39–55.

———. "Open Admissions: Design for Failure?" *Politics and Education* 1 (Summer 1978):8–13.

———. "Social Control, Social Mobility, and the Eastern European Jews: An Analysis of Public Education in New York City, 1880-1924." Ph.D. dissertation, Columbia University, 1975.

———. "Undermining Hierarchy: Problems of Schooling in Capitalist America." *Monthly Review* 29 (October 1977):20-36.

———. "We Are Climbing Carnegie's Ladders: The Development of a National System of Higher Education in the United States." Unpublished paper, 1979.

Goren, Arthur A. *New York Jews and the Quest for Community: The Kehillah Experiment, 1908–1922.* New York: Columbia University Press, 1970.

Gossett, Thomas F. *Race: The History of an Idea in America.* New York: Schocken Books, 1965.

Gottschalk, Louis. *Understanding History: A Primer of Historical Method.* New York: Alfred A. Knopf, 1950.

Gouldner, Alvin W. *The Coming Crisis of Western Sociology.* New York: Equinox Books, 1971.

Graeber, Isacque, and Britt, Stewart, eds. *Jews in a Gentile World.* New York: Macmillan, 1942.

Gramsci, Antonio. *The Modern Prince and Other Writings.* New York: International Publishers, 1970.

Greeley, Andrew M. *From Backwater to Mainstream: A Profile of Catholic Higher Education.* New York: McGraw-Hill, 1969.

Greer, Colin. *The Great School Legend.* New York: Basic Books, 1972.

Guralnick, Stanley M. *Science and the Ante-Bellum American College.* Philadelphia: The American Philosophical Society, 1975.

Guthrie, William B. *Socialism Before the French Revolution: A History.* New York: Macmillan, 1907.

Gutman, Herbert G. *The Black Family in Slavery and Freedom, 1750–1925.* New York: Pantheon Books, 1976.

———. *Work, Culture and Society in Industrializing America.* New York: Alfred A. Knopf, 1976.

Halpern, Ben. "America Is Different." In Sklare, *The Jews:* 23–39.

Halsey, A. H.; Floud, Jean; and Anderson, C. Arnold, eds. *Education, Economy and Society.* New York: Free Press, 1961.

Hammack, David. "The Centralization of New York City's Public School System, 1896: A Social Analysis of a Decision." Master's thesis, Columbia University, 1969.

Handlin, Oscar. *Adventure in Freedom: 300 Years of Jewish Life in America.* New York: McGraw-Hill, 1954.

———. *Race and Nationality in American Life.* Boston: Little, Brown, 1957.

———. ed. *Immigration as a Factor in American History.* Englewood Cliffs, N.J. Prentice Hall, 1959.

Hanson, W. Lee. "Who Benefits from Higher Education Subsidies?" *Monthly Labor Review* 93, no. 3 (March 1970):43–46.

Hapgood, Norman. "Jews and College Life," and "Schools, Colleges and Jews." *Harper's Weekly: A Journal of Civilization Begun in 1857* 62 (1916):53–55, 77–79.

Harris, Hannah Margaret. *Lessons in Civics for the Elementary Grades of City Schools.* Washington, D.C.: U.S. Government Printing Office, 1920. Printed as bulletin no. 18 of the Bureau of Education, 1920.

Hawgood, John A. *The Tragedy of German-America.* New York: G. P. Putnam's Sons, 1940.

Hays, Samuel P. "The Social Analysis of Political History." *Political Science Quarterly* 80 (September 1965):373–394.

Herberg, Will. "The Jewish Labor Movement in the U.S." *American Jewish Yearbook* 53 (1952):3–74.

Hicks, Granville; Gold, Michael; et al, eds. *Proletarian Literature in the United States: An Anthology.* New York: International Publishers, 1935.

Higham, John. *Strangers in the Land: Patterns of American Nativism 1860–1925.* New Brunswick, N.J.: Rutgers University Press, 1955.

Himmelfarb, Milton. "Secular Society? A Jewish Perspective." *Daedalus* 96 (Winter 1967):220–236.

Hinkle, Roscoe C. Jr., and Hinkle, Gisela J. *The Development of Modern Sociology: Its Nature and Growth in the United States.* New York: Random House, 1962.

An Historical Sketch of the State Normal College at Albany, New York and a History of Its Graduates for Fifty Years: 1844–1894. Albany: Brandow Printing Co., n.d.

Hofstadter, Richard. *Social Darwinism in American Thought.* Philadelphia: University of Pennsylvania Press, 1944. Rev. ed. Boston: Beacon Press, 1955.

Hofstadter, Richard, and Smith, Wilson, eds. *American Higher Education: A Documentary History.* 2 vols. Chicago: University of Chicago Press, 1961.

Hogan, David. "Education and the Making of the Chicago Working Class, 1880–1930." *History of Education Quarterly* 18 (Fall 1978):227–270.

Horowitz, David. "Billion Dollar Brains: How Wealth Puts Knowledge in Its Pocket." In *The Poverty of Progress: The Political Economy of American Social Problems.*, edited by Milton Mankoff, pp. 298–314. New York: Holt, Rinehart and Winston, 1972.

Horowitz, Irving Louis. "The Student as Jew." In *Sociology and Student Life: Toward a New Campus*, edited by Arthur B. Shostak, pp. 29–42. New York: David McKay, 1971.

———. *Professing Sociology: Studies in the Life Cycle of Social Science.* Chicago: Aldine, 1969.

Hourwich, Isaac A. *Immigration and Labor: The Economic Aspects of European Immigration in the United States.* New York: G. P. Putnam's Sons, 1912.

Howe, Irving. *World of Our Fathers: The Journey of the East European Jews to America and the Life They Found and Made.* New York: Simon and Shuster, 1976.

Hutchinson, Edward P. *Immigrants and Their Children, 1850–1950.* New York: Wiley, 1956.

Itzkoff, Seymour W. *Cultural Pluralism and American Education.* Scranton: International Textbook Company, 1969.

Jackson, Sydney. *America's Struggle for Free Public Schools: Social Tension and Education in New England and New York, 1827–1842.* Washington, D.C.: American Council on Public Affairs, 1941.

James, Edmund J., ed. *The Immigrant Jew in America.* New York: Buck and Co., 1907.

Jencks, Christopher, and Riesman, David. *The Academic Revolution.* Garden City, N.Y.: Doubleday Co., 1968.

Jessup, Walter A. *The Social Factors Affecting Special Supervision in the Public Schools of the United States.* New York: Teachers College, 1911.

———. *The Teaching Staff.* Cleveland: The Survey Committee of the Cleveland Foundation, 1916.

Kaestle, Carl. *The Evolution of an Urban School System: New York City 1750–1859.* Cambridge: Harvard University Press, 1973.

Kane, Michael B. *Minorities in Textbooks: A Study of Their Treatment in Social Studies Texts.* Chicago: Quadrangle Books, 1970.

Karier, Clarence; Violas, Paul; and Spring, Joel. *Roots of Crisis: American Education in the Twentieth Century.* Chicago: Rand McNally, 1973.

Karp, Abraham. *Golden Door to America: The Jewish Immigrant Experience.* New York: Penguin Books, 1977.

Karpf, Maurice J. *Jewish Community Organization in the United States.* New York: Bloch, 1938.

Karpp, Mortimer. "Vocations of College Men, 1849–1934: A Study of the Alumni of the College of the City of New York." *The Personnel Journal* 13 (October 1934):158–168.

Katz, Michael B. *The Irony of Early School Reform: Educational Innovation in Mid-Nineteenth Century Massachusetts.* Boston: Beacon Press, 1968.

Kautsky, Karl. *Are the Jews a Race?* New York: International Publishers, 1926.

Kessner, Thomas. *The Golden Door: Italian and Jewish Immigrant Mobility in New York City, 1880–1915.* New York: Oxford University Press, 1977.

Keyes, Charles Henry. *A Study of Acceleration and Arrest.* New York: Teachers College, 1911.

Klaperman, Gilbert. *The Story of Yeshiva University: The First Jewish University in America.* London: Macmillan Co., 1969.

Klapper, Paul, ed. *College Teaching: Studies in Methods of Teaching in the College.* Yonkers-on-Hudson: World Book, 1920.

Kober, Adolf. "Emancipation's Impact on the Education and Vocational Training of German Jewry." *Jewish Social Studies* 16 (January and April 1954);3–32, 151–169.

Kozol, Jonathan. *Death at an Early Age: The Destruction of the Hearts and Minds of Negro Children in the Boston Public Schools.* New York: Bantam Books, 1967.

Kuhn, Thomas S. *The Structure of Scientific Revolutions.* Chicago: University of Chicago Press, 1962.

Kuznets, Simon. "Economic Structure and Life of the Jews." In Louis Finkelstein, ed., *The Jews.* 3rd ed. Vol. 2. New York: Harper and Bros., 1960.

Laidlaw, Walter. *Statistical Sources for Demographic Studies of Greater New York, 1910.* 2 vols. New York: The Federation of Churches, 1913. (In Special Collections Division, Butler Library, Columbia University.)

Laqueur, Walter, and Mosse, George L., eds. *Education and Social Structure in the Twentieth Century.* New York: Harper Torchbooks, 1967.

Laslett, John. *Labor and the Left.* New York: Basic Books, 1970.

Lazonick, William. "The Subjugation of Labor to Capital: The Rise of the Capitalist System." *Review of Radical Political Economics* 10 (Spring 1978):1–31.

Lenin, V. I. *Imperialism: The Highest Stage of Capitalism.* New York: International Publishers, 1939.

Leon, Abram. *The Jewish Question: A Marxist Interpretation.* Mexico: Ediciones Pioneres, 1950. Reprint, New York: Pathfinder Press, 1970.

Leroy-Beaulieu, Anatole. *Israel Among the Nations: A Study of the Jews and Anti-Semitism.* Translated by Frances Hellman. New York: G. P. Putnam's Sons, 1895.

Leslie, W. Bruce. "Localism, Denominationalism, and Institutional Strategies in Urbanizing America: Three Pennsylvania Colleges, 1870–1915." *History of Education Quarterly* 17 (Fall 1977):235–256.

Lestchinsky, Jacob. "The Economic and Social Development of American Jewry." In *The Jewish People, Past and Present.* Vol. 4. New York: Martin Press, 1955.

———. "The Position of the Jews in the Economic Life of America." In Graeber and Britt, *Jews in a Gentile World:* 402–416.

Levin, Nora. *While Messiah Tarried: Jewish Socialist Movements, 1871–1917.* New York: Schocken Books, 1977.

Levine, Israel E. "Coeds on the Campus." *The Alumnus* 48 (October 1952): 8–10.

Liebman, Charles S. "Orthodoxy in American Jewish Life." *American Jewish Yearbook* 66 (1965):21–92.

Lipset, Seymour Martin. *Political Man: The Social Bases of Politics.* New York: Doubleday, 1959.

———, and Bendix, Reinhard. *Social Mobility in Industrial Society.* Berkeley: University of California Press, 1967.

Lyman, Stanford M. *Chinese Americans.* New York: Random House, 1974.

Mahler, Raphael. *A History of Modern Jewry 1780–1815.* New York: Schocken Books, 1971.

Mahoney, John J. "Training Teachers for Americanization." U.S. Bureau of Education bulletin, no. 12 (1920).

Maller, Julius B. *School and Community: A Study of the Demographic and Economic Background of Education in the State of New York.* New York: McGraw-Hill, 1938.

Mankoff, Milton, ed. *The Poverty of Progress: The Political Economy of American Social Problems.* New York: Holt, Rinehart and Winston, 1972.

Marcus, J. *An Index to Scientific Articles on American Jewish History.* Cincinnati: American Jewish Archives, 1971.

Marx, Karl. *Capital.* Edited by Frederick Engels. 3 vols. New York: International Publishers, 1967.

———. *A Contribution to the Critique of Political Economy.* Moscow: Progress Publishers, 1970.

———. *The German Ideology.* New York: International Publishers, 1947.

———. *Grundrisse.* Translated by Martin Nicolaus. Middlesex, England: Penguin Books, 1973.

———. "On the Jewish Question." *Karl Marx: Early Writings.* Edited and translated by T. B. Bottomore. New York: McGraw-Hill, 1963.

———, and Engels, Frederick. *Selected Works.* New York: International Publishers, 1968.

Masserman, Paul, and Baker, Max. *The Jews Come to America.* New York: Bloch Publishing, 1932.

McGurk, Josephine H. "History of the Department and School of Education of the College of the City of New York." Master's thesis, CCNY School of Education, 1934.

Memmi, Albert. *The Colonizer and the Colonized.* Boston: Beacon Press, 1965.

———. *The Liberation of the Jew.* Translated by Judy Hyun. New York: Orion Press, 1966.

Mendelsohn, Ezra. *Class Struggle in the Pale: The Formative Years of the Jewish Workers' Movement in Tsarist Russia.* London: Cambridge University Press, 1970.

Merton, Robert K. *Social Theory and Social Structure.* 2nd ed. London: The Free Press of Glencoe, 1957.

———, et al. *Reader in Bureaucracy.* London: Collier-Macmillan, 1952.

Metzker, Isaac, ed. *A Bintel Brief: Sixty Years of Letters from the Lower East Side to the Jewish Daily Forward.* New York: Ballantine Books, 1971.

Michels, Roberto. *Political Parties.* Translated from the Italian by Eden and Cedar Paul. London: Collier-Macmillan, 1962.

Mills, C. Wright. *Power, Politics and People.* Edited by Irving Louis Horowitz. New York: Ballantine Books, n.d.

———. *The Power Elite.* New York: Oxford University Press, 1959.

———. *White Collar.* New York: Oxford University Press, 1951.

Mitchell, Juliet. *Women's Estate.* New York: Vintage, 1973.

Moore, Wilbert E. *Social Change.* Englewood Cliffs, N.J.: Prentice-Hall, 1963.

Mosenthal, Philip J., and Horne, Charles F. *The City College: Memories of 60 Years.* New York: G. P. Putnam's Sons, 1907.

Murdoch, Katherine. "A Study of Race Differences in New York City." *School and Society* 11 (January 1920):147–150.

Myers, Gustavus. *The History of Tammany Hall.* New York: Dover, 1971.

Natanson, Maurice, ed. *Philosophy of the Social Sciences: A Reader.* New York: Random House, 1963.

Naylor, Natalie A. "The Antebellum College Movement: A Reappraisal of Tewksbury's *Founding of American Colleges and Universities.*" *History of Education Quarterly* 13 (1973): 261–274.

New York, New York. City College Archives. Morris R. Cohen Library, The City College of New York. *Alumni Register,* 1853–1931, The College of the City of New York. Edited by Donald A. Roberts, 1932.

———. By-Law on Curriculum, 1901.

———. *The City College of New York Register,* 1906–1926.

———. *The City College Quarterly.* Vols. 1–16.

———. Executive Committee Minutes, June, 1872.

———. Minutes of the Board of Trustees, 1878, pp. 19–21; 1882, pp. 10–11, 35–36; 1910; 1920.

———. *School of Education Bulletin,* 1911–1913; 1916–1927.

———. Special Collections.

New York, New York. Columbia University Archives. Columbiana Collection. Columbia University *Bulletins,* 1897–1898, 1903–1904, 1905–1906, 1910, 1915, 1919–1920.

New York, New York. Municipal Reference Library Archives of the City of New York. "Civil Lists." *The City Record,* July–December, 1905; January–June, 1915; January–June, 1925; July–December, 1925.

Newcomb, Theodore M. "Attitude Development as a Function of Reference Groups: The Bennington Study." *Readings in Social Psychology.* Edited by Eleanor E. Maccoby, Theodore M. Newcomb, and Eugene L. Hartley. New York: Holt, Rinehart and Winston, 1958.

Newcomer, Mabel. *The Big Business Executive: The Factors that Made Him, 1900-1950.* New York: Columbia University Press, 1955.

Nicolaus, Martin. "The Theory of Labor Aristocracy." *Monthly Review* 21 (April 1970):91–101.

Nieves, Josephine, and the Puerto Rican Studies Task Force, *Puerto Ricans in United States Higher Education*. New York: Centro de Estudios Puertorriqueños, May 1979.

Ossowski, Stanislaw. *Class Structure in the Social Consciousness*. New York: Free Press, 1963.

Page, Charles Hunt. *Class and American Sociology: From Ward to Ross*. New York: Octagon Books, 1964.

Palmer, A. Emerson. *The New York Public School*. New York: Macmillan, 1905.

Parkes, James. *The Jew in the Medieval Community: A Study of His Political and Economic Situation*. London: Soncino Press, 1938.

Pauling, J. K. "Educational Influences: New York." In Bernheimer, *The Russian Jew in the United States*: 183–199.

Perkinson, Henry J. *The Imperfect Panacea: American Faith in Education 1865-1965*. New York: Random House, 1968.

Podhoretz, Norman. *Making It*. New York: Random House, 1967.

Potts, David B. "American Colleges in the Nineteenth Century: From Localism to Denominationalism." *History of Education Quarterly* 11 (Winter 1971):363–380.

———. "College Enthusiasm as Public Response, 1800–1860." *Harvard Education Review* 47 (February 1977):28–42.

Poulantzas, Nicos. "On Social Classes." *New Left Review*, no. 78 (March–April 1973):37–54.

Powell, Reed. *Race, Religion, and the Promotion of the American Executive*. Monograph no. AA-3. Columbus: College of Administrative Science, Ohio State University, 1969.

Ravitch, Diane. *The Great School Wars: New York City, 1805–1973*. New York: Basic Books, 1974.

———. *The Revisionists Revised: A Critique of the Radical Attack on the Schools*. New York: Basic Books, 1978.

Reports on the Course of Instruction in Yale College by a Committee of the Corporation and the Academical Faculty. New Haven, 1828. Reprinted as "Original Papers in Relation to a Course of Liberal Education." *American Journal of Science and Arts* 15 (1829):297–351. (Referred to as the Yale *Report.*)

Richman, Julia. "A Social Need of the Public School." *Forum* 43 (February 1910):162–169.

Riis, Jacob. *How the Other Half Lives: Studies Among the Tenements of New York*. New York: Sagamore Press, 1957.

Rischin, Moses. *The Promised City: New York's Jews 1870–1914*. New York. Corinth Books, 1962.

Rivkin, Ellis. *The Shaping of Jewish History: A Radical New Interpretation*. New York: Charles Scribner's Sons, 1971.

Rosenfeld, Max. "Schappes on Morris Raphael Cohen." *Jewish Currents* 34, no. 7 (July/August 1980):24–33.

Rosenfeld, Morris. *Selections from His Poetry and Prose.* Edited by Itche Goldberg and Max Rosenfeld. New York: Yiddisher Kultur-Farband, 1964.

———. *Songs of Labor and Other Poems.* Translated from the Yiddish by Rose Pastor Stokes and Helena Frank. Boston: Richard G. Badger, 1914.

Rosenfield, Leonora Cohen. *Portrait of a Philosopher: Morris R. Cohen in Life and Letters.* New York: Harcourt Brace, 1948, 1962.

Rosengarten, Isaac. "The Jewish Teacher in the New York Public Schools." *Jewish Forum* 1 (July 1918):319–330.

Rosenthal, Erich. "Acculturation without Assimilation? The Jewish Community of Chicago, Illinois." *American Journal of Sociology* 66 (November 1960):280–288.

Rosenwaike, Ira. "Interethnic Comparison of Educational Attainment: An Analysis Based on Census Data for New York City." *American Journal of Sociology* 79 (July 1973):69–77.

Rubinow, Isaac M. "Economic and Industrial Condition: New York." In Bernheimer, *The Russian Jew in the United States:* 101–121.

Rudolph, Frederick. *The American College and University.* New York: Vintage Books, 1962.

Rudy, S. Willis. *The College of the City of New York: A History.* New York: City College Press, 1949.

Sachar, Howard Morley. *The Course of Modern Jewish History.* New York: Dell, 1958.

Sanger, Margaret. *Woman and the New Race.* New York: Brentanos, 1920.

Sartre, Jean-Paul. *Anti-Semite and Jew.* Translated by Goerge J. Becker. New York: Schocken Books, 1965.

Saveth, Edward N. *American Historians and European Immigrants, 1875–1925.* 1948. Reprint. New York: Russell and Russell, 1965.

Schappes, Morris U. *A Documentary History of the Jews in the United States, 1654–1875.* 3rd ed. New York: Schocken Books, 1971.

———. *The Jews in the U.S.: A Pictorial History, 1654 to the Present.* New York: Citadel Press, 1958.

Schmidt, Sarah. "From Ghetto to University: The Jewish Experience in the Public School." *American Educator* 2 (Spring 1978):23–26.

Schneider, Linda. "Workmen and Citizens: American Nationality and Workers' Consciousness, 1870–1920: Three Case Studies." Ph.D. dissertation, Columbia University, 1975.

Schwartz, Leo W., ed. *The Menorah Treasury: Harvest of Half a Century.* Philadelphia: The Jewish Publication Society of America, 1964.

Scott, Donald. "The Social History of Education: Three Alternatives." *History of Education Quarterly* 10 (Summer 1970):242–254.

Seligman, Ben B. "The Jewish Population of New York City: 1952." In Sklare, *The Jews:* 94–106.

Sewell, William H., and Armer, J. Michael. "Neighborhood Context and College Plans." *American Sociological Review* 31 (April 1966):159–168.

Sewell, William H., and Shah, Vimal. "Parents' Education and Children's Educational Aspirations and Achievements." *American Sociological Review* 33 (April 1968):191–209.

Sexton, Patricia Cayo. *Education and Income: Inequalities of Opportunity in Our Public Schools.* New York: Viking Press, 1964.

Shannon, Fred Albert. *The Farmer's Last Frontier, Agriculture: 1860–1897.* New York: Farrar and Reinhart, 1945.

Shepard, Richard F. "30 Alumni of Townsend Harris High Recall Glory Years as Elite Scholars." *The New York Times,* December 7, 1973, p. 431.

Shostak, Arthur B. *Blue-Collar Life.* New York: Random House, 1969.

Silverman, Rabbi J. "The Hebrew Educational Fair and Its Bearing on the Immigrant Question." Extract from a lecture delivered at Temple Emanu-El December 1, 1889. *The American Hebrew* (December 6, 1889):119–120.

Singer, David. "David Levinsky's Fall: A Note on the Liebman Thesis." *American Quarterly* 19 (Winter 1967):696–706.

Sklare, Marshall. *America's Jews.* New York: Random House, 1971.

———. *The Jews: Social Patterns of an American Group.* Glencoe, Ill.: Free Press, 1958.

Slater, Mariam K. "My Son the Doctor: Aspects of Mobility Among American Jews." *American Sociological Review* 34 (June 1969):359–373.

———. "Rejoinder to Dr. Cahnman." *American Sociological Review* 34 (December 1969):936.

Sloan, Douglas. "Harmony, Chaos and Consensus: The American College Curriculum." *Teachers College Record* 73 (1971):221–251.

Smith, David N. *Who Rules the Universities? An Essay in Class Analysis.* New York: Monthly Review Press, 1974.

Smith, Timothy L. "Immigrant Social Aspirations and American Education, 1880–1930." *American Quarterly* 21 (Fall 1969):523–543.

Spencer, Herbert. *The Study of Sociology.* 1874. Reprint. Ann Arbor: University of Michigan Press, 1961.

"Statistical Summary by States." *American Jewish Yearbook* 3 (1901–1902):126.

"Statistics of Jews." *American Jewish Yearbook* 5677 (1916–1917):279; 5699 (1938–1939):556–557.

"Statistics of Public High Schools: 1917–1918." Bureau of Education bulletin, no. 19 (1920).

Steinberg, Stephen. *The Academic Melting Pot: Catholics and Jews in American Higher Education.* A Report Prepared for the Carnegie Commission on Higher Education. New York: McGraw-Hill, 1974.

Stern, Bernhard J. *Historical Sociology: The Selected Papers of Bernhard J. Stern.* New York: The Citadel Press, 1959.

Supple, Barry E. "A Business Elite: German-Jewish Financiers in Nineteenth-Century New York." *Business History Review* 31 (Summer 1957):143–177.

Suttles, Gerald D. *The Social Order of the Slum: Ethnicity and Territory in the Inner City.* Chicago: University of Chicago Press, 1968.

Sweezy, Paul, and Baran, Paul. *Monopoly Capital.* New York: Monthly Review Press, 1966.

Synnott, Marcia. *The Half-Opened Door: Discrimination and Admissions at Harvard, Yale and Princeton, 1900–1970.* Westport, Conn.: Greenwood Press, 1979.

TenHouten, Warren, et al. "School Ethnic Composition, Social Contexts, and Educational Plans of Mexican-American and Anglo High School Students." *American Journal of Sociology* 77 (July 1971):89–107.

Thernstrom, Stephen. *Poverty and Progress: Social Mobility in a Nineteenth Century City.* New York: Atheneum, 1973.

Thompson, E. P. *The Making of the English Working Class.* New York: Vintage, 1963.

Thorndike, Edward. "The Teaching Staff of Secondary Schools in the United States." U.S. Bureau of Education bulletin, no. 4 (1909).

Trotsky, Leon. *On the Jewish Question.* New York: Merit Pamphlet, 1970.

United States Bureau of the Census. *Historical Statistics of the United States from Colonial Times to 1970.* 2 vols. Washington, D.C.: U.S. Department of Commerce, 1975.

Updegraff, Harlan. "Teacher Certificates Issued Under General State Laws and Regulations." U.S. Bureau of Education bulletin, no. 18 (1911).

Van Denburg, Joseph. *Causes of the Elimination of Students from the Secondary Schools of New York City, 1906–1910.* 1911. Reprint. New York: AMS Press, 1972.

Veysey, Lawrence R. *The Emergence of the American University.* Chicago: University of Chicago Press, 1965.

Wald, Lillian D. *The House on Henry Street.* 1915. Reprint. New York: Dover, 1971.

Walton, John C. "Requirements for the Bachelor's Degree." U.S. Bureau of Education bulletin, no. 7 (1920).

Warner, W. Lloyd, and Srole, Leo. *The Social Systems of American Ethnic Groups.* New Haven: Yale University Press, 1945.

Waxman, Chaim. "Bringing the Poor Back In: Jewish Poverty in Education for Jewish Communal Service." *Forum* 35 (Spring/Summer 1979):133–143.

Weber, Max. *On Law in Economy and Society.* Edited by Max Rheinstein. Translated by Edward Shils and Max Rheinstein. New York: Simon and Schuster, 1967.

———. *The Protestant Ethic and the Spirit of Capitalism.* Translated by Talcott Parsons. New York: Charles Scribner's Sons, 1958.

———. *The Sociology of Religion.* Translated by Ephraim Fischoff. Boston: Beacon Press, 1963.

———. *The Theory of Social and Economic Organization.* Edited by Talcott

Parsons. Translated by A. M. Henderson and Talcott Parsons. 1947. Reprint. New York: Free Press, 1964.

Wechsler, Harold S. *The Qualified Student: A History of Selective College Admission in America*. New York: John Wiley and Sons, 1977.

Weinryb, Bernard D. "Jewish Immigration and Accommodation to America." In Sklare, *The Jews:*4–22.

Weinstein, James. *The Corporate Ideal in the Liberal State, 1900–1918*. Boston: Beacon Press, 1968.

————. *The Decline of Socialism in America, 1912–1925*. New York: Vintage Press, 1967.

————. "The Left, Old and New." *Socialist Revolution* 10 (July-August 1972):7–60.

Whittemore, Richard F. W. "Nicholas Murray Butler and Public Education, 1862–1911." Ph.D. dissertation, Teachers College, 1962.

Who Was Who in America, 1897–1942. Vol. 1. Chicago: Marquis, 1943.

Whyte, William F. *Street Corner Society*. 3rd ed. Chicago: Chicago University Press, 1955.

Wiebe, Robert H. *The Search for Order: 1877–1920*. New York: Hill and Wang, 1967.

————. "The Social Functions of Public Education." *American Quarterly* 21 (Summer 1969):147–164.

Wiener, Leo. *The History of Yiddish Literature in the Nineteenth Century*. 1899. Reprint. 2nd ed. New York: Hermon Press, 1972.

Williams, Eric. *Capitalism and Slavery*. New York: Capricorn Books, 1966.

Wirth, Louis, *The Ghetto*. 1928. Reprint. Chicago: University of Chicago Press, 1969.

Wood, Joseph S. "A Comparison Between the Courses of Study at the College of the City of New York and Yale University." January 1902. (In City College Archives.)

Woodward, C. Vann. *The Strange Career of Jim Crow*. 2nd ed. London: Oxford University Press, 1966.

Woolston, Howard Brown. *A Study of the Population of Manhattanville*. In *Studies in History, Economics and Public Law*. Vol. 35. New York: AMS Press, 1909.

Yaffe, James. *The American Jews: Portrait of a Split Personality*. New York: Random House, 1969.

Yuditzky, A. *Jewish Bourgeoisie and Jewish Proletariat in the First Half of the Nineteenth Century*. (Yiddish). Kiev: Institute for Yiddish Culture at the Ukrainian Scientific Academy, 1931.

Zweigenhaft, Richard. "American Jews: In or Out of the Upper Class?" *Insurgent Sociologist* 9 (Fall 1979–Winter 1980):24–37.

Index